The Bluebird Effect

# The Bluebird Effect

## UNCOMMON BONDS WITH COMMON BIRDS

### JULIE ZICKEFOOSE

HOUGHTON MIFFLIN HARCOURT

BOSTON   NEW YORK

For information about permission to reproduce selections from this book, write to Permissions, Houghton Mifflin Harcourt Publishing Company, 215 Park Avenue South, New York, New York 10003.

www.hmhco.com

*Library of Congress Cataloging-in-Publication Data*
Zickefoose, Julie.
  The bluebird effect : uncommon bonds with common birds / Julie Zickefoose.
     p. cm.
  Includes bibliographical references and index.
   ISBN 978-0-547-00309-2
1. Birds—Behavior—United States—Anecdotes. 2. Bird watching—United States—Anecdotes. 3. Birds—Wounds and injuries—Treatment—Anecdotes. 4. Wildlife rehabilitation—United States—Anecdotes. 5. Human-animal relationships—Anecdotes. 6. Zickefoose, Julie—Anecdotes. 7. Naturalists—United States—Anecdotes. 8. Wildlife rehabilitators—United States—Anecdotes. 9. Birds—United States—Pictorial works. I. Title.
  QL682.Z53 2012
  598.07234—dc23      2011036692

*Book design by Melissa Lotfy*

Printed in China
SCP 10 9 8 7 6 5 4

*For Ida Zickefoose. Thank you for your love of words, and for letting me bring those things into the house.*

*For DOD, who knew a little something about everything.*

*For Bill, my heart's archer, and for Phoebe and Liam, sweet arrows flying.*

# Contents

# Acknowledgments

A LITTLE PETTING ZOO at Maymont Park, Richmond, Virginia, perhaps 1964. I'm very young, barely able to reach over the woven wire fence. A large tom turkey stands on the other side, feathers raised into an enormous sphere, his fleshy red, white, and blue wattles and doodads fully engorged, wanting whatever a petting zoo turkey wants. Corn? A hen turkey? Me?

"There. Pet the turkey's head. Feel how warm it is," my father says. I still remember the jolt of pure empathy that coursed through me upon laying my hand on the bird's bare head. To my surprise, he didn't flinch, peck me, or turn away. The warmth of his skin awakened something deep and primal, a realization that, despite his bizarre appearance and feathered armor, there was someone in there, someone I could understand.

I thank my father, C. D. Zickefoose, for giving me that and countless other moments with birds, for knowing what to feed an orphaned dove, blue jay, grackle, or robin, and for leaving me to figure out the rest. Thanks to my mother, Ida, for letting me bring them inside, for letting me dream by myself in the woods and ride miles into the Virginia countryside on bicycle or horseback. I know now, having my own kids, that you worried the whole time, Mom. Thank you for never clipping my wings. And thanks to my sisters, Nancy, Barbara, and especially Micky, for being incredible human beings, and for looking after Mom. And to my brother, Bob, for doing all the things Dad dreamt of doing.

*Bird Watcher's Digest* has published my writing and art since 1986 and brought it to tens of thousands of kind and enthusiastic subscribers. I thank Elsa, Bill Jr., Bill III, Andy, and Laura—the entire Thompson family—and their editor emeritus Mary Bowers for helping me reach this audience. As my writing has matured from simply expounding on the beauty and wonder of birds to grappling with more complex issues of human-bird interaction, I thank *BWD* for continuing to grant me a voice.

My husband, Bill Thompson III, editor and publisher of *BWD*, is intertwined in these stories in myriad ways, whether he's checking bluebird boxes, transporting an avian client, supporting me in baby bird season, hauling out the ladder for a hummingbird rescue, or suffering the stench of vulture vomit in the company van. He's got my back when I drop everything to help a bird, and he has lived many of the stories in this book. For his love, his vision and guidance; for bringing me out to this splendid pocket of Appalachian Ohio and putting a roof with a bird-watching tower over my head; and most of all for giving me the chance to be a mother to things without feathers, I am forever in his debt.

Phoebe, fifteen, and Liam, twelve, my things without feathers, you give me hope for the world with your delighted appreciation of nature and empathy for the small and helpless. Phoebe's helped me feed doves, waxwings, hummingbirds, chimney swifts, and phoebes; Liam has given our charges the love every young thing needs, and both have been troupers, growing up gracefully with parents of many interests. May you both eclipse your parents; may art, music, and insatiable curiosity be your shadows.

*Shaking in flight*

My editor, Lisa White, has been unfailingly kind, deft, subtle, and patient through the five years it has taken to produce this book. In an age when more and more of us read from screens, I am deeply grateful to see my paintings and words on pages, in the heft of a hardcover. I'm grateful to my agent, Russell Galen, who helped shape the book's concept. And I thank my Web wizard, Katherine Koch, for giving wings to my online aspirations. Jeanne Saunders, as always, dwells in my heart.

National Public Radio, delightfully personified by the anchor Melissa "Bird Friendly" Block and my editor, Ellen Silva, has been generous in airing my stories on *All Things Considered*. Enormous listener reaction to the hummingbird and macaw stories helped convince me that there was a book here.

Because these stories span decades, I'm indebted to a small village of people who have helped along the way. In Connecticut, Robert Braunfield shared my love of birds, woke me to the everyday miracles going on in bluebird nest boxes, sharpened my artist's eye, and supported me in a thousand ways. Susan Cooley, the last best boss I'll ever have, gently launched me into conservation work. Richard and Esther Goodwin gave me shelter in a miraculous sanctuary, and the time and freedom to be simply a naturalist. Rufus and Charlotte Barringer did the same. I thank the dozens of volunteers who helped me post and patrol least tern and piping plover nesting beaches, but two stalwarts stood out: Andy Griswold and Tom Damiani.

For their insights about the great woodpecker will-o'-the-wisp, I am indebted to James Tanner, Nancy Tanner, Thomas Murray, Don Eckelberry (who also lent a mentoring eye to my artwork), Virginia Eckelberry, Clifford Shackelford, John Dennis, Dennis Garratt, and especially Jerome Jackson, whose naturalist's skills and integrity I strive to emulate. Paul Johnsgard, Matt Mullenix, Paul Tebbel, Vickie Henderson, and Cyndi Routledge all informed my writing on sandhill cranes. I'm indebted to Alan Poole not only for his osprey observations but also for a decade of collaboration on my illustrations for the Birds of North America project. Thanks to Paul Spitzer for encouraging me to enter osprey time. I fondly remember time spent with "Madame Osprey" Anne Gaylord and George and Nancy Terpenning of Old Lyme. Sylvia Halkin kindly reviewed the cardinal chapter. For his poignant turkey vulture story, I thank Charles Kennedy.

For gifting me with a Savannah sparrow and many boxes of Christmas pears, I'm grateful to Doreen Lammer. I thank Kandy Matheny and Sandy Fredenburg for the nestling phoebes, Don Noland for Libby the mourning dove, Lori Hall and Sherri Killen for the miraculous hummingbirds, and Rosetta Dalison and Gwen Kelby for the life-altering batch of baby swifts.

So many of the birds I try to help come to me broken, and I'm grateful for the friendship and incredible skill of the avian veterinarian Robert Giddings, who was willing to fix mine for nothing. The Ohio Wildlife Center, under the leadership of Dr. Donald Burton, takes in thousands of wild things each season, and I'm deeply grateful for the dedication and compassion of Lisa Fosco, Kristi Krumlauf, Stormy Gibson, and OWC's two hundred volunteers. Along with OWC staff, the avian rehabilitators Astrid MacLeod and Connie Sales have enlightened and guided me in caring for tough cases.

Scott Weidensaul continues to set writing standards to which I can only aspire, and is a true friend besides.

For bringing real jazz to my life, in both human and musical form, I thank my late father-in-law, Bill Thompson, Jr.

I thank Bill Thompson III, Wendy Eller, Jeff Eller, and Craig Gibbs of the Rain Crows for musical nourishment; and Chet Baker, Boston terrier, for unwavering love. Most of all, I thank the birds: foundlings and teachers both.

JZ
May 28, 2011

# Foreword

FOR LITERALLY as long as I can remember, I've been fascinated by birds. Some of my earliest memories are of watching the cardinals and nuthatches at our winter feeder, being dazzled by their colors and sounds.

It's a fascination I never outgrew, and although my job as a writer and a researcher has taken me to distant corners of the world and given me the opportunity to see some of the most exotic birds on the planet, the allure of those backyard birds has never waned.

If anything, I've come to understand how little we know about even the most common birds — not only how they live, the migrations they make, the social fabric in which they exist, but also, at an even more mysterious and fundamental level, how they perceive the world around them. I've also wondered, more than once, how a wild bird perceives us, we strange bipedal primates that have reshaped every aspect of their landscape.

But few of us — even those of us who spend our days and devote our lives to the study of birds — interact with birds in quite the way that Julie Zickefoose does. Zick's avian experiences are not the run of your typical mill. Although I've handled and banded thousands of hummingbirds, for instance, I have never had one snake its long exploratory tongue up my nostril. Throughout her life, Julie's been dealing with birds on a much more direct, sometimes startlingly intimate level than most people—as a biologist, rehabilitator, artist, and conservationist.

The result is a trove of stories, stretching back decades, through which she explores the relationship between human and bird. Some of these relationships were intense but transitory, like a cat-injured sparrow brought back to independence by grit and daily massages, while others have occupied her life for longer than her husband and children. For twenty-three years, Zick was the owned—at least as much as the owner—of a chestnut-fronted macaw named Charlie. I am proud to say that I was nipped by Charlie (and happy that he didn't draw blood), and I can attest to the deep, strange, tightly entwined bond between those two.

In *The Bluebird Effect: Uncommon Bonds with Common Birds,* Julie lays out the ways in which her life and those of many birds—swallows and swifts, wrens and chickadees, woodpeckers and raptors, and many others—have intersected. By and large, these are not glamorous, rare species but the kinds of common backyard birds the rest of us see every day—cardinals and titmice, ospreys and robins—and to which we usually pay little more than passing attention.

To Julie, however, these daily encounters are windows into a sovereign principality—a world that overlaps ours but which is strikingly different, at once alien and familiar. They illuminate the grip that birds hold on her own life, and her attempts to reconcile our own connections and responsibilities to birds—from tiny plovers that nest on the same beaches where we sunbathe and play volleyball, to huge cranes that some people see as majestic symbols of American wilderness, and others as "sirloin on the wing."

*after a nap*

In the pages that follow, you'll also find hundreds of Julie's incredible watercolors and pencil sketches. More than almost any other contemporary artist, Zick has the ability to capture the spark of a living creature—the gift for translating motion and color into line and form, while retaining the essence of the bird.

What you won't find in this book, thankfully, is the kind of soupy, woolly-minded treacle that tends to bubble up when someone is speculating on the emotional lives of birds. Zick is commonsensical, viewing her avian subjects with the pragmatic and unsentimental eye of the naturalist, even when what she sees is keenly moving.

She remembers what we often forget: that much of what underpins our passion for birds is a one-way street. Just because they can raise us to heights of joy and transcendence—by the glint of morning sun off the brassy hackles of a golden eagle in flight, through the ringing harmonics of a hermit thrush's song at daybreak, or the explosion of sound and motion as ten thousand snow geese leap simultaneously into the air—we are mere observers, watching from the wrong end of the binoculars.

Roger Tory Peterson once noted that *love* is probably the wrong word to use for our connection with birds, since love is a reciprocal emotion—and birds don't repay our feelings. But what makes *The Bluebird Effect* such a rare and important book is how Julie provides from her own unusual life plenty of examples of times that birds do reciprocate—the "uncommon bonds" of its title, when birds appeared to repay her passion and concern with, if not love, then trust and what may even be gratitude.

Birds are not little automatons. The notion that

they are merely feather-clad bundles of stimulus/response programming, which has long been the view of science, shortchanges the complexity that biologists like Julie observe in avian lives, and which research is beginning to unveil.

But if birds are not rigidly coded robots, neither are they little people. If Julie's stories illuminate the fact that birds have a richer, deeper, more nuanced emotional life than scientists had long been willing to credit, her experiences also show very clearly that birds do not always (or even often) react to the world in ways we recognize as "human."

In the end, birds and people are both profoundly similar and profoundly different. With its lyrical words and lovely images—all backed by Zick's observant eye, biologist's instinct, and nature geek curiosity—*The Bluebird Effect* helps, at least a little, to bridge that gulf.

Scott Weidensaul

August 2011

# Introduction

ITHACA, NEW YORK, is cold and gray through much of the winter and early spring, and the spring I came to the Cornell Lab of Ornithology to give a talk was no exception. As a child who staggered out of the Henrico County Public Library with head-high stacks of bird books, I thought—no, I knew—I'd attend Cornell, to trace the hallowed footprints of Louis Agassiz Fuertes, Arthur Allen, and Fredrick Kent Truslow, the men who'd written the words I committed to memory. Alas, in my Cornell interview, I was told that my math SAT scores weren't up to par to be accepted as a biology major, that I should probably be a journalist or a writer instead. So, being a pliant yet obstinate high school senior, I didn't even apply.

At Harvard, I couldn't compete with premedical students in biology, so I declared a major in biological anthropology and figured out how to take independent studies on bird behavior without having to take (flunk) organic chemistry. I wrote my way through college. I wanted so badly to become an ornithologist, but by all standard measures my brain wasn't organized right to fulfill what I'd thought was my destiny. I didn't want to cut birds up, measure them, or reduce them to mathematical equations (the trend in ornithology at the time). Heck, I couldn't do that. Five years later, I didn't want to be in academia anymore. I wanted to be in the field, to work with birds, to save them when they needed saving. I wanted to do something with them, to understand them, and the best way to do that seemed to be by helping them, watching them, sketching them, and writing down what they did. The writer Alice Sebold said, "It's very weird to succeed at thirty-nine years old and realize that in the midst of your failure, you were slowly building the life that you wanted anyway."

So thirty-two years after leaving the Cornell University admissions office with my head hanging, having since parlayed a passion for birds into a crazy quilt of

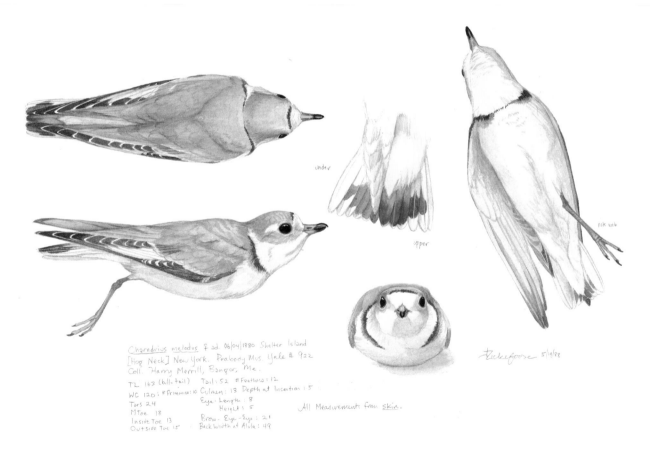

Introduction ✦ xix

a career, I'm staying in Ithaca with my friend Alan Poole, a real ornithologist, and he's arranged for me to speak and show my paintings at the Lab of Ornithology, which is about the most exciting thing I could think of, having all this ancient, stored-up emotion about the place. He's on the telephone in the other room, trying to tell his daughter what I do. He starts off on a couple of different tacks and finally says, "She's a storyteller. That's what she is." And it's true.

This book is many things—a sketchbook, a journal, an attempt to understand other beings—but it is not a dispassionate recitation of scientific truths about birds. It's a series of stories that I hope will pull back a curtain on their minds. I've worked with many species of birds in many capacities in my life as a naturalist, bird painter, and songbird rehabilitator. I included only those birds for which I had a satisfying story to tell. Each species has its own chapter. In order to be one of the twenty-five, a given species needed to come into my sphere several times, or in a particularly meaningful or instructive way. Many of the birds I write about came to me orphaned or injured. Others I've spent time studying and sketching in the wild. Some are ones that I've worked to manage, like piping plovers, least terns, and eastern bluebirds. One is Charlie, the macaw who is sitting on my shoulder as I write, who has been preening my eyelashes and sticking his rubbery tongue in my ear for twenty-three years. And one is just a will-o'-the-wisp, a giant woodpecker with its powerful ivory bill sunk deep in my psyche.

This book is as much about my process of learning about birds as it is about them. You will find me naming some of the birds and, when I know their sex, referring to them with the pronouns *he*, *she*, and *who* rather than *it* or *that*. They are birds, not people; I know that. But for me they are not merely objects of study or admiration. Birds, as I know them, are individuals. One scarlet tanager may behave completely differently from another; one piping plover will not react the same way to the same stimulus as his neighbor might. Birds have unique (for lack of a better word) personae, highly idiosyncratic reactions to the same stimuli. Like people, each one is different.

As I looked through my journals, I struggled to translate them into something readable, wondering whether or how to allow my life and viewpoint to intrude on the central narrative. Because virtually all the revelations about birds that you'll find here are anecdotal, and because most of them have come of my personal experience with birds, I couldn't excise myself; I wouldn't know where to begin. And so some of the stories, such as the saga of becoming a mother to four orphaned hummingbirds, unfold in the form of a journal, just as my understanding of them blossomed with each passing day. As much as I wanted birds to be its focus, I

Robin Day 18 (the day after
his surgery for neck gash)
His sixth day in captivity
He had lost all fear by the
third day.

He will come when called,
Would much rather sit on top
of his cage than in it (a
universal avian characteristic)
He likes his mealworms
beheaded. Diet: Mealworms
Puppy Chow soaked w/ Nutrical
Raw lean beef
Lactobacillus
Nekton Vitamins
Sips of Nutrical & water w/ each feed
Whatever else I can catch:
earthworms, crickets, caterpillars.

realized that the book might turn out to be a memoir whether I willed it or not. And so it has.

Someone who's never raised orphaned songbirds can have little concept of what's involved in making them ready to fend for themselves. I hope, through these writings, that I'll give you a glimpse of the work required. I hope that you'll view wildlife rehabilitators with new eyes, and know a little more of what's behind the "warm and fuzzy" image most hold of them. We're anything but bunny huggers; we need to be flint-hard at the core. We do what it takes to get these birds out the door and back into the wild, and we're not going to fall down on the job just before the finish line. There's too much invested. The reward is in understanding how a bird thinks, how it develops, and how it might react to any given situation. It's an understanding so deep that it goes beyond words. That empathy with wild birds is my pay for a job very few choose to take on.

In thinking about this book, I thought about some of my favorite nature books. I found out a lot about Bernd Heinrich as I explored his writings about ravens and owls; about Konrad Lorenz as I read about jackdaws, dogs, and geese; about Jane Goodall, though the subject was chimpanzees; about Elizabeth Marshall Thomas as I learned about dogs and cats; about Sy Montgomery as I followed her search for pink dolphins and moon bears. Their writings are personal, deeply human as well as humane. In the end, I find these people as interesting as their subjects. And I realize that it is in the zone where birds interact with people that I write my best stuff: I am a storyteller, always looking for a line into our common thoughts. I live for the moment when my gaze meets a bird's—that exchange of awareness of the "who" in each of us, the spark of understanding leaping from the bright bead of its eye to mine.

It's that spark gleaming in the cupped hand of my own experience that I want to bring to you. I want to tell you their stories.

# Spring Songbirds

## PEEKING INTO THE NEST

Feet clenched in fear.
That's the hallux in front.

# The Bluebird Effect

I HAD KNOWN this day would come, had been thinking about it a lot lately, but I wasn't truly prepared for it. Mr. Troyer didn't come in for his mealworms this afternoon, February 16, 2000. His widow, if widow she be, is already consorting with another male, the same day Mr. Troyer disappeared. He came to the kitchen window to remind me about his mealworms this morning, and this afternoon he is simply gone, erased, replaced. Such is the nature of songbird bonds, even long-standing ones. Bluebirds can't live forever, after all, and this one, I know, was at least eight years old, and probably closer to nine: a Methuselah among bluebirds.

He wasn't banded, but he had been marked just the same, by the quick talons of a sharp-shinned hawk, on May 19, 1993. It was at that moment that he became more than just another bluebird to me, that our lives were knit together, that I began to know him as an individual.

Bill and I had been gardening all day, and dusk was approaching. My notes from that day:

*Bill saved the male bluebird from a sharpie who barreled between the forsythia and garage, picked the male bluebird off the clothesline pole, and carried him, shrilling, for a distance before Bill's yelling scared the hawk into dropping him!*

*Oh! I picked him up and checked him over, finding nothing that
would keep him from flying. He sat sleeked and terrified on the
TV antenna for about 40 seconds before flying to the orchard.
He looked OK. His mate just sat on the wire, stunned. If Bill
hadn't heard a robin scolding and thought fast, the bluebird
just would have been gone in the morning.*

This was not the considered action of a well-informed naturalist—though Bill more than qualifies. This was the same
primitive response that snatches a toddler off a curb as a taxi
sweeps by. Denying a sharp-shinned hawk a well-earned meal
is not something we routinely do or recommend. There was no
thought involved, and thus no excuse to be made for my husband's intervention. I think back on that moment as pivotal, though I couldn't
have known it at the time. People speak of the "butterfly effect," describing
the unknown consequences of a seemingly irrelevant action. Taken to its extreme, one flap of a butterfly's wings in Brazil might alter the atmosphere sufficiently to cause a tornado in Texas. Though I couldn't know it, this moment,
for me, would herald eight years of the bluebird effect.

When the sharpshin dropped the bluebird, I picked him up. His tiny chest was
heaving, his bill was wide open, and bright beads of blood dotted his left bicep
and breast. Carefully, I spread both wings, stretched his legs, and blew a stream
of air on the feathers on his breast to part them and search for wounds. Finding
nothing gashed or broken, I smoothed his feathers and released him. His brood
was due to fledge in four days, and he had work to do.

For two days, we didn't see much of him; he sat mopily in the wooded border,
left wing drooping. But then his parental instincts won out over his discomfort,

and he helped his mate see the brood out of the box. But there was a marked difference in his demeanor. This once skittish bird seemed to have completely lost his fear of us, and he'd bathe merrily in the birdbath as I weeded less than ten feet away. On my hands and knees, I could feel the spray flying from his fluttering wings. A bird will not bathe if it feels the least bit threatened, because wet feathers spell vulnerability to predators. Clearly, he no longer regarded me as a threat. Could he view me as a protector after the hawk incident and actually feel safer when I was near? I thought back to other similar instances. One concerned barn swallows and can be found on pages 46 and 47; another involved a woodpecker.

A female hairy woodpecker who visited our peanut and suet feeders hit our large plate-glass window twice in the winter of 2000. The second time, she was knocked almost cold and lay sprawled on the lawn, vulnerable to attack from a predator. My heart sinking, I picked her up, checked her for broken bones, and, finding her intact, gently placed her in the crotch of a thick pine tree to recover. I checked on her several times over the next two hours and was glad to find her preening, then flying back to the feeding station for a snack. Her mate remained as shy as ever, as befits a hairy woodpecker, but the female showed not the slightest fear of me from that day on, feeding calmly as I filled feeders only a few feet away. Was she still stunned or had she

2/10/93 She was investigating the boxes above her          mate took off to the north

reclassified me to "nonthreatening" in her mental catalog? I know it's unfashion-able to conjure words like *trust* in a discussion of animal behavior, but as much as my mind circles around this and similar incidents, it keeps running into the same conclusion.

Having forged this bond of trust, however mysterious, with the rescued blue-bird, I took renewed interest in the course of his life. After all, he was instantly identifiable, with his drooping left wing. He was to nest with the same mate in the east box for the next three seasons, successfully fledging eighteen young. When the male bluebird nesting in our front yard suddenly disappeared, on March 16, 1996, I was surprised to see the injured male making forays from his eastern terri-tory into the front yard. Little matter that he had a mate building a nest in the east box. He waved his wings at the widowed front yard female, who, seemingly ener-gized by his presence, began gathering nesting material.

Singing vigorously, he encouraged her to build again in the front yard box. The widow had other ideas. She flew around the corner of our house to a box on the west side and began to build in it. Savagely, the droop-winged male attacked her and drove her back to the front yard box. Again and again she attempted to build in the west box, and each time he drove her back to the front yard. He went so far as to enter the west box and toss her nesting material on the ground!

I was mystified at his behavior, until I realized that he may have wanted both his mates in sight at once. From the front yard box, he could keep an eye on the east box. The west box, where the widowed female wanted to nest, was blocked by our house; there was no sightline between it and the east box. If he was to have a chance of squiring two females and holding two territories at once, he had to keep an eye on both at all times. When the widow finally gave in and took a bill-ful of possum fur to the front yard box, he rewarded her with a soft caterpillar. His aggression ceased, and peace reigned. I marveled at this vehement demonstration of his preferences; it spoke to me of planning and forethought, an awareness of the way nest box placement played into his plan to raise broods with two females at once.

With greatly reduced help from him, the injured male's first mate raised a brood of five in the east box. But his affections clearly had been won by the widowed front yard female. When, on June 16, 1996, a new male arrived to woo the east box female, the two-timing male had little argument. He settled in with the front yard female and conceded his first mate to the interloper. He'd had two broods by two females at one time, though, a rarely achieved feat in the bluebird world.

Now that they were an official pair, the droopy-winged male and the widowed female seemed to need a name. I decided on the Troyers, after the Amish bluebirder and inventor Andy Troyer. He had sent me a nifty slot box and PVC baffle to try out, and it was here that the pair settled. The name Mr. Troyer fit the injured bluebird somehow; like Andy, he was intelligent, with a zest for life. He came to know our schedule and would appear like magic at breakfast, lunch, and dinnertime, peering into the appropriate windows with a gentle reminder that he'd like to eat, too. In the morning, when I was rising from bed and dressing, he'd perch on a cast-iron bell just outside the window and watch for me to raise the blind. When the two set to their mealworm feast, Mr. Troyer always let his mate eat her fill before feeding himself.

The pair seemed set on making bluebird history. While in 1994 and 1995, Mr. Troyer had managed to raise a total of only fourteen young with his first mate, in 1996, with the widow by his side, his production took off. That season alone, fourteen young in three broods fledged from the Troyers' box. (One of those was an orphan that I slipped into the box.) The 1997 season saw thirteen young in three broods, and 1998 resulted in seventeen fledged from four broods—a first for me in Ohio. There was a downturn in 1999, when all but one of the Troyers' second brood died of bacterial enteritis; still they managed to fledge nine that year in three broods. Carefully paging through my notes, I found that Mr. Troyer had fathered and fledged no fewer than sixty-seven young in his eight years of nesting in our yard, an awesome output for a droopy-winged bluebird.

I have to take some credit—or blame—for this production, for it was unique among the fifteen bluebird boxes on our farm. Thanks to the close relationship we enjoyed with the pair, the Troyers were heavily subsidized with mealworms that I doled out onto the deck railing. Feeding them was easy and fun, and I enjoyed having the Troyers heckle me for food as I went about my chores. Spurred by this abundance of food, Mrs. Troyer usually had her first clutch complete by April Fools' Day, even as snow flew around the little slot box. In 1998, the banner year of four broods, I fed the pair as

June 25, '97

There's almost always a bluebird topping the old farm bell—the male fledgling preens while his sister sits in the shade underneath. They've just hatched. It's 95° and the sky is white.

many mealworms as they could eat. And I learned a lesson at their expense.

By the time their fourth and final brood of the year had fledged, at the astonishingly late date of September 14, 1998, the Troyers were clearly done in. Neither had followed a proper bluebird molting schedule, gradually replacing their feathers in late July through September. Instead, they looked like bad taxidermists' mounts. Mr. Troyer lost his tail all at once, and every feather on his head, and Mrs. Troyer didn't look much better. It was a wonder they were able to fly, much less feed their young. I realized that I had overtaxed their systems by offering too much food and encouraging them to raise one too many broods. I'd thrown their metabolisms off, and I clearly hadn't done them any favors. The fact was that they didn't need all those mealworms; the superabundance of food brought on overproduction and exhausted their energy reserves.

Sept. 14 1998 after four broods, the last fledging this day,
the Troyers look terrible, with three tail feathers
between them. In the frenzy to breed, they've missed
the midsummer molt.

Not only that, but I would find out later that mealworms are quite high in phosphorus, which can upset a bird's calcium balance and lead to a deficiency of this all-important mineral—a clue to why their feathers looked so shabby. All that fall, I watched and worried as cool weather came on and the Troyers still wore their shabby summer feathers. To my great relief, their smooth autumnal plumage finally emerged, and the Troyers looked good by mid-October. I resolved never to do that to any bird again and quit offering mealworms in anything but cold, wet, or icy weather.

By the spring of 1999, I realized that Mr. Troyer was getting old. A house sparrow had cornered him in his box and pecked the back of his head bald: another identifying mark for the bird who'd become a beloved neighbor to me. We tackled the house sparrow problem, trapping the offending pair, and the Troyers carried on with their fourth season together. It wasn't to be their best; that was the year bacterial enteritis killed all but one of their young in the second brood. After the Troyers abandoned her, I took her in and fed her until she was strong enough to be fostered into another box. Wisely, they switched boxes for their third brood, nesting on the west side of the house. That's the best way to avoid an infectious disease, I thought. I rinsed the first box with bleach and settled back to watch. I hoped Mrs. Troyer was pleased to finally occupy the box she'd chosen and been dissuaded from using three years earlier.

Five healthy young fledged from their third brood of 1999, and then construction started on an addition to our house, which effectively eliminated the Troyers' territory. Great gaping pits and piles of earth replaced their lush lawn and flower garden habitat. The Troyers wisely quit the premises. They'd appear first thing in the morning, a few fledglings in tow, and sit atop the chimney, surveying what had once been their yard. Then they'd fly off down the orchard to parts unknown. I felt terrible about it and promised them that we'd rebuild their old home better

Oct 8 03
The more I draw
from life the
harder it hits me;
There is not a
chance of getting it
even remotely right
unless the bird's
right in front
of me!

than ever once the addition was completed in the winter. I hoped they wouldn't desert us altogether, though I couldn't have blamed them if they did.

On a fine September day in 1999, the Troyers returned and asked for a handout as if nothing had ever happened. Their box was back up in the front yard, and they inspected it. From then on they were regulars, navigating the construction moonscape with aplomb. All winter they stayed around, accepting mealworm snacks at sunup and sundown, and disappearing deep into the woods during the day.

Spring crept on and buds started to swell, and the Troyers' thoughts turned to nesting once again. Mr. Troyer spent increasing periods sitting on and near the box, singing intermittently and waving his wings on fine mornings. What a trouper, what a life he'd had, I thought, and marveled that he was ready to start perhaps his ninth season of nesting, to feed and fledge yet more young. He was the first bluebird to nest on our farm, moving in the same spring that we did and nesting in the first box we ever put up. He'd weathered floods and drought and ice storms, construction and excavation, a sharpshin attack and a sparrow drubbing, and who knows what other vicissitudes that I hadn't had the privilege of witnessing. One summer he'd taken ill and developed a sneeze and cough, and he became sluggish and stopped feeding his young. I worried him through that, trying to figure out how to administer an antibiotic in his mealworms, but against the odds he recovered and carried on.

We'd intervened so often on his behalf that I suppose it was open to question whether Mr. Troyer was truly a wild bird. He should have been dead in 1993, and would have been, but for Bill. That was fifty-three young and seven years ago. Through it all, he taught me the ways of a bluebird, the thought processes of which he was capable, the dispassionate hedging of bets that led him to abandon a sickly brood and try again. I was desperately fond of him, his old droopy wing, and his bald spot.

The last time I saw him, he was perched on the front door awning, peering in the kitchen window at me as I played with our new baby, Liam, on the floor. "Mealworms? Aren't you forgetting my mealworms?" he seemed to say. Dutifully, I put them out, and he and Mrs. Troyer feasted. That afternoon, he was gone. The smooth, gunmetal blue male sharpshin who often strafed the yard might have borne him off without a trace, plucked him in the woods, littering the duff with bright azure feathers as he stoked his own frantic fire. I would never know what happened to Mr. Troyer.

That same afternoon, Mrs. Troyer was being escorted by a new male, a sleek, young thing, traces of juvenile plumage lingering about his throat, snappy and boisterous in movement and song. How quickly she allowed her mate to be replaced! They were a pair the same day. I should be more like her, I thought, willing to fast-forward to the next act. I suppose if my allotted span were less than a decade, I'd be better at it, but we humans have time to mull and grieve and reflect on a life well lived, no matter how small. I had held him in my hand, helped his young through rain and cold, changed his nests when parasites threatened, fed him in bitter cold and snow, spoken to him nearly every day for seven years.

I thought about human intervention and the debates around bird feeding. I have colleagues who view bird feeding as the equivalent of turning wild birds into backyard pets. I know birders who have never opened a bag of sunflower seed. Knowledgeable bluebirders maintain that bluebirds don't need a mealworm subsidy to thrive and raise young, and I know that, on the whole, they are right. When a week of cold rain hits in midsummer, soaking the adults and making it impossible for them to find food, many trail operators simply clean the starved nestlings out of the houses so the adults can start again. I, on the other hand, travel box to box with tweezers and mealworms, and feed the young birds through the hardship. It's not easy, and it's going overboard, I know, but I am compelled to do it, and I don't apologize for it. I feel responsible for these birds who have chosen to nest in my boxes.

My thoughts jumped to the larger issue: where would bluebirds, as a species, be without human intervention? When the long-term decline of bluebirds became evident in the 1960s, the nationwide move to provide housing for them was the largest single-species conservation effort ever launched. Thanks to pioneers like Lawrence Zeleny, who worked hard to make their plight known; thanks to thousands of dedicated bluebird trail operators across the nation and to state and national outreach organizations like the North American Bluebird Society, eastern bluebirds have rebounded. Their upright silhouettes mark telephone wires and fencerows across America.

In my experience with Mr. Troyer, I created a microcosm of the larger picture. By waving our arms at one hawk, we'd unwittingly allowed fifty-three more young bluebirds into the world. I'd had the privilege of chronicling the long and productive life of a single bird, whom I'd never have recognized had he not been marked by the hawk. I'd learned a valuable lesson about nearly loving birds to death with too much of the wrong food. My little girl, Phoebe, had known the magic of providing for wild birds who would come to within an arm's length when she called to them. We had intervened, and we were much the richer for it. One bluebird had made the world a more beautiful place for us, and his memory, a small azure flame, burns in my heart.

# Tree Swallow

## The Early Bird Wins My Heart

MARCH 23: He sits on the old phone line running into the house, the one I wouldn't let the telephone company crew take down when they finally buried our line. Yes, it was unsightly and no longer necessary, but where would the tree swallow rest when he came back each spring? Where would the barn swallows line up to chatter like wind-up toys? Where would the bluebirds arrange their nestlings' fecal sacs like a string of dubious pearls? I look up at the indigo and white bird on the wire. His small, flat head turns side to side as I walk directly under him, talking to him, congratulating him on another migration completed. He peers down and chirrups like a friendly parakeet. Our tree swallow is back.

I haven't always been such a fan of tree swallows. As a nascent bluebird land-lord in the early 1980s, I saw them as rivals for the few nest boxes I was able to maintain. I hated to see a pair, three, or even four tree swallows gang up on an eastern bluebird, driving it to the ground and sometimes even injuring or killing it. So ferocious was the competition for nest boxes that I had to pair them wherever I mounted them, lest the swallows outcompete the birds I really wanted. Such was the case in Connecticut, where tree swallows are abundant. I had to move to southern Ohio to realize how much I missed them. In 1992, we knew of only one

location in our county where tree swallows nested, in a flooded backwater with lots of hole-riddled dead trees. Over the ensuing twenty years, tree swallows have dramatically expanded their breeding range, likely a response to the increasing popularity of bluebird nest box trails. They are now firmly established through-out Ohio and breeding as far south as the Carolinas. Not only that, but in 2006 they began to take advantage of Ohio's longer breeding season to double-brood in my nest boxes, something that was unheard of in New England. The leopard may not be able to change its spots, but, given time, the tree swallow can push out two broods in a single season.

Tree Swallow,
just hatched—
a surprise
wild turkey
feather in
the nest.

18

Everything in the tree swallows' makeup seems to be geared to taking over scarce nesting cavities. They appear in March, inspecting cavities before flying insects may be widely available, clinging to life by eating things such as hard, waxy bayberries and even sedge and bulrush seeds. Still they rush to nest and lay eggs, and I worry about the adults when the temperatures dip below freezing. Sometimes tree swallows pile up together in nest boxes, sharing their body warmth, waiting out the cold in a torporlike state. And they will bask in periods of sunshine. But what will they find to eat? With years of observation behind me, I don't fret quite as much now.

In southern Ohio, it's fairly common for tree swallows to lay a full clutch of five or six eggs, then be forced to abandon them temporarily when the weather turns foul. Our birds head en masse to the Ohio River, where they subsist on aquatic insect hatches until the weather warms and their usual insect prey becomes abundant again. I've learned to trust them to return.

The mysteries locked in the heads of swallows, in their pearly pink eggs, are greater and deeper than we can fathom. I've seen this scenario time and time again. A pair of tree swallows arrives in March, builds a nest through April, then lays eggs in May. Cold, wet weather arrives, the flying insect supply dwindles to nothing, and the birds vanish, leaving their partially incubated eggs cold in the nest. My first instinct is to remove the nest, to allow the birds to start over. And yet, knowing something of swallows, I hesitate and leave the clutch. A week goes by; the eggs lie cold. I envision the squirming embryos stilled, killed.

But a clutch of tree swallow eggs, partially incubated, then left untended for a week, will still hatch. Not all may survive, but most of them will hatch. The tree swallow knows that; the bluebird knows it, too. I've documented it on our farm time and time again: the "abandoned nest" with its stone-cold eggs suddenly reclaimed when sunshine and warm temperatures return. It defies reason, and yet it

happens. First, do no harm: I caution people who call or write with questions about their nest boxes to trust the birds to know what they're doing, no matter how screwy it seems to us. So many well-intentioned landlords throw out cold eggs, unaware of the birds'
greater plan, and thinking, as humans usually do, that we know best. Only occasionally is that true.

And so I reflect on my tree swallow wars—when I favored bluebirds over them, when I thought I knew what was right—with a tinge of shame. It has taken me years to realize that in only two instances can I justify species discrimination, and that's when European starlings or house sparrows (both invasive exotic birds) take over a nest box meant for native species. Deciding, on the other hand, that a bluebird should take precedence over a tree swallow is like stating that a tulip is a better flower than a daffodil. It's an arbitrary choice and has no basis in reality. Living without tree swallows, I came to miss them terribly, and the turtlelike head of a swallow, poking out of one of my nest boxes to watch me as I walk up, always splits my face in a grin. Each spring, we buy bags of white chicken and goose feathers from craft stores, tossing them up into the mild air, listening for the snap of a swallow's bill as it snatches the prize from the sky. Our tree swallows have lavishly lined nests, and studies in Michigan have shown that the more feathers line a tree swallow nest, the more young fledge from it. Insulation is the key to survival if a bird would nest in cruel April.

The swallows come to know us, some even to trust us. Sometimes a female won't budge off her eggs after I open the box, and I can gently move her with my finger to get a count, then close the box and leave her still sitting. Their liquid twitters, like paper clips being shaken in a little tumbler, define early spring just as much as clear light and bursting buds, periwinkle skies and high, hazy clouds. Skies with tiny triangles swooping, twittering, jingling—skies graced with tree swallows.

Tree swallows have taught me that birds, their distribution and behavior, are much more fluid than we realize. That a species's range can expand many hundreds of miles in a few years; that the incubation period of their eggs can fluctuate from twelve to twenty-two days, depending on the weather. That almost nothing where birds are concerned is set in stone. They are creatures of change, creatures of air, their only charge to adapt to a capricious environment in the best way they can.

# Speaking of Starlings

IT'S TEMPTING to dismiss the European starling as a nuisance; a greedy, filthy pig of a bird, known only for the myriad ways in which it inconveniences or disgusts us. In winter, when they're gobbling down the suet dough I mix up for the birds I want at my feeders, I think of a starling as nothing more than a capacious digestive tract propelled by a set of triangular wings. Input, output; they wolf down my homemade bird food, process it, and deposit it seemingly seconds later all over my porch.

And yet . . . catch a starling in spring sunshine, glowing with oily green and purple, tiny buff stars (the "starlings" of its poetic name) running down its back and under its tail. Look for the turquoise glow at the base of its corn yellow bill. And as soon as it perceives that it is the focus of your interest, it will be gone. If starlings know anything, they know how we despise them. There is a mind under that sloping forehead, behind the small, glittering eyes set low by the corners of its bill.

On a busy street in Marietta, Ohio, only a block from the *Bird Watcher's Digest* office, I stop for a red light and watch a starling on the wire overhead. It is flying repeatedly down to a spot in the middle of the intersection. I wonder what food could so entice it to dodge traffic again and again. Drawing closer, I see it walking

Three years later I finally have another brood of starlings to paint.
Healthy and mite-free, and in a much more salubrious spring - warmer and
perfectly sunny but moist. The chick bears a strong yeasty odor from its
already - funky, damp nest. No organized fecal sacs and a lot of liquid
in the droppings foil the adults' attempts at hygeine. I'm impressed at the
strength of its grip. Dawn is long and yellowish, voice a reedy squeaky chirp.
Rt. Eye has just opened today. It is already taking an interest in its surroundings.
What a huge chunk of gargoyly chick to enjoy! I hold it in my palm to keep it warm.

12:50-1:40 pm May 6 2008 Day 8. Phew! A strong, pungent, metallic, almost snakelike odor
emanates from the chick today. Stroking the top of its head elicits gapping, and I feed
it moistened parrot chow 3x, taking away 3 huge fecal sacs in 50 min

tight circles around another starling, just killed. It steps aside as the cars roar past, then returns to the dead bird's side. It can only be the starling's mate. An hour later, I see the bird, still sitting on the wire, still watching what is now just a paste of feathers, unrecognizable to any but its mate.

In the course of painting the development of a nestling, I spent two weeks regularly raiding a starling nest in a plastic martin gourd in our yard. I'd take the baby out at the same time each morning, sketch and paint it from life, then re-place it in its nest. I was impressed with the sheer heft and size of the nestling, compared to all the other birds I'd worked with. It had a strong, rank, horsy odor, and I wondered at the reports that starlings make good eating, making a mental note never to try one. But what impressed me most was the palpable intelligence in this creature as it changed over the course of two weeks from a formless blob of pink protoplasm to a feathered youngster. One eye slit opened on Day 7, and the bird turned its head from side to side, taking in its surroundings and acting on the information it was able to collect. Unlike any other week-old bird I'd worked with, it seemed to be hatching a plan to escape, its mind well ahead of its still-helpless body.

On its eighth day, the nestling figured out that I'd feed it as I worked, and it gobbled down moistened parrot chow, snuggling into my hand for warmth. On the ninth day, it shivered pitifully, for it was still devoid of feathers, just a large pink dollop of guts, topped by enormous yellow clown lips. The drawing stage of the portrait finished, I cradled it to my chest as I painted its likeness. It stopped shivering and asked for food. It would have been easy to fall for this creature, as homely as it was, for the consciousness that glimmered behind its eyes. Mozart kept a pet starling that could whistle parts of his concertos, with its own improvisations and additions. When it died, three years later, he held a funeral, with invited guests in full mourning dress. His eulogy speaks of the composer's sense of loss:

A little fool lies here
Whom I held dear—
A starling in the prime
Of his brief time
Whose doom it was to drain
Death's bitter pain.
Thinking of this, my heart
Is riven apart.
Oh reader! Shed a tear,
You also, here.
He was not naughty, quite,
But gay and bright,
And under all his brag
A foolish wag.
This no one can gainsay

And I will lay
That he is now on high,
And from the sky,
Praises me without pay
In his friendly way.
Yet unaware that death
Has choked his breath,
And thoughtless of the one
Whose rime is thus well done.
              —June 14, 1787

I kept a starling for several weeks, having agreed to release it for a friend who, with a little instruction from me, had hand-raised it. (I had decided to devote myself to a robin and a catbird instead.) Einstein, as she named it, enjoyed riding on my shoulder as I moved around the house and yard, and I liked the bird, even when it would suddenly insert its closed bill into my ear canal or (worse) my nostril. It would then gape widely, turning its bill into a miniature but very powerful speculum and eliciting a startled yelp from its caretaker. This is the same behavior starlings employ when looking for grubs in a lawn: stab, gape, gobble; stab, gape, gobble. I'm not sure what it was looking for in my nose and ear; perhaps simply the drama of my reaction.

Einstein's release was a fairly swift endeavor, compared to those of other songbirds I'd raised. The starling set to poking about in the lawn with gusto. On its first full day outside, I heard a tap on the studio window. Einstein was standing on the windowsill with a shiny nickel in its bill. When I emerged from the house with my palm full of mealworms, Einstein dropped the nickel into my hand. Though the nickel didn't go far in paying for the fifty thousand mealworms it took to feed the young starling, I certainly felt richer for my brief contact with this brainy bundle of fat and feathers.

Starlings invest a great deal of care in their broods, and they are not as prolific as their numbers might suggest. In Ohio, they are single-brooded, laying eggs in April and investing all their time and attention in the young through the end of May. Comparing notes with purple martin landlords, who spend much of their time battling interloping starlings, I learned that if an Ohio starling has not laid eggs by June 1, it is not likely to attempt nesting at all that season.

I found their strategy interesting in its contrast to that of most other garden birds I'd studied. While open-cup nesters such as field and chipping sparrows leave the nest at the impossibly tender age of one week, and robins stay as long as

fourteen days, cavity-nesting birds such as bluebirds remain in the nest for an average of eighteen days. Starlings hang on for as long as twenty-one to twenty-four days—longer even than tree swallows or purple martins. Why should this be? The answer seems to lie in their post-fledging behavior.

Young starlings, in sharp contrast to sparrows and bluebirds, burst from the nest completely feathered, with substantial tails, and flying well. From that moment on, they accompany their parents as the adults forage. While sparrows, warblers, robins, and bluebirds "stash" their offspring in thick cover, returning to feed them dozens of times a day, starlings take the kids along. It's easy to see them in June, soot gray fledglings trundling behind their parents on emerald lawns, voicing a harsh and insistent *krrrr!* Such early mobility in the young birds heralds an unusually short juvenile dependency period—as little as one day, or as long as twelve days—when the parent birds feed their young, gradually decreasing the subsidy until the fledglings are on their own. At this point, juvenile starlings gang up in flocks, presumably learning about food, predators, and life as they go. Could this aspect of their biology be an Achilles' heel?

Inconceivable as it may be to those of us who wave flocks of starlings off with a broom as they denude a suet feeder or a fruiting dogwood, starlings are declining across much of Europe and are red-listed (designated a species of highest conservation concern) in the United Kingdom. Changes in the survival rate of first-year birds seem to be the single greatest factor in the decline, with food availability a major contributor. Since starlings so closely follow human-altered landscapes, using artificial structures as nest sites and lawns as feeding grounds, things as simple as changes in turf management, new pesticides, and watering regimes could have a large impact on starling foraging success.

There are many in North America who express the desire to see the starling exported back to its native Europe by the container load on a slow boat. We still have far too many. But the species's precipitous decline in Europe could herald an ecological change that as yet escapes our perception. I'm of two minds on starlings; half of me respects their rough-and-tumble spunk and their piercing intellect, while the other half bemoans their negative impact on native nesting birds like flickers, red-headed woodpeckers, and bluebirds, whose cavities they usurp every spring. It would be ironic should starlings be decimated in their native land, leaving North America as their population stronghold. Are we ready to be the global keepers of a species we despise, a bird we poison and roust wherever it attempts to roost?

As much as we try to spurn it, the starling hangs on to our structures and our way of life. With a gift for mimicry, it renders startling imitations of car alarms, barking dogs, yelling children, clanking machinery, and sundry birdsongs in its rapid-fire monologues. As much as I enjoy their songs and their portly presence on my lawn, I stop at allowing starlings to take over our flicker and purple martin nest boxes. I try to throw out their nesting material as soon as it appears. One spring I got lazy, and a pair of starlings went so far as to lay a clutch of pale blue eggs in the flicker house.

Now, throwing nesting material out of a birdhouse is one thing, but throwing starling eggs out is tough. There's life in each little capsule, and discarding eggs bothers me. Still, I told myself I'd do it. Right after I finished the laundry. I pinned the clothes up on the line, enjoying the fresh breeze and the rare, warm, early spring sunshine. The starling sang from a telephone wire overhead, whistling and barking, grunting and wheezing, the way starlings do. I loved listening to his ever-changing bird station.

It was peaceful out there, just me, a basket of wet clothes, and the starling. Our toddler, Liam, was teetering on the edge of abandoning his afternoon nap, but I'd fought him down this time, and I had a couple of hours off-duty. He was napping. His bedroom window was right over my head. And I heard his voice. "Mommy? Mommy?"

Ack! So much for downtime. But the soft, sweet voice had come from my right, from the pointed bill of the starling perched on the telephone wire. Mouth agape, I listened, smothering amazed laughter. As a little experiment, I called softly to him. "Mommy?" The starling paused, then answered, "Maa! Maa!" in Liam's voice. My plans to toss his nest and pale blue eggs into the weeds evaporated on the spot.

The talking starling and his mate raised five sooty nestlings in our flicker box. When they finally left the nest, I took the box down. I liked that starling, but we don't need any more of them here. A starling comes around every spring, singing hopefully about the place, but he's going to have to come up with something else to amaze me if he's to get back in my flicker nest box. I keep glancing at the eaves, expecting a dew-spangled spider web that reads, "TERRIFIC!" or "RADIANT!" or "SOME STARLING!" to appear. Some people say the animals talk at midnight on Christmas Eve. I don't know about that. Here, it happened about noon, on a sunny spring day.

# Chickadee

## Tough Tit

I THINK OF CHICKADEES—Carolinas are the ones with which I've had the most experience—as tiny corvids. They're like mini-jays, with much the same appetites, intelligence, boldness, and abilities—wrapped in tiny, fluffy packages. Chickadees are not necessarily as nice as they are cute. My friend the humorist Al Batt says he thanks God chickadees aren't the size of hawks. Nobody would go outside. Open a nest box with an incubating chickadee, and it may hiss, then strike like a snake, hitting its beak against the nesting material with enough force to give you pause. My heart always races, and I jump, repeating the mantra, "It's only a chickadee. It can't really hurt you." Offer it a finger, and it may give you a good bite before quitting the premises, though. Chickadees are scrappers.

I began to awaken to the true nature of chickadees when I got a bright idea that turned out in practice to be a dumb one. I thought I might mount two nest boxes on the same pole, one atop the other. The top box had a one-inch hole, meant for chickadees, and the bottom box had a one-and-a-half-inch hole, intended for bluebirds. I thought I was a pretty slick nest box landlord when my plan unfolded perfectly. Carolina chickadees claimed the bottom box, and eastern bluebirds built a grass nest in the top one. The chickadees were building their moss nest while the bluebird was laying eggs just above. And one by one, the bluebird eggs disappeared as they were laid. Finally, I set up watch on the box and saw one of the chickadees disappear into the bluebird box, perhaps to make sure no more eggs had been laid.

There wasn't much left to do but remove the bluebird box, leave the chickadees undisputed rulers of their neighborhood, and relocate the bluebirds. Who'd have thought a sweet little chickadee would remove bluebird eggs? I thought back to several other occasions when I'd had mysterious egg disappearances in bluebird nest boxes. Since all my boxes are baffled with two-foot lengths of six-inch stovepipe, snakes and mammals could not be at fault. When a sprig or two of moss would appear in the pirated nest, I'd have a clue as to the perpetrator. (Carolina chickadees like to use green moss in their nest foundations.) In most cases, the chickadees never moved in; they just removed the bluebird eggs. It's possible that chickadees remove eggs from the nest boxes they're simply considering for takeover, or to lessen competition for food within their territories. Lesson learned. I'd make no more bird condos.

It's hard to say whether the behavior birds exhibit in artificial nest boxes (especially two mounted one right on top of the other) is a true reflection of what goes on in natural cavities, so I give chickadees the benefit of the doubt. They're nowhere near the egg pirates that house wrens are, but it's clear that they have the potential to be home wreckers—something few of us who are dazzled by their black-capped charm at our feeders might suspect.

We put a box up in the orchard in 2005 just for Carolina chickadees. The entrance hole is only one inch across, which rules out anything but chickadees and house wrens as nesters. It stood empty that year, suffering the attempts of a downy woodpecker to hack into it, but on April 9, 2006, I was elated to find that

A Carolina chickadee cleans out her upstairs bluebird neighbors. Whoops. Stacking the nest boxes wasn't a good idea after all.

the inside front of the box had been laboriously chipped away, making a three-quarter-inch-thick layer of fine splinters on the bottom of the box. Only a chickadee could have gained access to do this—a natural, albeit unnecessary excavating behavior. Over the wood splinters was laid a four-inch carpet of dry green moss. Atop the moss layer was a fine, buff mass of plant down, filamentous inner bark, and deer and rabbit hair—the softest bedding imaginable. I thought of the Jedd bird, in *Dr. Seuss's Sleep Book*, whose bed is: "the softest of beds in the world, it is said."

By April 24 the nest was complete, with a deep cup, almost a tunnel, of plant down, fur, and feathers cradling six rufous-flecked eggs. Female chickadees carefully cover their eggs with a flap of this soft bedding whenever they leave the box during the laying period, a bit of calculating behavior that I find quite endearing. It doubtless keeps the eggs warm, and it may also reduce egg destruction by house wrens.

For the first couple of years that I had a nest box trail, in the early 1980s, I would check chickadee boxes and find no eggs, then be amazed to find a complete clutch of six or even seven eggs the very next day, already under incubation. I learned to feel gently down through the layers of fur and fiber for the smooth domes of the eggs. The cinnamon-speckled white eggs are so tiny and fragile that it's easy to poke a hole in them with an errant fingernail—you really can't be too careful. They're much too small to handle safely with big, clumsy fingers. Looking for eggs, I've learned to peel the flap of fur away from the nest cup like a blanket, rather than risk breaking an egg by trying to feel for it. I find myself wondering how a bird weaves such a blanket with only a bill as a tool, and marveling.

Though spring is my busiest season, with birding festivals and speaking engagements all around the country, I was particularly anxious to be home when the orchard chickadees hatched in early May 2006. I wanted to paint portraits of the chicks each day as they grew and developed. This series of nestling paintings is a self-guided, intermittent project I've been working on for years. I had done the math, and I knew this clutch of six eggs was due to hatch on Saturday, May 6, while we were working at a nature festival in West Virginia. We would get back late Sunday, and I knew I'd have to get with it the next morning in order to document as much of their lives as possible.

The softest of nests— a Carolina chickadee's. Goldenrod fiber, rabbit hair, green mosses and the fluff of milkweed and dogbane — the seven eggs gleaming in the deep tunnel of softness. I've never found parasites in a chickadee nest.

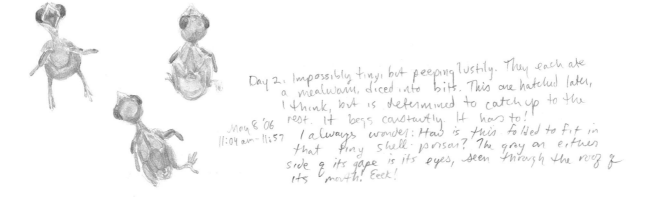

Day 2. Impossibly tiny, but peeping lustily. They each ate a mealworm, diced into bits. This one hatched later, I think, but is determined to catch up to the rest. It begs constantly. It has to!

May 8 '06
11:04 am – 11:57 I always wonder: How is this folded to fit in that tiny shell: poison? The gray on either side of its gape is its eyes, seen through the roof of its mouth. Eeek!

Sure enough, the eggs are replaced by squirming pink flesh when I open the box on Monday morning. Oh, they are impossibly tiny. I am delighted to find one that looks as if it had hatched a day later than the others, so for the first session I take two — the tiniest one and a medium-size chick. From the start, the smallest chick is active and vociferous, peeping loudly and standing up on its tarsometatarsi to beg. You'd better beg hard, I think. Does it know it is the runt? Does it know that its life depends on competing successfully with its larger siblings? Helpless to resist its nearly ultrasonic call, I dice up a small, tender mealworm and feed it with forceps. The older chick lies quietly. It is visibly larger and better filled out than its sibling, and it doesn't peep or beg. On this first day, I paint both the smallest chick and a larger sibling, and trust that I've recorded a two-day-old and a three-day-old chick for my project.

Chickadees hatch naked, and I am surprised to find no body down and only a small crown of down atop the head. Perhaps this is why the nest is the softest and warmest imaginable, why the chicks snuggle at the bottom of an eight-inch tunnel of feathers, fur, and plant fuzz. Birds hatching in open-cup nests are much downier; baby house finches, for instance, wear halos of bluish white head and body fuzz that cover them in their open nests like down comforters.

As I draw the nestlings, I think about what it is that makes them chickadees. They are very round and compact, with short necks and cobby bodies. Something I notice on Day 4 is the strength and coordination of their feet. I've never lifted a nestling that young that clung so well to the nest material, and even took some with it. Of course, grown chickadees make their living by clinging and hanging upside down. Any flights they make are fairly short—flits, really—from tree to tree. Locomotion and foraging have much to do with the legs and feet in chickadees. I am amused to see the nestlings occasionally flipping over on their backs in the nest as they beg for food, and just as quickly righting themselves with their hefty legs.

It is a stunning exercise, to be in on every day of a chickadee's development. I put the chick in a little plastic tub lined with tissues, observe it carefully, and paint it from life. Then I return it to the nest, to take it out at the same time the next day. It changes so much from day to day that I can hardly believe it's the same chick I had the day before. Unlike many other species I've worked with, this chick doesn't peep or beg. When I suddenly sneeze, I say "Excuse me!" in a small voice, and its bill flies open. I guess I sound like a chickadee to it. I stuff four tender white mealworms into its gaping bill. By feeding my subjects abundant, age-appropriate food, I try to return the favor of their temporarily modeling for me.

By May 11, it has turned windy, cold, and rainy, with the temperature dropping through the lower fifties by afternoon. It's dogwood winter, as they say in West

Day 3 · May 8 '06

This is the larger sibling of the chick in the three studies below. I have been slipping the runt a few extra tender mealworms when I replace the model chick each day. I want them all to thrive.

Virginia, cold laid over snow-white blossoms. I begin to worry about this brood. The weather forecast is for rain for the next six days. When I take the chick back to its nest, I feed as many of its siblings as will open their bills, then leave a stash of tender, newly molted white mealworms on the roof of the box for the adults to dole out. They accept my offering unhesitatingly. In anticipation of the cold spring rains that always seem to come when young birds are in the nest, I have laid in a supply of three thousand mealworms. I have a feeling I will be subsidizing a number of birds in the coming week. I do this by duct-taping plastic jar lids to the tops of the nest boxes and filling them with mealworms. The hard part of this painting project is worrying about my subjects, who become more precious to me with each passing day, as models and as individuals.

I'm increasingly intrigued by the smallest chick, which apparently is mysteriously and profoundly retarded in its development. At ten days old, it is still naked, an anomaly among its rapidly feathering nestmates. Its wings look like a seven-day-old's, but its body is the size of a five-day-old's. It has no spinal or cervical feather tracts showing, and yet its wing feathers are bursting their sheaths. I wonder and worry what will happen to it when the other four are ready to fly. Most of all, I'm amazed that it has survived this long. It begs more aggressively than its nestmates, as if trying to make up for its obvious shortcomings by ingesting as much food as possible.

I pass the next few days trotting out to replenish the mealworm cup and painting both normal and stunted nestlings. It rains steadily until May 17, when the temperature finally creeps into the upper sixties. By now, at Day 12, the normal chick I'm painting can perch on my finger. I take the runt in to paint at the same time, and it wraps its lilac-colored toes around its sibling's leg. How sweet! Its siblings look like fully feathered, clown-lipped versions of their parents; this one looks like a six-day-old. What will become of it when they fledge?

I have to stop my painting project when the chicks reach Day 13, because I risk frightening them from the nest before they're ready to fly. I wonder and worry about the runt. Is it still growing, however slowly? On Day 17, I can no longer stand the suspense. Silently, I open the box, and, with one finger, I count chickadee heads deep in the fur-lined tunnel of their nest. All five are present and warm to the touch. I close the box and hope that they will fledge late, giving the runt time to catch up.

On Day 23, the box stands empty, but the two fecal sacs still in the nest are soft and wet. I imagine they're from the runt, doubtless the last to leave. I envision it hopping on the ground, its parents still tending it, until it is finally able to fly. How I wish I could know what finally became of it. If the parents' dedication to its care continued after fledging, it had a good chance of finally becoming a chickadee. They'd pulled the brood through a soaking, cold week of dogwood winter, suffered my ministrations, and accepted my subsidy. I felt a part of them, happy that I'd contributed to their survival.

Seeing chickadees flit back and forth for what seems like an endless succession of sunflower seeds and peanut bits at my feeders, I wonder how much they depend on winter feeding stations. A study of Carolina chickadees showed that fully 7 percent more birds survive the winter when they have access to feeders. Like many birds, chickadees split their diet down the middle in winter, half being vegetable, the other half insects and their eggs. In summer, 90 percent of their sustenance derives from invertebrates. I've watched a Carolina chickadee land on

I watch, horrified but rapt, as a Carolina chickadee tears into a luna cocoon. It flies away with the pupa before I can see how it processes it. What a load of food for a rainy winter's day! I imagine that would be akin to my running with a 50 lb. sack of sunflower seed.

a twig and begin tearing at a large bullet-shaped, brown wad of leaves that I hadn't even realized was a silkworm moth cocoon until the bird showed it to me. Faced with a large prey item like a pupa, a chickadee will hold it in its toes and tear off bits — the miniature hawk image, complete.

In winter, Carolina chickadees are subordinate to the larger, stronger tufted titmice, which kick them out of their territories. The chickadees, in their turn, kick the smaller kinglets off their turf. It's a tough world out there, and these tiny, fluffy, deceptively cute scraps of energy are built to survive in it.

# Barn Swallow

## Old Friends and Eggshells

LITHE BIRDS of navy and rust, all wing and tapered tail, barn swallows seek out human-made structures for nesting, the bigger the better. Living cheek to jowl with barn swallows gives us the chance to appreciate their adaptability and ingenuity, should we choose to welcome them. Barn swallows inhabit my earliest childhood memories from my birthplace in South Dakota. I recall a salvo of alarm calls and the arrowlike swoop of birds overhead when I'd enter our garage. My parents left it open all summer so the barn swallows could nest there. Most people would deny them access, to keep them from dropping detritus on the cars, but my father loved them and encouraged them to nest in the rafters. Raised on a farm in Iowa, he missed country life, and I think nesting barn swallows brought a little, beautiful bit of it back for him.

Recently, barn swallows have entered not only garages and barns but large home-improvement stores. And they've entered the collective human consciousness as birds of remarkable intelligence. In multiple, unrelated instances in the United States and Japan, barn swallows have learned to hover before the motion-activated electric eye units that open and close sliding glass doors in warehouses and "big box" home-improvement stores. When the doors open, the birds enter

the protected interiors of the buildings to build and tend their nests, and exit to forage for flying insects in the same way. In a Home Depot in Maplewood, Minnesota, barn swallows have returned every year since 2000, opening and closing the garden center doors at will by hovering directly in front of the infrared beam of the electric eye. One assistant manager who locked the doors earlier than usual one evening was beset by swallows who swooped at him and protested vociferously until he unlocked the doors again. The colony had increased beyond a dozen pairs by 2009. Chances are good that offspring of the original pioneers are now exploiting this predator-free environment, having learned from their parents how to gain access (and, perhaps, how to bully store employees into keeping a bird-friendly schedule).

My family moved from South Dakota to a suburb of Kansas City, Kansas, and there were barn swallows in the garage on Wenonga Road. I remember sun hitting off the cement driveway, and the black, swooping fleurs-de-lis of swallows against a bright sky. Too soon, we moved to Virginia, where towering trees all but cut off our view of the sky, and I would spend the rest of my school years without barn swallows to watch.

Throughout my childhood, though, on our yearly trips to Iowa to visit relatives, my favorite time of all was evening on my uncle's farm near Hampton. We'd sit in Adirondack chairs as the Iowa sun, a defeated but still fierce orange ball, sank behind the grove. And we'd watch the barn swallows come out to catch flying insects in the low light, pumping smoothly over the lawn, arresting themselves in air with quick snaps of their bills, then resuming their tireless and ravishingly graceful flight. My aunt and uncle weren't bird watchers, but they loved to watch swallows, and they made time in the evening just for that. Surrounded by family in the dying light, the mingled scent of corn pollen, cattle, and hogs rising around us, we sipped 7UP from jewel-toned aluminum tumblers, watching in silent reverence the almost supernatural grace of barn swallows. For a bird-worshiping child, it didn't get any better than that. I hoped fervently that I'd live among swallows again someday.

Upon graduating college and leaving the last in a series of noisy little apartments in and around Cambridge, Massachusetts, in 1981, I promised myself that I would always live in the country, where crickets and katydids, owls and whip-poor-wills would sing me to sleep, and the din of traffic and sirens could fade away into memory. I fetched up on a sanctuary in East Haddam, Connecticut, owned by The Nature Conservancy. To my joy, there were barn swallows nesting in my landlord's garage. Like my father had, my landlord always left his garage open for the swallows; as one of the founders of The Nature Conservancy, Dick Goodwin lived gently on the earth. But he didn't much like droppings on the hood of his little pickup truck, so I climbed a ladder and hung an old umbrella upside down under the barn swallows' nest to catch the mud and droppings. I wanted to improve relations between this venerable conservationist and the birds I loved so much.

After that simple act, the barn swallows, formerly innocuous neighbors, were deeply suspicious of me. They didn't like the umbrella so close to their nest, and they remembered who had placed it there. To my dismay, they singled me out for persecution, swooping and clicking their bills next to my ear at the low points of their dives. *Kiveet! Kiveet!* they'd shrill, and pester me until I drew far enough away from the garage to defuse their aggression. I noted with bemusement that they had no such objection to my landlords; the Goodwins could walk in and out of the garage with impunity. Didn't the swallows understand that, in hanging the umbrella, I was trying to help them? No, they remembered that I'd climbed up to their nest and hung an oddly shaped thing under it, and they would hold a grudge indefinitely. Or so I thought.

One afternoon, as the swallows' chicks were nearing fledging age, I came home to pandemonium in the garage, a ruckus far more frantic than their usual objection to my getting out of my car. The resident swallows, joined by a number of other birds attracted to the commotion, were swooping and calling anxiously. The lanky loops of a five-foot black rat snake slithered smoothly along one high rafter. It was headed for the swallows' nest, and it would certainly clean out the plump nestlings if they didn't jump to sure injury on the garage floor below. I sized up the situation and gathered my courage. I've never much liked catching large snakes over my head while standing on a ladder. Maybe there's a word for that little cluster of phobias. *Stepnophidiophobia* works; I just coined it. If what one is frightened of is truly, ridiculously scary, is it fair to call one's fear a phobia?

I ran to the house and grabbed a pillowcase off my bed—always my preferred nonpoisonous-snake-carrying apparatus. I decided that a long-handled iron rake would be handy, too, given the size of the predator and its station high above the garage floor. I tucked the pillowcase into my pants and moved the ladder into position beneath the barn swallow nest. The snake froze, watching me. The swallows ceased their frenetic motion and landed in the rafters, watching the scene in eerie silence. I eased a rake tine into one of the snake's loops and carefully pulled it away from the rafter. It did not want to give up its perch, but, presented with a choice between coiling around the rake and falling, it chose to follow my suggestion. I lowered the rake into the pillowcase and shook the snake off the tines. A hushed twitter arose from the barn swallows as this icon of pure terror disappeared from view. Still they perched and watched.

I looked up and made eye contact with the birds. "There. I've got him now, and I'm going to take him for a ride down the road. He won't be back to eat your babies this year." I knotted the writhing pillowcase, folded the ladder up, and put it away. Still the swallows sat, their eyes glittering as they cocked their heads to watch me go. From that moment on, they never swooped at me again. I could walk beneath their nest with perfect impunity. The umbrella incident was forgotten or perhaps forgiven, replaced in their memory, I believe, with my removal of the snake. Could gratitude be part of a bird's emotional makeup? It was clear to me now that they could distinguish individual people and remember grievances and kindnesses alike. And, as I was to learn many years later, they could recognize people out of context, far from home.

I'd lived in the little cottage in Connecticut long enough to have built up some nice compost to use in my garden. I had brilliant jewel-toned nemesia and alyssum, valerian and other early spring flowers in bloom, and I fed them all with a top dressing of rich compost from the pit out back of the garden. There were coffee grounds and lettuce stubs, orange peels and rotten tomatoes, old carrots and cantaloupe and eggshells, to name just a few of the things that, through the magic of decomposition, had become plant food. In the spring, I rarely approached the compost pit without frightening a bird up off the refuse. Female prairie warblers, blue-winged warblers, redstarts, and blue-gray gnatcatchers were among those who haunted the pit. Even the gnatcatchers grubbed around in the compost, but for what?

I kept bluebird boxes all around the property, and half of them filled up with tree swallows. Early in the spring, I kept spooking tree and barn swallows out of the front flower bed. It's not often one sees a swallow on the ground, and their presence here was a mystery that needed to be solved. I stationed myself behind the curtain inside and waited for the swallows to alight. The birds weren't gathering nesting material, as I'd originally suspected. They were trundling around, picking up and avidly eating pieces of eggshell from the compost I'd spread among the flowers. Apparently, birds that feed on flying insects have a high requirement for calcium, and eggshells satisfy that need.

A light went on in my head. I began saving eggshells and baking them in a low oven until they started to brown around the edges, just to make sure they harbored no harmful bacteria from the eggs. Then I'd spread them on a big flat rock out in the yard, where the swallows had room to approach and take off. There would be no more grubbing in the flower bed for my swallows.

When we moved to Ohio, in 1992, I brought my eggshell-feeding habit with me. I'd bake the shells, crush them, and spread them on the paving stones that led up to the front door. A small flock of barn swallows keyed in to the bright white

offering and put our sidewalk on their feeding route. Years passed and our children were born, and it was time to put in a real sidewalk: a tricycle road, a place to draw with chalk and bounce a basketball. The swallows seemed to like feeding on the wide gray concrete path. When the trike and tractor traffic got too heavy, and the swallows had a hard time settling to feed, we started tossing handfuls of eggshells atop the garage roof. It was the perfect solution, because it gave the birds the remove they needed to feel comfortable while we went about our business in the yard below. Now, we could eat at the picnic table and watch the swallows scuttling around on the garage roof, picking up eggshells and gulping them down.

The flock has grown, and now there are as many as seventeen barn swallows visiting our garage roof four or more times a day. Over the years, we've put many small platforms up under our eaves, trying to entice barn swallows to nest there. One pair built a nest but never laid eggs. The more I watch barn swallows, the more convinced I become that they prefer nesting colonially, in large structures that afford many nest site options. We'd love to leave our garage open for them, but the raccoons would take the invitation just as readily. So try as we might, we've never had nesting barn swallows. We have to borrow them from our neighbors.

It's been twenty years since we moved to southern Ohio and started building a relationship with area barn swallows. They've learned our rhythms, and we've learned theirs. From early May to late August, they come in for eggshells first thing in the morning, a couple of times in the afternoon, and at dinnertime, arriving as a flock and leaving together. They come from the northwest and head back the same way. If the eggshells on the garage roof have all been eaten up or washed away by the rain, the swallows swoop conspicuously around the yard until they succeed in catching our attention. We obediently drop whatever we're doing to replenish the supply. Without much of a stretch, you could call it begging. Starting the lawn mower brings an almost instant escort of swooping swallows, as they forage for insects that are scared up by the roar and vibration. I've yet to figure out how they know I'm mowing. Can they hear it from where they live? And where in the blue yonder *do* they live? There is a large barn within sight of our home, but there are no swallows using it; the farmer keeps it shut tight all summer until the hay comes in.

You wouldn't think it would take a curious amateur ornithologist fifteen years to figure out where a flock of swallows might be coming from. But I figured it out only in August 2007. I was driving along a country road about four miles by car from home. There are two buildings that host barn swallows there: a cow barn and an open machine shed. As I drew alongside the machine shed, I noticed a line of swallows on the wires beside it. There were about twenty birds in the flock. I can't describe what happened next without raising the hair on the back of my neck. I slowed to a crawl, counting swallows through the windshield. They craned their necks and looked down at me. A jolt of recognition shot through me to them, and back again. "It's *you!*"

As one, the birds lifted off the wire and headed southeast, flying high and strong. A smile spread across my face. I knew where they were going. My old car leapt forward as I gunned the engine. The swallows beat me home and were swooping low over me as I came up the sidewalk. I glanced at the garage roof. The eggshells were almost gone. I took a handful out of the big jar in the garage and threw them with all my might onto the shingles. It felt good to know where my old friends lived.

# Carolina Wren

## Kitchen Sink Ornithology

LIVING IN THE MIDDLE of nowhere, working from my home studio, I have to confess that I'm fond of e-mail. I've got an all-but-defunct account that I check sporadically, just to make sure there's not something important buried in the piles of spam that drove me away from it in the first place. And there, glimmering in the dross, was a week-old nugget from Louisiana State University's resident ornithologist-artist John O'Neill, inviting me to show some paintings at an upcoming ornithological meeting. The concept behind the show, he explained, was to showcase work by ornithologists who also paint. My first reaction? He must be thinking of someone else. I'm no ornithologist; I'm a naturalist, a bird painter. But I was touched by the generosity and apparent looseness of John's definition of an ornithologist, and I gladly accepted his invitation.

Then I sat back and thought for a bit. Well, maybe I am an ornithologist. I do study birds, each and every day, in between meeting illustration and writing deadlines and fetching Popsicles for the kids. There's a pair of binoculars in every room of the house, sometimes three, and they are as necessary to my everyday life as water and air. I just had to interrupt this sentence to train them

Female
Blackburnian
arrives
May 18 2009

on a female Blackburnian warbler in the birch outside the studio window. To find a pen and write that arrival down in my nature notes.

This, I think, is the heart of science. Seeing a Blackburnian warbler is nice, but it really doesn't mean much unless I write it down. *(May 18, 2009. Arrived: Female Blackburnian in the birches. Had seen only males until today.)* Suddenly, there's context and meaning in this chance observation. Male Blackburnians come through first, a week or two before the females. When I start seeing females of these northern nesters on the move, I know spring migration is winding down. But I wouldn't know that if I hadn't been watching and writing for thirty years.

Nothing is beneath an alert naturalist's notice. There is always something new to be discovered, some context that will make a birding experience more meaningful. Since my childhood in the suburbs of Richmond, Virginia, I have loved Carolina wrens. Their ringing duets and spritely movements straight-arm winter away. Even those who love them may not know that these little birds are the only species of a large tropical genus, *Thryothorus*, that makes it up into the States. Go to Costa Rica, Brazil; watch the riverside wren, the buff-breasted wren, and see if those white eyebrows and brilliant melodies strike a familiar note. Like their tropical congeners, Carolina wrens stay in pairs the year around, and they holler back and forth to each other through the dense underbrush, often duetting, their notes so closely spaced that they seem to come from a single bird: a single bird with two heads, ten yards apart. It's a great way to stay in touch when you can't see each other, the avian equivalent of a cell phone.

"What are you doing?"

"Grubbing around for wood roaches. And you?"

"Not much. Just wanted to hear your voice."

"Well, I'm here, but I may flit up to check the nest now."

"Need company?"

"Sure."

So might go the conversations of mated pairs of *Thryothorus* wrens the New World over.

As an AWOL undergraduate and field assistant at the National Institute of Amazonian Research (INPA) in Manaus, Brazil, I sometimes had the unhappy duty of preparing study skins of birds that had been mist-netted in various types of rainforest habitats. Tears mingled with powdered borax as I raced the equatorial heat to skin, preserve, stuff, and sew up the feathered pelts of the euphonias, antbirds, woodcreepers, manakins, wrens, and others that the graduate student to whom I was indentured was collecting. As I skinned and sorted through the organs of these tropical birds, I noticed things, things I could never have learned without opening stomachs and skulls. And, being a naturalist at heart, I couldn't help but be fascinated, and add what I observed to the body of knowledge I was building about the birds on the wing. Cleaning the skulls of various species of *Thryothorus* wrens, I noticed that they are very brainy birds. Though I never weighed or measured, they seemed to have almost twice the brain mass that a sparrow of similar body size might. Over the years, I've seen ample evidence of this braininess in their everyday behavior.

When we moved to our southeast Ohio property, in 1992, we had no nesting Carolina wrens. We'd hear them singing in back of some of the broken-down outbuildings on the road to our place, but our lone house on its naked lawn held little allure for these denizens of underbrush and toolshed. Not until we planted shrubs and trees, not until the orchard grew up to briar and rose, not until the white-footed mice chewed portals in the scabrous wooden garage door were we graced with Carolina wrens. This took eight years, a little planting, and much laziness on our part.

In the summer of 2001, I watched our pioneering pair of Carolina wrens raise

their first brood in a rotted stump in the orchard. To my delight, they then began prospecting in the garage. I'd see them flutter up whenever I'd enter the garage and assume they'd blundered in by chance. Slow to catch on, and thinking they were trapped inside, I kept hoisting the heavy door open for them, until I saw one cock its tail, look me in the eye, bob once, and slip out a mousehole in the closed door. They had figured out where the entrance was long before I had.

By then, it was June, and the black rat snakes were active, and the wrens may have judged the garage a bad risk for eggs and young. I saw one trying to wedge rootlets and leaves in the kink of a gutter pipe under the house eave, right by the front door. The nesting material kept falling down. "Hold on. I can help," I said to the wren. "You just watch." And it waited on the gutter as I ran for a stepladder, some wire, and a little copper bucket. I wedged the pail atop the gutter pipe and wired it securely under the eave, with just an inch or two clearance, weatherproof and snakeproof. The wren watched. Even as I was climbing down the ladder, I saw it fly to the bucket, peek inside, fly down to strip the moss from the bases of my bonsai trees, and begin filling the pail with nesting material. The pair worked furiously, and by nightfall they had a nest roughed out in its copper bottom.

I watched and wrote, climbed up to the bucket to peer inside. Even amateur ornithologists should confirm their suspicions. A wren brought a tiny spider to the nest on the morning of June 16. Out came the stepladder. Four new pink hatchlings writhed in the nest. *The Birds of North America*, my favorite comprehensive life-history reference, cites the average age of fledging as 12.2 days in Alabama, with a range from 10 to 16 days. I watched, waited, wrote. On the morning of July 4, at the ripe age of 19 days, four fledgling Carolinas made minor ornithological history as they leapt from the bucket, three days behind the latest recorded fledging.

There was more to learn. With the 2002 nesting season, I had another surprise coming. I knew that thryothorine wrens were thought to be monogamous, year-round. The ornithological term is *genetic monogamy*. In other words, they're programmed on the cellular level to be faithful. I always saw the pair together as they foraged, in snow or sun. They roosted in the bucket or the garage all winter, protected from the elements. They built a nest in a plastic grocery bag hanging from a nail in the garage, laying two eggs by March 25. Peace reigned. Then, on March 29, 2002, a third wren appeared in our yard. This event was heralded by furious singing. Two wrens rolled on the ground, ferociously pecking at each other's vents (ouch!) and clutching each other's faces with sharp claws. A third bird stood to the side, singing vigorously. I watched, fascinated, ready to intervene should the fight prove deadly. All three disappeared behind the garage. Quiet fell. The interloper, apparently alone, was vanquished, or so I thought.

A week later, the two eggs were still cold in the garage nest. Then, on April 11, I spooked an incubating female off a second nest in the mess I call my recycling center, really just a mound of plastic grocery bags full of other plastic grocery bags. Four eggs hatched on April 26, the young wrens soon peering, bright-eyed, from their plastic-insulated lair as I went to and from my car. At the same time, only fifty feet away, I saw one of the wrens begin to refurbish the old bucket nest under the eave. Well, maybe the male is going to use that for a roost, I thought. Wrong. On May 5, I saw an adult take a tiny spider to the bucket. Hold on a minute. There was an active nest with nine-day-old young in the garage! Out came the stepladder. Five tiny new hatchlings writhed in the bucket nest. A huge grin spread across my face. I had seen the male wren take food into the garage, return to the mealworm feeder, and take food to the bucket nest. That third wren that showed up at the end of March must have been a lone female. He was hosting two females on two nests at the same time!

Thomas M. Haggerty, in his *Birds of North America* account, reports a case of suspected polygyny in northwestern Alabama, with two females nesting in the

CAROLINA WREN 🖋 59

territory of a single male. The male assisted at the first nest but not the nest of the second female. *Suspected* is the operative word here, because, like Dr. Haggerty, I can't be absolutely sure there's not a fourth wren sneaking around in the picture. Because the literature states that only the female Carolina wren incubates (only she develops a brood patch), and because there were eggs being simultaneously incubated in both nests from April 21, when incubation started in the bucket nest, through April 26, when the garage nest hatched, I knew there had to be two females present. I knew that the resident male's territory encompassed both the garage and the eave where the bucket hung. I suspect that the same male fertilized both clutches, and I'm certain he tended both nests, since I watched him take food from the mealworm feeder into the garage, then reenter the feeder and take food to the bucket nest.

My interpretation of events goes like this: a single pair of wrens built the early nest in the garage, and the female laid two eggs. While she was completing the clutch, a second female arrived, took over the garage, built another nest, and drove the original female out to the bucket nest. The male, seeing a chance to send his genes out nine times over, took that opportunity to redefine monogamy. Mating with both females, he housed both on the same territory. He did feed young in both nests, until the garage nest fledged on May 8 and the garage female took those four young into the woods. Then, he turned his attention full-time to the bucket nest. A serial monogamist, to put it kindly. And the vent pecking between the two tussling birds—likely females? A scientifically recognized bird's way of trying to interrupt insemination is removing sperm from the interloper's cloaca. I envisioned a clandestine tryst between the resident male and the interloping female, interrupted by his original mate. *Give me back his DNA, you hussy!* Yeow! I was thankful that I could envision no human parallels for this specific behavior.

The bucket nest fledged on May 17. The five young were in the nest at nightfall and out on the ground beneath it, only eleven days old, the next morning. Clustered together, bills out, they looked like a single clump of soft cocoa brown feathers. The parents, seeing us watching them through the foyer window, gave a signal, and the clump exploded, tiny wrens buzz-bombing low over the flower beds. They bivouacked at the fishpond. Both adults led them toward the woods. An adult would fly to a fledgling's side, linger a moment, then fly to the next logical perch, and call. The fledgling would immediately launch for that perch, landing neatly beside the adult. One baby, still lacking its tail, could fly only half as far as the other four. The adult took it to the woods in a series of shorter flights, leading it in much shorter stages. Brains.

Since that day, thirty-five (and counting) baby Carolina wrens have been raised in the copper pail, and we've watched the fledglings flutter out time and time again, adding motion and music to our lives. There were five nestlings in the summer of 2008, and they lined up on the downspout before making their first stuttering flights into the world. Well, four of them did.

When Carolina wrens leave the nest, they don't mess around. One minute, everything's quiet; the next minute, baby birds are shooting out of the nest like popcorn. The parent birds work in shifts, calling and encouraging the young to hop and flutter to the nearest deep cover. Somehow, the adult birds keep them all together and feed them for the next three weeks, as their wings strengthen and their foraging skills develop.

So I was alarmed to find one baby wren, all bright eyes and yellow clown lips, still perched by the bucket after its four siblings had gained the safety of the woods. Surely a parent would return for it. One hour, then two went by, and the fledgling was hungry, chirping constantly for help. Oh, dear. I did not want to be a teenage wren's mother for the next three weeks. I listened—nothing from the silent woods. By now, the family could be hundreds of yards away. What to do?

It was time for a little technology. I grabbed my iPod, which is fully loaded with the songs and calls of nearly every North American bird. I ran to the edge of our woods and dialed up the song of the Carolina wren. *Please, please, let this work.* I played it at full volume. No response. Desperate, I dialed up the alarm call of the wren and blasted it down into the silent tangle of raspberry and sumac. *Danger! Danger!* the recording shrilled in wrenspeak. An adult wren shot right past my head, flying straight toward the forgotten baby in the copper bucket. The recalcitrant fledgling buzzed out to meet it. Baby wren: last seen, headed toward the safety of the woods, in the company of a parent. Nature geek: smiling broadly.

The intrigue, the interventions, and the observations will continue. At this point, who could stop? Catfights, a two-timing male, abandoned babies to be rescued . . . the drama keeps coming. Carolina wrens are tiny birds who live large. No, I don't look much like an ornithologist; I look more like a mom who, binoculars always at the ready, dashes between window, kitchen sink, washing machine, and computer. But, in the spirit of amateur ornithology, I send this story out to Dr. Thomas M. Haggerty, because we also serve who watch and write.

*Taking the last baby to the woods*

# Summer Work

## DRAWING, RAISING, AND SAVING BIRDS

July 4  Day 18
They're lethargic today—but better
by afternoon. They definitely
do better on an all insect
diet.

# Hummingbird Summer

IN THEORY, at least, I like being a licensed wildlife rehabilitator. I like much of the practice of rehabilitation. Then there's the responsibility. In Ohio, part of the requirement for getting your permit is allowing your home telephone number to be put on a list that is given to every veterinarian, wildlife official, extension office, and nature center in the state. Needless to say, it's a bit of a leap, personally and professionally, to become a wildlife rehabilitator. There are times when there's nothing better to be in the whole world. When a cedar waxwing you've raised drops out of the sky and lands on your arm, then whirls off to join its flockmates, for instance, it's a really good thing to be.

In practice, it can be harrowing. In June and July, the months that rehabilitators know as "baby season," the telephone rings several times an hour, and each caller has a unique problem that, should I allow it, might become mine. The particular difficulty is that I work with songbirds, which are much more labor-intensive than larger birds. There are a lot of raptor rehabilitation facilities around but very few places that will take songbirds. The simplest reason is that raptors need to be fed once a day. Most of the songbirds that get in trouble are orphaned nestlings, and they need to be fed every twenty to forty-five minutes, dawn to dusk, for a period of weeks. Try to imagine your life as it would look while feeding something every twenty minutes, and you have the short answer to why so few people are willing to work with songbirds.

I dread hearing the phone ring in summer, but I always pick it up because I can help the vast majority of the callers without ever having to handle the bird. In many cases, they've found a feathered fledgling that is supposed to be out of the nest and hopping around on the ground, one that's being tended by its parents and just needs to be put back outside so it can live out this vulnerable but necessary part of its life cycle. Because I travel a lot, have a family and a career, and I need to do things other than feed baby birds, I do what I can to help over the phone. I try to redirect injured birds to the facilities where they can be helped. Occasionally, though, there are calls that demand immediate action, calls that change my life.

It's July 9, 2003. Two calls come in rapid succession, both from Reno, Ohio. One woman has found two nestling hummingbirds in an intact nest on the ground following a powerful thunderstorm. I tell her to tie the nest back up in the sweet gum from whence it came and call me in an hour if the female hummingbird hasn't returned. I hang up the phone, and another call comes in, from another woman in Reno with exactly the same story. "Didn't we just speak?" I ask. No, it's a second nest, with two baby hummingbirds inside. I instruct her to do the same thing, but her front yard is such a mess that she can't tell from which tree it might have fallen. As I'd done with the first caller, I give her directions to my house.

As it turns out, neither hummingbird mother was able to relocate her young, and both nests, their precious cargo intact, are on my kitchen table within two hours. When I see the first one, my hand flies up to cover my mouth and I gasp. I know, intellectually, that hummingbirds are small, but these two nestlings are so very tiny. After all, they've hatched from eggs no bigger than black-eyed peas. They're in pinfeathers, and their eyes are winking open and closed. They're breathing hard and fast. The birds in the second nest are a few days older than the first two, with all but their head feathers out of the sheaths. Four baby hummingbirds, where before there were none. I've never even seen a baby hummingbird up close, and now they're mine to deal with.

I am reeling from the thought that these unutterably dear little birds will die unless I figure out how to take care of them. I imagine them, clinging to the walls of their soft, walnut-size homes as their nests suddenly became space capsules, hurtling downward to a hard landing. I know, looking at them, that my life has suddenly and irrevocably changed, as it would have had I opened my front door and found a newborn baby crying on the stoop.

## What to Feed Them?

By chance, I have on hand a jar of powdered hummingbird maintenance diet, the kind that's used in zoos and aviaries. I'd ordered it when I'd taken in an adult ruby-throated hummingbird, who had hit a window and broken her wing. I thought I'd keep her until I knew whether the wing would heal. If it wouldn't, I told myself, I'd euthanize her, because a hummingbird who cannot fly can no longer be a hummingbird. By the time I knew she was permanently grounded, I had fallen for her bright eyes and indomitable spirit. My

The far hummingbirds rode their lichen-covered cradles to the ground when the boughs broke.

resolve to do the right thing ebbed away. I no longer knew what the right thing might be. Lily lived in a large glass tank next to my drawing table, set up with delicate twigs, a handicapped-accessible feeder, a shallow bathtub, and clean paper towels. She chipped in alarm when she saw a hawk, and she scolded vigorously whenever anyone but me entered the studio. Her zest for life was barely dimmed by her infirmity. When she finally died, as grounded hummingbirds inevitably do, I missed her terribly. Her spirit, so much larger than her tiny, broken body, had imbued the studio. I buried Lily in a bed of cardinal flower and salvia and stored the seventy-nine-dollar jar of powdered hummingbird diet in the refrigerator, saving it against the time when I might need it again.

Remembering Lily and thanking my lucky stars that I had saved her food, I mix up some solution and drizzle it along the sides of the tightly closed bills of

plasticene holds her perch in place.

Lily: I could give her everything but flight, and that's what she needed to be a hummingbird again.

the nestlings. They swallow eagerly. I try a variety of sounds to stimulate them to gape as they would for their mothers. A rapid peeping does the trick—orange gapes fly open, and their heads pump like sewing machine needles as they glug down the nectar. They practically swallow the eyedropper in their eagerness. To my amazement, I can see their newly full crops ballooning out on the left sides of their necks, like pea-size water blisters. It's easy to tell when they've had enough.

And yet I worry. Is a diet formulated for maintaining adult hummingbirds sufficient to keep nestlings healthy and growing? I'd read that female hummingbirds take tiny insects to their young—gathering aphids and gnats, robbing spider webs of their catch. Protein is an essential ingredient in the diet of any young bird. I think hard about how to get some live animal protein into the nestlings, since the protein in the powdered formula is derived from soybeans. When has a hummingbird ever eaten a soybean? I hit upon the idea of beheading and squeezing mealworm larvae, like miniature toothpaste tubes, and offering the pastelike substance on the blunt end of a toothpick. The extra protein seems to agree with the nestlings. As they get older, I pick out freshly molted, tender white mealworms, dice them up, and give each bird a few bits with every formula feeding. Although I'm flying by the seat of my pants, I learn afterward that the powdered formula alone would have provided insufficient nutrition for the growing nestlings. Successful hummingbird rehabilitators (at the time, I hadn't known there were any!) add live insect protein, usually in the form of pulverized fruit flies, to their nestling formulas.

## Setting the Motherclock

The first day of being a stand-in hummingbird parent is a little rough, remembering to drop everything every twenty minutes, cut the head off a mealworm, squeeze it out, and warm their formula. By the end of the day, my natural moth-

erclock sets itself, and I automatically
head for the glass tank where the nestlings wait in their nests, bills agape,
for their next meal. I've had the hummingbirds for two days when my daughter's seventh birthday arrives. I clean the
house, cook dinner for sixteen people,
wrap a dozen presents, and make and decorate a cake shaped like a dolphin. I can't
find the blue food coloring, and I can't
go to the grocery store to get some
with my hummingbird guests in tow,
so I tell Phoebe it's an Amazonian
freshwater dolphin and dye the frost-
ing pink. She seems happy with that.
In between, I feed the hummingbirds
twenty times. While I'm giving them their
last evening feeding, Phoebe unwraps all the
presents I bought for her, including her
new roller skates. I miss the whole thing.
It's hard to hide my disappointment. Even
so, I realize that no seven-year-old ever
had a better present than four baby hummingbirds to help care for. Should she
choose to be a naturalist, she will instinctively know things that only living with
wild creatures can impart. Things I know in my bones, things they have taught
me—things she will know, too.

By Saturday, July 12, on their fourth day with me, almost all their pinfeather

The head pumps
rapidly as the baby
tries to swallow the
eyedropper. The crop is a
translucent pouch—it's
easy to tell when he's
full.

sheaths have burst, and the nestlings really look like birds. They are immeasurably easier to feed, having abandoned the sewing-machine motion for quiet gaping, allowing me to slowly drop the nectar into their gullets. It's a good thing, too, because the pump-and-dodge behavior was getting them covered with the sticky, protein-rich nectar solution, and I had to swab them down with wet Q-Tips after each meal. They're looking natty and clean now, save for a bit of stickum around the gape. A new shipment of mealworms arrives, and I tear the tender white worms into millimeter-size pieces and give the birds one worm each per feeding, washed down with nectar. I grow more confident in my ability to provide for them every day and am beginning to allow myself to fall in love with them. Like a mother of identical quadruplets, I can tell each one from the others, by its behavior and preferences if not by its looks. These are hours well spent.

## Life in the Nest

I think about what it must be like to be crammed into a tiny, thick-walled nest with a sibling for three weeks, the space getting tighter and tighter. Hummingbird nests, being constructed mainly of plant down and cobwebs, stretch considerably as the nestlings grow, but they remain a tight fit. One hummingbird cannot preen without the consent and accommodation of the other. Often, a nestling that's trying to preen or scratch itself winds up preening or scratching its nestmate instead.

The birds are crawling with feather mites, so many that, when I inadvertently touch the nest branch or the edge of their tank, twenty or more swarm up my arm. Looking like tiny, animated periods, the mites make me itch intensely. I can only imagine how they feel to the hummingbirds. I can't dip or treat the birds, so I hope that, when they fledge, they'll leave the majority of their mites in the nest. I take the empty nests and microwave them as soon as they're vacated, and the napkin beneath the nests looks as if it's been peppered.

The most trying time for the roommates comes when the wing feathers shed their sheaths. Then, the major occupation of the birds is exercising their wings. They climb up to cling to the nest rim, wings beating in a translucent blur. Only one of the two (hummingbirds always lay two eggs) may exercise at a time. The exercising bird's wings hum, and it chips excitedly. Its nestmate hunkers down as low as it can, shutting its eyes and sounding an annoyed, low-pitched growl as it is buffeted hard about the head by its sibling's wings. (Nestlings almost always face the same direction while sitting in the nest.) As soon as the buffeter is finished, the buffetee climbs to the nest rim to give tit for tat. I decide, watching the birds barely tolerating each other, that the ferociously independent and irascible temperament of ruby-throated hummingbirds must find its genesis here, in twenty-five days of enforced confinement with an annoying nestmate.

And yet they seem to be eager to imitate each other. Like that of other birds I've observed, I suspect that much of hummingbird learning is based on instinct but also on observing others. I am amazed to find them copying each other's feeding style. When one bird learns to stop pumping its head and lets me drizzle nectar into its open gullet, its nestmate immediately follows suit. One of the nestlings, my favorite for its clean plumage and alert demeanor, often refuses to gape for me, preferring to slowly lap nectar out of the dropper. When I come in to feed them one afternoon, a younger baby from the other nest is sitting by this bird's side. I try to feed my favorite, and it refuses to gape. When I offer the dropper to its companion, it, too, refuses to gape. I have to laugh. There is so much more going on in their tiny heads than I give them credit for.

## Fledging Day

It's Monday, July 14. Because they need to be fed so frequently, and it's an hour roundtrip to town, I have to take the birds with me to the store when we finally run out of human food. I put them in a plastic pet carrier and into the grocery basket, with Phoebe and Liam riding in a big plastic, carlike apparatus up front. It's cumbersome but workable. I feel sorry for the hummingbirds, clinging to their nests through the bumps and jolts and sudden appearance of pineapples and boxes of Cheerios all around them. Two of the nestlings take this opportunity to become fledglings, and I thank the stars they're in a carrier with its top fastened. I shudder at the thought of getting a baby hummingbird out of the rafters of a cavernous food warehouse. The birds are clinging to the paper towels in the carrier, buzzing their wings madly, as I labor through the shopping and loading. As soon as I get home and put the frozen food away, I'll have to start preparing their aviary. If they're ready to fly, they'll need a place to practice.

July 15 is a hard day's labor, retrofitting the glassed-in room where my macaw, Charlie, lives, for hummingbird occupancy. I move Charlie's cage out, tape newspaper over the walls, and affix some fine birch branches around the room. Finally, I move the hummingbirds' covered tank into the aviary and remove the top. One baby lifts off its nest in a single smooth motion, flies two feet, and lands on my arm. I am almost limp with delight, to be a landing pad for this brave hummingbird child. A second bird rises and makes a perfect landing on a birch branch. The other two, younger birds will sit in their nest for another day before they work up the courage to leave. I spend most of the next day sketching and painting the youngest nestling. It's a lovely thing to have a hummingbird nest stuck in a jar full

Young hummingbirds explore with their tongues, tasting everything they wonder about.

of paintbrushes, a living, pulsing almost-fledgling sitting in it, looking back at me.

It is a time of observation and contemplation for me, watching to see what makes a hummingbird what it is. Hummingbird nestlings explore everything, surprisingly enough, with their tongues, which they can extend like fine rice noodles, almost twice the length of the bill. If baby hummingbirds are curious about an object, they taste it. I cannot think of another bird that explores in this way, but most birds' tongues can't be extended much beyond the end of the bill. I wish I could peek into a woodpecker nest; I would bet that young woodpeckers use their long, bony-spined tongues in the same way. In the spring of 2010, I will get the answer when a pair of pileated woodpeckers excavates a nest in our orchard. From a pop-up blind near the nest tree, I will watch in delight as the two nestling woodpeckers run their tongues over everything they explore, just like the hummingbirds did. It's bad enough to have a hummingbird run its tongue up your nostril while you're trying to feed it; I'd hate to have a woodpecker try that.

Such exploratory behavior is a presage of their time of independence, which is coming all too soon. Fledging would be a tricky time without the aviary, that's for sure. As it is, I'm climbing atop the counter to feed the birds on their high twig perches. I'm thankful to have this confined space where they can fly but not fly away. Were I to let them go outside, I'd never be able to reach them, and I doubt

I'll be able to train them to come to me as I do most songbirds. I wonder how a hummingbird could grasp the concept that its big earthbound foster mother can't fly to the top of a tree to feed it. Every other songbird I've raised has come to me for food after release, but hummingbirds seem so flight-oriented, so different, so independent, that I'm apprehensive about release day.

I wonder if I'm underestimating them. I've got nothing to go on but instinct; I've got no model to copy here. I can only keep my eyes open and let the birds teach me how this will unfold. Even through the work and worry of being a hummingbird mother, I know I'm being pelted with diamonds. I've got an eight-by-ten-foot glassed-in room at home with four hummingbirds flying around inside it. For the next few weeks, they're mine to care for, to sketch, and to paint. How lucky can you get?

JULY 17. The last hummingbird—the youngest one—fledges today. Its uppity sibling, with its spotless plumage and persnickety feeding behavior, fledged on the morning of the sixteenth, at an estimated age of twenty days. Now they're all hanging around on high perches in the aviary, preening and exercising. I still pop in to feed them every hour. Except for growing, flying, and gaining strength, I'm not sure what this period holds. *The Birds of North America*'s ruby-throated hummingbird account states that fledging occurs around Day 20 and that the female hummingbird feeds her young for another four to seven days after fledging. That would make their age at independence twenty-four to twenty-seven days. I wonder if, and how, that can be correct. For a bird with a specialized foraging technique (hovering while probing flowers, catching flying insects in the air), a four- to seven-day dependency period seems very short. Wouldn't it take longer than that for a hummingbird to learn how to feed itself? Could this all-consuming nurturing exercise I've embarked upon hold part of the answer?

Fuchsia
"Gartenmeister
Barstedt" - a huge
favorite of the hummers
and me! This, from the
greenhouse   November 3, 2009

## Aviary Life

JULY 18. I decide to hang a hummingbird feeder filled with protein formula from a branch in the aviary, just in case one of the birds wants to try using it. I feed them all day, every hour. They're flying more today. I try spraying them with a fine mist of rainwater. They preen and fluff and look much better after their bath. I'll bathe them every day, until they shine. This evening, I sketch them preening and resting. It's such fun to be in the company of four hummingbirds that have no fear of me, that come to probe at the bright flowers on my shirt and poke their bills in its buttons. They're like fairies — fairies that poop constantly. I have to shield my painting from the intermittent warm patter of their droppings. What I can't wipe off, I incorporate into the painting. It occurs to me that hummingbirds would make charming but really lousy house pets. This evening I'm called away, and for the first time I let them go almost two hours between feedings. When I get home, I rush to the aviary and find them all peeping loudly. I'm hurrying to feed each bird, the most insistent one first, when I hear a humming sound behind me. The oldest bird, a rusty-tinged fellow I call Adventure Joe, is hovering at the little feeder I'd hung this morning. You go, Joe! Finally! A warm flush of pride and accomplishment washes over me. I've been feeding each of these four birds on average every half hour from dawn to dark for nine days. That's one hundred and twenty feedings each fifteen-hour day, over one thousand feedings all told. I'm weary, but, like Adventure Joe, I can taste the sweet nectar of independence.

However delightful raising hummingbirds is, it is like being under house arrest. Having to drop everything and feed them every thirty to sixty minutes certainly shapes one's day. Now that they've fledged, I can't take them in the little plastic pet carrier, so I can't leave the house for more than two hours without starving them. Our home is a half-hour from town, so a roundtrip kills an hour.

That gives me an hour to do my grocery shopping, banking, kid taxiing, all the things I do in town. No matter what I do, the hummingbirds are always in the front of my mind, needing to be fed. I'll be so glad when they're all feeding themselves.

I think about how to introduce them to life at large. I'll put different styles of feeders up, bring in cut flowers and hanging baskets and planters for them to investigate. I've got a fuchsia crawling with whiteflies that they'll love for both nectar and insect food. They watch gnats, fruit flies, and flour moths with the greatest interest, snapping at them when they come close. I can't wait until they're skilled enough to snap up whiteflies. I'll bring in some aging bananas and grapes. If only it were tomato season. I could feed a small army of hummingbirds off the fruit flies that swarm my countertops in canning season.

## Small Tragedy

JULY 19. I walk into the aviary to find the last-fledged bird on the floor. I had seen quite a bit of chasing between it and its assertive nestmate, heard a light impact on the glass door earlier. The injured bird's left wing is swollen around the wrist and doesn't work properly. All I can do is confine the bird to a small tank and hope that the injury resolves; it's too small to splint, even if I knew what the problem was. The other three birds are flying like little helicopters, eagerly checking out the flowers I bring in for them, sipping occasionally from the feeder. The injured nestling sits still, left wing drooping. How can a hummingbird injure its wing and ever hope to fly again? These minuscule gossamer wings, which have to describe figure eights to propel the bird up, down, back, and sideways, must be perfect in every particular. I'm so distraught I can hardly sleep this night.

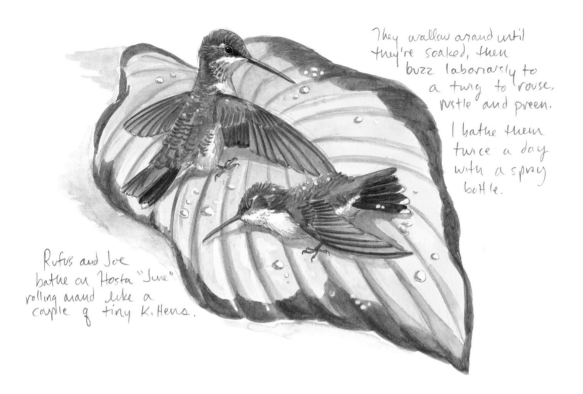

They wallow around until they're soaked, then buzz laboriously to a twig to rouse, rustle and preen.

I bathe them twice a day with a spray bottle.

Rufus and Joe bathe on Hosta "June" rolling around like a couple of tiny kittens.

As it turns out, I am right to be deeply concerned. Though I will do my best to support him, keep him clean and well fed, this injured bird will never fly again. I will keep him until November 24 — four and a half months of support and care — when I finally euthanize him. Without variety or exercise, he'd simply wear out, run down like a little clock.

The most heartbreaking part of nursing grounded hummingbirds — and this is the fourth I've kept since I started practicing bird rehabilitation, in 1982 — is watching them rage against their condition. The hummingbird temperament has no provision for enforced inactivity. An injured hummingbird knows what it should be doing: hovering, zipping from flower to flower, investigating anything that piques its curiosity—and it will try again and again to do it, until it wears all the feathers off its wings and bleeds from the stubs, until it flips over on its back, buzzing like an angry bee, and has to be righted ten times a day. A life of stasis is no life for a hummingbird, and I gently explain that to people who contact me for advice. "Make sure the injury is irreparable, that there's no chance the bird will regain its power of flight. As soon as you know that, euthanize it." Would that I could take my own advice. My heart is an intractable organ, and my head is no match for it.

By July 21, I've finally got them all named. The injured bird becomes Buzz, since that's all he can do now. His arrogant sibling, the one who stopped gaping first and chased Buzz into the aviary glass, is Bela. Adventure Joe is the eldest, first out of the nest and first to try self-feeding. Rufus, his nestmate, is heavily marked with reddish brown, retiring and shy. I need to name them if I'm to release them and keep track of them afterward. Naming them honors their distinct personalities, proclivities, and idiosyncrasies. Mostly, though, I need to name them because I'm their mother.

## Graduation

I begin bringing commercial hummingbird feeders into the aviary. I wash them thoroughly before introducing them, and one is beaded with water. Bela flies over to inspect it, feeds at one of the ports, then rubs his breast against the feeder's droplet-dotted surface. I dash outdoors to get a couple of hosta leaves and spray them with water. Within seconds, Bela is down and rolling like a minuscule green mallard in the puddles on the quilted leaves. Adventure Joe and Rufus crane their necks in wonder, then helicopter down to join him. It's a hummingbird bathing orgy. I chortle in delight at the bizarre poses the birds strike as they revel in their first real bath. Who would imagine that hummingbirds would lie down on their breasts and scoot along like penguins, roll on their sides, or close their eyes and rub their faces on the damp leaves like luxuriating cats?

By the time they're twenty-nine days old, the fledglings are all sipping sporadically at the small plastic feeder. I'm supplementing them with dropper feedings, and I notice that Rufus and Adventure Joe are always hungry, always peeping for subsidy. Testosterone has kicked in. Bela is dominating the feeder, guarding it from the other two fledglings, locking feet in flight and twirling to the floor with any other bird that tries to feed there. He's chasing them around the aviary. He performs a shuttle display flight to a birch leaf on one of the twig perches, zooming side to side in a perfect (and clearly instinctual) precopulatory display. He lands and tries to copulate with the leaf. Though his throat is still clear white, he's indubitably male, and he's messing up my peaceable kingdom in the glassed-in room. He's already driven Buzz into the glass door and grounded him forever. It's from this hard lesson that I decide to invest in an outdoor, nylon-screened tent for all future rehabilitation projects. I can't take the chance that Bela will injure one of the other birds. It's time to release them.

Release Day is July 29, 2003. It dawns bright and clear. All three hummingbirds, even shy Rufus, are feeding themselves. Both Joe and Bela are performing shuttle displays and mounting birch leaves, proof of their maleness. Rufus is spatting with both of them, and I'm encouraged by his newfound moxie. I remove the screen from the aviary window and crank it all the way open. This does not go unnoticed. Within seconds, Bela darts into the open air, returns to the room, and suddenly is gone, headed out to the orchard. Adventure Joe follows, feigning interest in some spider webs in the corner of the open window, then making a beeline out over the house chimney. I'm breathless with the speed of their exit. Rufus follows within seconds. He hovers, then vanishes to the orchard. The little aviary is suddenly, oddly silent. Buzz spins in a little circle around his broken wing, wanting so badly to follow the others. Just like that, it's over.

*Adventure Joe comes back.*
*July 29, 2003*

## Return of the Prodigals

I wander around the house, newly free but oddly empty. What was I doing with my days before there were hummingbirds to care for? I decide to do some laundry. There's always laundry, and there's been more of it piling up since this hummingbird summer unfolded. Shadows are getting long as I emerge from the basement with a load of wet clothes to hang out. I'm arranging them on the line when I hear a familiar peep. In the line of clothespins, no bigger than one of them, perches Adventure Joe. Phoebe, who's helping me, skedaddles up to the house to fetch a dropper full of nectar. Joe gapes widely, and I fill his crop. He looks tired, his eyelids are droopy, and he is famished. When he's full, he buzzes off to perch high in a birch tree. My mind races. Maybe they're not old enough to be on their own. Maybe I've released them too soon. I trot around the yard, listening. There's a peep from a birch tree on the opposite side of the yard. It's Bela. He's hungry, but he ignores the dropper I wave at him, swooping down to feed at the cardinal flowers like he's been doing it all his life. I'm delighted at the sight. I wonder, panicked, where Rufus could be. I can't find him, and I know he'll be needing me.

I go out to pick string beans for our dinner, and there is a peep from the garden fence behind me. It's Rufus, begging. I'm beyond delighted to see him at last. By now, I have a vial of nectar in my pants pocket, and I roam around the yard like a sheepdog, listening for my flock. Near sundown, Bela finally comes and perches on a low trellis on the back deck, where I give him a few drops of nectar. He's clearly not hungry; he's been at the garden flowers all day. I'm knocked back with the wonder of it all—that these birds could disappear into the clear blue sky, then come to find me in the vast yard, peeping to get my attention. It's behavior that I would anticipate from any other hand-raised bird, but somehow I didn't expect it from these hummingbirds. When they took off, I thought they were gone.

It's becoming ever clearer to me that the existing ornithological literature on ruby-throated hummingbirds is woefully inadequate. *The Birds of North America* states that female ruby-throats feed fledglings for four to seven days after they leave the nest. My foundlings left the nest at Days 20 and 21. By the literature, they should have been independent by Day 27, but they were incapable of sustained hovering flight by then, and they spent most of the day sitting around begging for food. They're thirty-three days old now, and it's clear that they aren't through with me, nor I with them. In the end, I feed them out in the yard until Day 37. Corresponding with hummingbird rehabilitators in

2007, I learn that most don't recommend release until Day 41. I wish I'd known that in 2003! Even though I fed them well past the supposed age of independence as stated in the literature, I'd jumped the gun on my birds' release. No wonder they'd hunted me down, peeping!

Far be it from me to cast aspersions on the observational skills of field ornithologists. There can't be a more difficult species to observe than a hummingbird, and following just-fledged birds to see how long they're subsidized by their mothers would be virtually impossible in the field. I can only surmise that the literature on the ruby-throat's age at independence is based on best guesses rather than direct observation. If captive-raised hummingbirds are any indication, the female hummingbird may feed her fledglings another two weeks longer than we surmise.

Released before they were ready, the hummingbirds came back to find me. Why was I so flabbergasted at that? Why did I so underestimate them? You'd think, having raised them, that I'd expect them to return for feedings just like the mourning doves, bluebirds, robin, wood thrush, catbird, rose-breasted grosbeak, cedar waxwing, and other birds I've raised. And yet somehow I thought that, being hummingbirds, they'd fly out the window and be absorbed into the vast population, jockeying for a place at the feeders with the other hundred and fifty or so hummingbirds that slurp down a half gallon of nectar each day. I didn't know how I would ever pick them out of the throng. But they aren't up to the jostling and poking and bickering, and they see a much better way to get their feet wet in the world.

## Hummingbird Mother

They've set up little duchies around the yard—Joe and Bela hanging out in the backyard willow, retiring Rufus in a vine tangle on a hill to the east—and they sit and wait until I emerge from the house, then peep and come to me to be fed. And it turns out that I find them in this vast, eighty-acre sanctuary just as their mother would—by their voices. I am hard-wired to listen for their peeps, just as they are to utter them. Mowing on the riding tractor, I have a hummingbird escort. They buzz my head and sit tight as I thunder past, spraying grass bits and exhaust. To them, it's perfectly normal that their mother would climb on a tractor and cut the grass. They're unperturbed, and still seek my company. I ponder this as I round the yard again and again. I wonder if the other birds are taunting them: "Yer mud-dah rides a lawn tractor!"

They know me, know my voice, my names for them. They have observed that I can't fly up to them as their own mother would, and they have the sense to come down to eye level to be fed. They know that I live in a big house and that I pop out to pick beans and weed the flowers and hang clothes. They listen for my voice in the house and come to the window where they can watch me. They peep and I call back; they beg and I feed them. They regard me as their mother, a strange, huge, earthbound, flightless mother, but a source of sustenance and even comfort. This is deeply fulfilling to me. It is knowing what they know that utterly beguiles me, that has me humming with joy along the invisible lines that connect us.

## Late Summer

In the end, I have only four days of hourly feedings with the orphans, but that is more than enough. Locating them in the outdoors, and waiting for them to locate me, is nerve-racking and takes almost all of my time. Gradually, I increase the interval between feedings until I feel the birds are able to sustain themselves. By August 2, their thirty-seventh day of life, I'm feeding them just before they go to roost at night, and not at all during the day. Bela hangs by the front door, sitting picturesquely in the little bonsai trees I keep. Rufus lives in a Russian prune hedge, shuttling between there and a trumpet vine tangle on the east hill. Ad-

Bela takes
a rain bath,
inches from
my face.

venture Joe hangs out in the front flower beds, guarding the red crocosmia blossoms. I hang a small feeder of protein solution by each one's haunt, and they feed themselves. Rufus still comes to sit and peep on the garden fence whenever I pick beans, and sometimes I feed him. Adventure Joe and Bela spend much of their time in spectacular aerial dogfights, perhaps because their chosen duchies are so close together.

AUGUST 3. It rains all day this day, and I see Bela and Joe rain bathing until they are shiny and slick. They can fly even when sodden, which is more than I can say for most songbirds.

AUGUST 6. I'm seeing Joe and Bela many times each day. Joe has become skittish and rockets off when I approach, but he uses his protein feeder all day. Bela came down during dinner at the picnic table and prodded the orange Sun Gold cherry tomatoes in my salad, then probed the printed flowers on my shirt. When I emerge from the house with his freshly washed and filled nectar feeder first thing in the morning, Bela zeroes in and feeds from it as I'm trying to hang it up. He's watching for me at first light.

AUGUST 8. Because they're getting wilder, it's harder for me to identify my foundlings immediately. But they blew their cover when I stood by the big hummingbird feeder on the front porch. All the wild hummingbirds scattered, but Joe and Rufus came right in, exploiting the suddenly vacant ports, and lacking any fear of this big pale animal they knew as their mother. I was able to examine them at leisure as they fed, inches from my nose. What a delight. They both look wonderful. They're forty-three days old now, and well beyond needing any subsidy. I decide to put protein solution out only in the morning. I've seen all three catching gnats in the air, and they should be able to subsist on natural nectar and insects, with an occasional sip of sugar water.

I wonder about the nature of the bond I forged with the three hummingbird orphans. Would any young hummingbird become attached to its caretaker, or is this dependency an artifact of the birds' having been hand-fed since they were in pinfeathers? I am rarely able to put a whole puzzle together, usually being given only a few pieces at a time. By the next summer, I have one more piece. On July 14, almost a year to the day after the four orphans came in, I get a call from a woman saying that a baby hummingbird has been found in a commercial green-

Sylvia hovers right in front of me, looking into my eyes. When I hold up my finger, she settles on it. What does she want? I believe it's me.

house and is in need of help. I drive to pick it up and find a newly fledged bird, bits of down still adhering to its head feathers. It is weak and debilitated from its long, hot ordeal. I put it in an empty glass aquarium and place a feeder with protein solution within reach. After I bring the feeder up to its bill once, it quickly accepts this food source and is self-feeding from then on. By the next morning it has picked up considerably and is buzzing around in the lidded tank. I put up my new fifteen-by-seventeen-foot nylon-screen tent in the yard and release the hummingbird into it, hanging a feeder in the center of the tent. I keep the foundling for six more days and am pleased to see it self-feeding with increasing confidence. I feed it once, when I take it in, but never handle it again. It's an altogether different upbringing than my four fledglings enjoyed the previous year.

I estimate the female fledgling, which Phoebe names Sylvia Salvia, to be around twenty-eight days old when I release her. I take her feeder and hang it conspicuously just outside the tent, then draw back the flaps and tie them open. She buzzes out and feeds, then settles in a birch tree. I dismantle the tent and replenish her feeder with fresh protein solution several times daily. And the oddest thing happens. Even though Sylvia is self-feeding, she seeks me out in the yard. She'll land on a low twig right by my face and peep. When I speak to her, she ruffles her feathers and preens companionably. I know that this behavior has little to do with food, because I've hand-fed her only once. She'll leave to visit the flower garden or her feeder, then return to perch near my face. As time goes on and she gains flight prowess, she'll hover in front of my nose, chipping irritably until I bring my finger up in front of my face. And she will land on it, fluff her feathers, and settle down for a good preen and talking-to. Seemingly satisfied, she'll then rocket away on some pressing hummingbird business.

I cannot describe how it feels to have a free-living, essentially wild hummingbird seek me out for companionship. I search for an answer to this delightful conundrum. I decide that, lacking a mother, she simply needs to make contact with someone she knows. And somehow, having a person speak lovingly to her fills that need. Perhaps she made the connection between food and me during her confinement in the tent, and she still associates me with that form of comfort and fulfillment. Whatever is going on, I know that I will never be through learning about how birds' minds work, even the tiniest ones.

## Epilogue

Everyone who met the three hummingbirds I raised and released in 2003 asked if I thought they'd return to our Ohio sanctuary the following spring. An image of the United States, the Gulf of Mexico yawning beneath it like a huge mouth, would pop into my head, and I'd hesitate before answering. Those baby hum-

April 17, 2004 - I've never seen two adult male ruby-throats sit touching shoulders. Could it be Rufus and Joe? Same twig, same feeder... perfectly tame... 7 months and an ocean crossing later, they've come home.

mingbirds would have to fly from southern Ohio to the Gulf Coast. There, they'd double their weight before launching themselves on an 18- to 24-hour, five-hundred-mile nonstop flight across the Gulf, trying to reach landfall in Mexico. If their wings stopped beating for more than a few seconds, if a storm hit, if a headwind sprang up, they'd fail, and there would be glittering green feathers in the flotsam. All I could say was "I sure hope they come back."

My three hummingbird orphans left on migration in September 2003, and I spent the winter wondering if they'd made it to Mexico, and the early spring wondering if they'd make it back home.

On April 17, 2004, my husband, Bill, stepped out, coffee mug in hand, to take in the morning sun. A male ruby-throated hummingbird zipped up, hovered in front of his face, then poked his beak between each pair of Bill's fingers. It was as close to a handshake as a hummingbird could manage.

Later that day, I looked out to see two male hummingbirds sitting shoulder to shoulder on a twig by our front door, one that had been their favorite as youngsters. I rummaged around until I found the small feeder they'd used the summer before and filled it with the protein-rich solution the three had been raised on. As I reached to hang it from a branch, three adult male ruby-throats wove through my arms and around my head, fighting to be the first to feed. Seven months and two ocean crossings behind them, my hummingbirds were home, right where they belonged.

# Osprey

## Hooked by Round Talons

AT FIRST I thought I might lose my mind. This was the third day I had sat, slowly fading my hair and clothes in the July sun, which bounced off the silvered dock and waves all around me. My spotting scope was trained on a nest full of ospreys: three young, with occasional cameos by the parents. And for the third day they did nothing. Sometimes they preened, sometimes they ate; they dozed and loafed.

It was tranquil, too tranquil, and I ached for some action. I have always loved to draw small birds, which rarely do any one thing for long. Now my sketchbook was full of loafing ospreys. My mind wandered to Jane Goodall, my idol since early childhood, patiently taking notes on the slightest move her animal subjects made. And slowly it dawned on me that I would have to enter fish hawk time, to shed my impatience and stop counting the hours, or I would never see the world through the yellow eyes of an osprey.

It occurred to me that the young birds must be hungry; they had had nothing to eat since the morning before. Their crops, normally comfortably rounded as though tennis balls lay within, were flat. I pulled a sun-warmed sandwich out of my pack, hoping the mayonnaise was still good, and forced part of it down while I watched.

Suddenly the female, who had been dozing, snapped to attention. Her lumpy form became all angles, and her eyes pierced the sky. Though I could not yet make him out, the male must have been on his way in, and from her demeanor I figured he must have a fish for his family. As one, the three young birds dropped their heads and began their wheedling pipe of hunger. He hovered for a moment overhead, the shredded head of his prize a fierce red in the blue sky field, and dropped to the nest in an exquisite one-footed landing, just long enough to release the fish to the quick bill of his mate. Over the long afternoon, as she patiently dissected and fed the fish to her young, I filled a sketchbook with images—eyeless, footless drawings, quick gestures and bits; toes and nostrils, even tongues, as I tried to understand how these strange, leggy hawks were strung together. Though I had fretted at first, I was now one of the legion of those who can't take their eyes off ospreys.

I was to spend part of two summers watching this massive stick nest on a Nature Conservancy salt-marsh preserve in Connecticut. A friend had approached me about illustrating a manuscript on his studies of ospreys. Reasoning that I needed to spend a lot of time sketching them from life to create believable drawings, I jumped at the chance to spend time with the great chocolate-and-white birds. Though the book illustration job never materialized, I'm grateful now that I spent part of two summers that way. Sitting under an osprey nest isn't something I could justify doing now that child care and career have taken the front seat in a busy life. If ever there were a period of my life when I could afford to enter osprey time, it was then. As I think about it, no other raptor would allow me to draw it in every phase of its life, cheerfully foraging, preening, mating, tending its young,

and fighting its battles while people swim, sail, and ski all around it, as I sat beneath the nest in witness. In its phlegmatic acceptance of us, the osprey seems almost to acknowledge its debt for safe, artificial nesting platforms. Yet we were very nearly its ruin.

In the mid-1970s, Connecticut's osprey population hit an all-time low. Eggs, shattered by the weight of the incubating hens, lay wasted in deserted nests, the females who laid them too contaminated by organochloride pesticides to produce normal shells. Ninety percent of the ospreys nesting between New York and

Boston vanished between 1950 and 1975, reports Alan F. Poole in *Ospreys: A Natural and Unnatural History*. New England was hardest hit. While DDT was used to control agricultural pests in other parts of the osprey's range, here the deadly chemical was sprayed directly on salt marshes in a misguided attempt to control mosquitoes. The silent mist settled on the ospreys' nests and on the grasses and water, where its molecules were quickly bound up in the fatty tissues of small fish. Larger fish, eating them, concentrated the poison. Ospreys hooked a deadly dose, for they eat solely fish. Osprey populations suffered a 31 percent annual decline in Long Island Sound in the 1950s and '60s. Reproduction fell to almost nothing. By 1974, one active nest remained in Connecticut.

Ospreys became bellwethers for the health of bird populations overall, as their nest failures due to eggshell thinning from organochloride pesticides were so spectacular and unequivocal. The lanky birds played a large role in alerting the public to the dangers of persistent pesticides. DDT was banned in 1972. Thirty-five years later, the New England population is still rebounding. Connecticut had 250 active nests in 2005; Maine boasted over 2,000. And yet there is still a long way to go for the bird's population to build up to historic levels. Ospreys were described as abundant, with Connecticut boasting perhaps 1,000 nests in the 1800s. The lower Connecticut River alone had 200 nests in 1938. Current limits on population appear to be fish abundance and predation, with great horned owls and raccoons leading the list of osprey predators.

On a clear August day, as I sit on the dock before the nest, I can see twelve ospreys in the air at once while newly fledged juveniles try their luck in a brisk northwest breeze. One clatters into a red maple, trying to land in the thin, leafy branches, and comes out again, a leaf impaled on one talon. He lands on a sturdy, dead snag and looks around ferociously before bending to tear the evidence of his ineptitude off his toe. I love watching these new fliers, as they show how difficult I always thought flying must be. Like kids sailing Sunfishes on choppy water, they screw up regularly and spectacularly. It is the young birds, too, that give me some insight into osprey consciousness.

A nest of ospreys, like that of most raptors, often holds young of graduated size and age. The third or fourth egg laid is usually smaller than the first two. That youngest bird is also the smallest, and it gets fed only when its siblings are full, and sometimes not at all. I watch the male drop a fish to the three, now well feathered and able to carve it up for themselves. Although I can't be sure, I've assigned them sexes according to their size and markings. Females are usually larger and marked with chocolate on crown and breast.

As always, the oldest female commandeers the prize. The second largest, a male, joins her and rips off a hunk of flesh for himself. The youngest shifts her feet, screams, then savagely bites a stick, tearing the bark and scoring the wood deeply. She will be lucky and will not starve, as youngest ones often do in lean years. Late in August, though, she is the last in the nest, and I watch her pick in a desultory way at a dried fish tail. Her siblings are mere specks in the blue, but she is stubbornly alone. Studies show that this is a vulnerable period for the smallest sibling, for this is when she should be learning to fish while being subsidized by her parents. In 1978, R. C. Szaro observed adult ospreys at Seahorse Key, Florida,

first it hangs over me, then

a juv makes a keening whoosee? as it makes several passes at the empty nest platform. It does not land.

dropping pieces of food into the water while their offspring practiced diving for them. This bird should have been learning to dive, feet-first, into the shallow waters of Niantic Bay.

Nearby lies a whole menhaden, but she cannot eat it, for it is aswarm with yellow jackets. She tries several times to drag it nearer, but their angry buzzing dissuades her. Were she more agile or confident, she might pick it up and airlift it to a nearby snag to finish it off. But she is resisting independence. She shakes her head and scratches her face with her huge black talons. Before long, her parents will leave for southern oceans, and she will have to put those great feet to use and beat the air with new wings.

As an artist, I find endless fascination in osprey architecture. I've had two ospreys in my hands, the most recent being one found dead and presumed shot. I hurried to the scene, hoping to find evidence. As any bird rehabilitator can tell you, raptors are still being shot for sport. But no bullet had felled this beautiful young bird. Its feet were charred and blackened, one hind toe and talon melted. Even its tail had been burned off. I looked up to see power lines just overhead.

The ornithologist Noble Proctor, who has consulted about raptor casualties with power companies, explained how it happened. A large raptor lands on a power line, not in itself a dangerous thing. As it teeters for balance, it lightens its load by defecating, sending a stream of whitewash behind. If this hits the ground wire, a charge leaps back up the stream, down the bird's legs to the perch wire, burning off the tail on its way and killing the bird instantly. The rounded breast and gleaming plumage speak of the bird's good health. If the world had to lose a young osprey, at least it had been quick.

Such a strong, lean, and sinewy bird! Its body is smaller in girth than a good fryer, but much longer. Its legs, though long and slender, are hard as iron, closely feathered like an owl's, the tarsi armored, ending in magnificent outsize, sea green feet. Fish scales still cling to the horny scutes on its toes, a detail that moves me inexplicably. The enormous talons, strongly hooked, are almost round in cross section, not concave on the ventral surface like those of other raptors. People frequently speak of ospreys "locking on" to an oversize fish and drowning, but the truth is that ospreys are perfectly able to release the talons when necessary. If their talons locked, how would they release the fish to turn it around and carry it head facing forward; how would the male be able to deliver fish to the female at the nest? Perhaps the smooth, rounded surface helps with that. The outer toe on each foot can swivel through 180 degrees, giving the bird a choice of a conventional three-toes-

Wing chord: 570 mm
Tail: 236
Tarsus: 70
Culmen: 28
10 primaries, 16 secondaries, 12 tail
Folded wings project 1½" beyond tail

Osprey *Pandion haliaetus* ♂ November 12, 1983
The male of a pair which nested for years at Harkness Memorial Park, New London, Ct; this bird was found standing on his mangled wings, and he died soon thereafter. (Summer). Ochre color of soles is fish oil. Scales still stuck to feet. Strong reek of fish.

forward grip, or two forward, two back. This trait, called "functional zygodactyl-ism," it shares with owls but with no other hawk.

The bird exudes an odor, not of death but of fish and its own pungent per-fume, that clings to museum specimens after decades of storage and identifies a feather found in the marsh grass with a single whiff. Its plumage is tightly scaled, with almost no down and a high, oily sheen. A plunge-diving bird like the osprey  can't afford to have absorbent down beneath its feathers; water would be forced in when it dove, and would soak it to the skin. An osprey rising from the water rouses itself like a wet dog, seeming to fly apart like a shaken mop.

One that has plunged several times in succession must spend an hour or more rearranging and drying its plumage before it tries again. Absorbent down would slow this process. Doubtless, the osprey's lack of down, along with the move-ments of its prey, sends it south for the winter. Most are gone from the Northeast by late October, when winds turn sharp and cold. They seek the warm shallows of southern oceans for the winter. I shiver in sympathy as I watch ospreys return to their New England nest sites in early March, often incubating eggs as the snow still flies. That has to be a rude contrast to the Gulf Coast and Mexico.

I turn the dead osprey over and part its feathers. The fish hawk's oil gland is huge, straddling the base of its tail like a pink saddle. Its life depends on oil, for without it the feathers would not repel the water when it dives. This bird was probably raised largely on menhaden, which had a good run in the Northeast in the summer of its birth. The oily members of the herring family, in fact, make up the bulk of North American ospreys' diet.

So much to learn by handling a bird . . . The osprey's nostrils are like nothing else I've seen: long and slitted, with grayish flaps of cartilage just inside. Further reading tells me that the flap is a valve that closes to prevent water from entering

in a dive! I am puzzled by the structure of the osprey's red-orange eyes, which would have faded to adult yellow by spring. They are large and protruding, and unprotected by the supraorbital ridge of bone that gives hawks, eagles, and falcons their stern, hooded glare. Within the eye, I expect to find a bony sclerotic ring, which stiffens the eyeballs of owls and many diving sea birds, but there is nothing in the vitreous humor. A thin, latexlike membrane holds the vulnerable orb in place, but there seems little to protect it from the impact of a dive. I think about this, reeling a mental film of the hundreds of dives I've witnessed. All the birds went feet-first into the water, letting their massive padded soles take the impact.

For all the cranial space taken by its goggle eyes, the osprey's brain is comparatively large. I'm not surprised. These birds are alert to subtle signals from us and uncanny in their ability to put aside their fear of us after deciding that we present no threat. When I first set my chair and scope up on the dock, perhaps sixty yards from the study nest, the pair circled, giving mild alarm whistles. Soon, though, they settled down to watch me, and after perhaps twenty minutes' observation, they completely ignored me. A few days later I reappeared with the same setup, to be met not with alarm but with placid indifference. And so it was for the season.

I had several conversations with the ornithologist Alan Poole, acknowledged worldwide as an expert on the species. Time and again he noted that osprey behavior is highly individual; in the preface of his book he quotes the ethologist Donald Griffin: "If one wishes to understand the behavior of animals, or still more if one is interested in their thoughts and feelings, one must take account of their individuality, annoying as this may be to those who prefer the tidiness of physics, chemistry, and mathematical formulations."

In 1984, when Griffin wrote this, the science of animal behavior was deeply bound to quantifiable analyses. Ospreys differ wildly in their individual responses to stimuli. Poole notes: "A very small segment of the population is hyperaggressive. When you have a bird with the size and equipment of an osprey, you have to pay attention to that. It's such fun to take green interns out who've never climbed a nest before. I'll say, 'This female's a little bad; you have to have a stick to hold up over your head,' and then there's this tremendous WHOOSH and they gasp and turn pale."

Dr. Poole points out that, being semicolonial, ospreys are in constant interaction with their mates and neighbors. The name of the game in osprey society is obtaining and holding a nest site. There is a continuous chorus of calls from ospreys nesting near each other. Poole describes

The dad e baby from the other nest Amazed to see me point the scope at them.

osprey colonies as "almost like a bar scene. Males are constantly testing to see who's available. They call and listen for the answer. Is her mate there? Is he calling aggressively? Is he flying up to you and chasing you out? Bingo is getting the female and the nest site."

Ospreys are constantly watching each other, testing and communicating their status, a rather unusual situation among raptors, which tend to nest singly.

"One of the things that jumps out at me," Poole relates, "is how ospreys are able to recognize individual humans and their boats. They're really good at pattern recognition. There could be a dozen boats out that they ignore totally, and then my little green boat comes out with a ladder sticking out over the end, and they go berserk. They know it's me coming to climb up to their nests and pester them.

"Their calls reach a pitch when we put our ladder against the nest pole and climb up. If there were a 'real' predator, like a harrier or a fox near the nest, they'd never calm down. But as soon as we finish our work and turn away from the nest they are instantly calmer. They stop the hysteria, the pitch and volume of the calls go way down. It's a routine for them." (Poole had between thirty and forty nests on Martha's Vineyard, Massachusetts, each of which he checked three times a week for five years.)

"They make a fuss when we're coming, a big fuss when we're in the nest, and then they breathe a big sigh of relief."

As I would show up day after sunny day to sketch the Niantic nest, neighbors whose houses overlooked the marsh would wander down to introduce themselves. I gave sketches to some of them. I liked these people who liked ospreys.

One neighbor told a story of the pair I was observing. "If I come out the front door and walk down to my mailbox, they don't say a thing. But as soon as they see me put my boots on, they start yelling. I put my boots on way up by the front door, but they know that means I'm going to take the boat out. My boat is moored right next to their nest, and they don't like my messing around there. And they yell at me from the minute I put my boots on until I'm out in the channel." Ospreys are able to pick up clues on our intent from close observations of our behavior, to make connections between our present and future actions. I looked over at the neighbor's house; it was hundreds of yards away. I marveled at both the ospreys' keen eyesight and the mental leap they had made in anticipating their neighbor's behavior. Many of the most telling observations of bird behavior are made by those who live among them.

Dad is sloopy

One volunteer who went out on the marsh to replace a fallen nest pole told me about the pair of ospreys that circled over

but a plane wakes him up

him, calling, the entire time he and his helpers were erecting the new platform. Within seconds of the final push to get it upright, the birds were on it. Their instant acceptance of artificial structures and the way they observe us as we build them show that the birds may understand more than we think of our doings and the direct benefits to them.

As a decadelong resident of Connecticut, I had to chuckle at a story related by an acquaintance, the ornithologist Tom Baptist. It is a perfect snapshot of both my former home state and the indomitable osprey.

> *In the fall of 2004, Audubon representatives approached Greenwich officials about the possible placement of a . . . pole and nest platform on the island in the center of Eagle Pond at the fabled Greenwich Point Park. The request was denied on the basis that the platform would degrade the quality of the view of the pond and its tall statue of an eagle, with its glorious wings spread wide, rising from the island in its middle. Well, local ospreys had their own opinion about the town's rejection of Audubon's request. [They] constructed this spring a large stick nest upon the wings of the eagle statue, and successfully fledged two young this summer from the new nest . . . The nest nearly obscures the entire eagle statue. The ospreys have nested on the statue every year since 2004.*

Go ospreys! Get your dive on.

And now there is another way to know something of individual ospreys. Trapped on the nest using a noose carpet, an osprey can be fitted with a small solar-powered backpack containing a radio that beams signals to a satellite, allowing the bird to be tracked wherever it goes with astounding accuracy. The bird's speed of flight, even its height above the ground, can be determined at any given moment. In some cases, the bird can be tracked to an individual tree where it may be roosting — within an accuracy of eighteen meters.

The osprey's backpack radio is programmed to take GPS readings hourly and then to transmit data at intervals of between one and ten days. Each radio is assigned a unique identification number and is monitored by a satellite tracking company based in Toulouse, France. The tracking company has satellites circling the earth, mainly collecting information from ocean weather buoys, and they pick

Now, having drawn
them flying, I wonder
how I could have drawn
them perching for so long.

up the birds' signals. Osprey researchers can connect to the company's database and extract their data using a password. And nobody's driving around in a Land Rover, radio antenna held aloft, listening to muffled beeps from the transmitter. It's possible for the osprey researcher Roy Dennis of the Highland Foundation for Wildlife to open his laptop on his desk in Scotland and receive information transmitted within the hour from Africa. He downloads a set of coordinates into the Google Earth mapping system, and an individual bird's migratory flight is mapped out on the screen before him. A record of an osprey's movements and behavior that has never before been imaginable emerges. The tracking shows that birds display amazing fidelity to their wintering sites once they've chosen them, fishing in the same favorite holes and carving their food on the same trees year after year.

Not only does satellite tracking technology illuminate a heretofore dark chapter of osprey life, but it can save lives as well. Similar technology is being used by the ornithologist Rob Bierregaard to track the migratory movements of ospreys on Martha's Vineyard. Through satellite tracking, Bierregaard found that the journeys of four out of four transmitter-bearing ospreys and dozens of banded individuals ended at fish farms in the Dominican Republic, where they were shot for taking advantage of easy pickings in man-made pools. Through direct contact with fish farmers and cooperation with conservation groups, which installed nets over the pools, he cut osprey mortality by 60 to 80 percent.

One well-traveled osprey, an adult female named Logie, has become famous, a star on BBC television. She nests in Scotland and winters on the coast of West Africa. I spent an afternoon reading Logie's story from her first autumn migration after being fitted with a transmitter, in 2007, following her via blog-style, dated entries over the treacherous, fish-free wasteland of the Sahara desert and deep into western Africa, ending up on the island of Roxa in Guinea-Bissau.

On the morning of the twelfth of March 2008, she awoke in her usual roost tree, then lined out flying north-northeast at an elevation of 258 meters. She was off! I read the posts on her journey north with increasing anticipation, saw her back across the Sahara, rejoiced when she finally reached water and caught a fish. (Researchers could tell she was feeding because the transmissions showed she detoured out over water, then perched for several hours in a tree, presumably devouring her catch.) Her migration from West Africa lasted forty-three days, and she flew at least 3,619 miles (5,824 kilometers) in twenty-seven days of active migration; she also spent sixteen days waiting out bad weather. Her best day's flight was 215 miles, and her shortest just 26 miles.

Logie was delayed by bad spring weather in Spain, and I worried along with all her fans as she fought to reestablish her bond with her waiting mate and take possession of her nest from an interloping female. In August 2008, her transmitter went dead, and, reaching that point in the narrative, I felt bereft. Roy Dennis, who'd been faithfully posting her whereabouts and welfare, advised that we'd all have to wait until spring of 2009 to know whether Logie was alive or dead. She never reappeared, so Dennis reluctantly concluded that she must have died early in her journey.

I was vividly reminded of how, over a period of years, my family and I became neurotically attached to my cell phone. Before I got it, I was incommunicado each time I left the house. Once everyone could keep constant track of me, my misplacing it or allowing its battery to die inspired panic in the ranks.

These are exceedingly interesting times for the student of birds, and ospreys are exceedingly interesting subjects of study. One tiny radio can forge a direct link between a bird and legions of people, can throw her into the light of our attention. What is everyday business to a fish hawk—crossing the Sahara desert, flying up and over a sandstorm, making 215 miles in a single day's flight, fighting *wheep wheep wheep* an interloping female for her traditional nest site—is an amazement to us. So much of what birds do simply to survive reaches into the realm of the unimaginable, and a proper awe for their adaptability and grit finds its place in our hearts.

I look back over my notes from what I now remember as my osprey summer. It is a sparkling August day, with a spanking northwester sending shots of sun off the wavelets. I've used the ospreys as my goof-off facilitators all summer. The sketches I bring home legitimize what has become my favorite pastime—hanging out with the osprey family. Humming, I pack a lunch and set off for Niantic. And there's no one home. I set up my chair and spotting scope. A few yellow jackets buzz around scraps of the last catch. Snowy egrets poke white holes in the marsh, and common terns flee the ratchety calls of demanding young.

But the osprey family, even the reluctant young female, has finally ridden the breeze south. I feel deserted and lonely. I guess I thought they'd say goodbye, hover above me, casting a last glance over their strong brown shoulders. Silly of me.

What a changed place this marsh is without them. It's like the empty set of a great play, a few stagehands crossing with push brooms. Nothing for it but to head home, I guess, and try to remember what I was doing before I was hooked by ospreys.

*great egret, leaving*

A very ticked-off
titmouse.

# Nobody Can Cuss Like a Titmouse

FOR MOST of my life, I've tried to fix broken birds. Like most children, I was tenderhearted, and I had no idea one had to have state and federal permits to handle wild birds. I just cleaned up what our neighbors' seventeen cats wrought, replacing baby birds in their nests, perching fledglings up higher in the shrubbery, trying to set broken wings with tape and Popsicle sticks, and raising those who had been orphaned. I learned a lot from my father, who was raised on a farm and knew how to nurture creatures. When I was in high school, we came up with a formula, fed through an ear syringe, that raised a nice, fat mourning dove. Dad knew that pigeons feed their young a milklike substance by regurgitation, and we went from there, using rolled oats, half-and-half, strawberries, and ground sunflower seeds.

Now, I have the pieces of paper that make such pursuits legal, and while I don't seek out broken birds, they come to me through word of mouth or calls to *Bird Watcher's Digest*. In mid-January, I got a call about a tufted titmouse that couldn't fly. The couple who brought it to me said they thought it had hit a window; they'd found it lying on its back on their patio. Its drooping wing and missing upper tail coverts made me immediately suspect cat damage. We continued to chat, and the couple mentioned that they owned two free-roaming cats but that they didn't bother birds. Such lovely people; I let that statement drop and allowed as how a sharp-shinned or Cooper's hawk might have injured the bird. Two things I know: hawks don't leave their prey lying on the patio, nor do windows grab birds from behind. It's an old story, and one I'm weary of. Even innocent-looking, fat, old cats kill birds.

This titmouse was bright and active but reduced to scuttling around on the floor of his cage, his left wing hanging. To figure out what might be wrong, I wet him to the skin and examined him carefully. My ears rang as he cussed me up and down. Nobody can cuss like a wet titmouse. In an ideal wing exam, one manipulates the bones of the wing and listens for crepitation, the sound of broken ends rubbing on one another. I had no chance of hearing anything over his earsplitting protests, but his wing bones checked out fine. I did find a massive purple and green bruise over the left scapula, which went a long way toward explaining why he was grounded. If bruising was all he had, and the scapula wasn't broken, this bird might just fly again. If the stars aligned, he might fly well enough to be releasable. It doesn't take much of an insult to the delicate bones, muscles, and nerves of a songbird wing to render it permanently useless. I decided to see what a small cage, a couple of weeks' rest for that wing, and about one thousand mealworms would do for him.

As the days went by, the titmouse got wilder and wilder. He began to ricochet off the bars of his cage when I entered the room, bing, bang, bong! He whistled *peter peter peter* and scolded me lustily. One night he whistled at 4:00 A.M. and my husband, Bill, leapt out of bed, thinking his cell phone was ringing!

Pussywillows!

February 9 1998
I am thunderstruck by the
difference between this fine adult titmouse
and the ragtag peanut—freeloaders just a
mile away at our feeder
A bright blaze of chestnut on his sides
velvety black mask, buttery smooth plumage
He glows with health

If things go well, there comes a moment in a bird's rehabilitation arc when you walk up to its cage and know it's ready to go. I had seen this one stretch both wings up over his back in a quiet moment, and I noticed him using the injured wing a little more each day. Now, twelve days later, he was hitting the sides of the cage so hard that I knew I had to release him before he damaged himself further. It's a delicate choice: I wanted to release him when he was sufficiently healed but before he lost his wild edge. So I closed the door of my little eight-by-ten-foot bird room and opened the doors of his cage. He shot out like a watermelon seed and clung to the screen over the window. He passed his test with flying colors. This titmouse wanted OUT!

Although I prefer to release birds where they were found, taking this bird back to the yard where he had been injured was out of the question. He deserved to

Jan. 24, 2008
A newly-released
titmouse gathers his wits in the
hedge, then makes straight for the peanuts!
What a bird!

live on a cat-free sanctuary, with the pampered titmice that frequent our feeders. I took him out into the yard, where he could see the feeders and the other titmice looping back and forth between the woods and the yard. Then I opened my hands. He rose up, higher and higher, with a slight twist to the left wing. He flew strongly, certainly well enough for a nonmigratory bird that needs only to flit from tree to tree. He flew all the way across the front yard and lit in the forsythia, where he fluffed his feathers, wiped his bill, and fluttered his wings. Three dark-eyed juncos darted over to keep him company. He flew farther, to a thick hedge, where he set to preening his disheveled plumage with that fussy, almost disdainful air of a bird just handled. I moved closer to try to get a photo of him setting things right, and he rose up and flew right over my head, back toward the feeding station. He paused a moment in a little birch tree, then flew straight to the peanut feeder.

If I hadn't seen it with my own eyes, I'd never have believed it. What a bird. He had the lay of the land all figured out within ten minutes of leaving my hands. People should get on with their lives so handily. When the feeder birds spooked, he rocketed into the woods with three other titmice. To this day, I peer at every titmouse I see, looking for a slight droop of the wing, a knowing glance. He's out there; I know it, and knowing that gives me a secret smile. Titmice 1, cats 0.

# Chimney Swift

## High-Maintenance Aerialist

IN A TINY COTTAGE in Connecticut, crowned by an ancient stone chimney, I lived with chimney swifts. A pair nested there each year, and, for about a month and a half each summer, I could hear the muffled roar of the birds' wings as they tended nestlings that first chittered and then yammered and then inexorably drove me to distraction with the harsh, scraping screech of adolescent chimney swifts being fed. The chimney acted as a sound chamber for the birds' slightest utterance. I loved the sleepy, continuous twitter of the family at night, even as the occasional ruffle of their wings woke me.

The birds were largely unseen, until a rainy day when I found three naked chicks rolling about in the cold fireplace, perhaps dislodged by the water streaming down the inside of the open chimney. I took them in, warmed them, and fed them, but I knew I was out of my league with these blind, naked nestlings. When the weather broke, I made a nest from a pasteboard strawberry box, climbed onto the roof, and lowered it on strings into the chimney, as close to the level of their original nest as I could get it. I tied it securely and went back into the house to listen. A whir of wings as an adult swift entered the chimney, the unmistakable scrabble of its claws on the side of the strawberry box, and the clamor of prodigals being fed. A huge grin spread across my face, one of wonder at the birds' flexibility in accepting my makeshift nest mixed with extreme relief at being freed from having to raise them myself.

I had no more significant contact with chimney swifts for the next twenty years. They were flying cigars; they were tiny bombers, chittering and swooping on trembling wings high overhead. I'd learned a little bit about them that I hadn't known; for instance, their incubation period is around twenty days—a very long time, especially for a bird that hatches altricially (blind and helpless). A chicken's incubation period is only twenty-one days, and chickens hatch covered with down, open-eyed, and ready to scratch and forage for themselves! And I'd always assumed that swifts nested colonially in chimneys, but further research revealed that one pair claims each chimney, despite what major reference books said. As many as forty nonbreeding birds may roost communally in a chimney occupied by a single breeding pair, a phenomenon that's not well understood and that contributes to the popular supposition that the birds are colonial nesters. For birds that nest literally in our living rooms, chimney swifts are poorly known.

From the strawberry box experience, I had an inkling that swifts were something more than an unknowable avian enigma, but I couldn't have guessed what was about to pan out on June 23, 2004, when the phone rang. A woman had a box of five tiny pink chimney swifts that had been knocked down when her neighbor's chimney was cleaned. The neighbor had called a chimney cleaning service when she heard strange noises in her flue. I had to wonder about a chimney sweep who would take an enormous steel brush to a flue occupied by swifts. Certainly a professional sweep knows what chimney swifts are; that they're the authors of the strange noises his client complains about; that his brushes will destroy their nests, breaking federal law. Perhaps that's the whole point of the exercise, to clean out that which annoys.

Homeowners often assume that a bird nesting in close proximity to their living space constitutes a health hazard, and they justify nest destruction on those grounds. Paul and Georgean Kyle, North America's leading advocates for chimney swift education and conservation, in a paper called "Environmental Tips for Homeowners and Professional Chimney Sweeps," state that a single chimney sweep has been known to kill as many as one hundred swifts in a season. A sooty little secret, one I hadn't thought much about before these small pink orphans came to me. It's a mistake to assume that everyone respects federal laws that protect native birds when there's money to be made.

The homeowner, perhaps feeling a bit of remorse for hiring a professional to come eliminate baby birds, called the squirming nestlings to the attention of her neighbor, a self-described "animal person," the kind of person who finds herself cleaning up after the thoughtless cruelties of others. I meet a lot of "animal people," most of them women, and I love them for the way they lead with their hearts, how they drop everything to help the helpless. There is a lot to know about caring for birds, and some birds are harder to provide for than others, which leads such kind souls to my door. If there were a scale of difficulty in raising birds, I'd give chimney swifts five stars, an Extreme rating, as I was to find out very soon.

I started out with five naked chicks, writhing in a shoe box lined with tissues. They were very young, perhaps four or five days old; another star on the difficulty scale. Before three days had gone by, I'd lost two; they'd languished and stopped gaping, and force feeding couldn't bring them back. A third bird died on the fifth day. But the two smallest chicks clung tenaciously to life as I blundered along, trying to do right by them.

So much of what makes chimney swifts hard to care for springs from their bizarre natural history. First, chimneys are very warm places in summertime; sun heats them, and at night, residual heat from the house travels up. I realized I'd need to provide supplemental heat from a lamp, keeping the swifts at a constant eighty degrees, which would aid their digestion and mobility. Second, chimneys are dark and full of soot. Fortuitously, chimney swifts' eyes are sealed shut until they're fourteen to eighteen days old, in contrast to those of open-cup-nesting songbirds, whose eyes open before a week has passed.

Perhaps because chimneys constitute visual deprivation chambers, young chimney swifts show no contrasting gape flanges or mouth lining colors. Instead, their parents find them by sound and touch. And, being blind for most of the nestling period, they react only to tactile or auditory stimuli. I nudge the silent nestlings, and they chatter and gape and gobble up what I offer them. I blow on them, and the same thing happens. In their world, an arriving adult announces itself with a whir of wings, and a stream of air rolled over a fluttering tongue simulates the event. They remind me of the naked, blind, pink animals that live in caves, input-limited creatures to whom light and vision mean nothing.

Chimney swifts lead vertical lives; they perch clinging to chimney walls. Even the nestlings' feet are incredibly strong. It's almost impossible to disengage one from any surface without peeling each toe off. It's no wonder—their lives depend on clinging strongly. In a chimney, falling from the nest or one's perch onto the bricks is a death sentence, and they hang on like they mean to stay. They climb from their tiny nest well before they're feathered and cling, shuffling around on the sheer wall with fluttering wing stubs.

Young chimney swifts never grow down feathers; they proceed from naked skin straight to pinfeathers, like woodpeckers do. This is another hallmark of birds that grow up in warm, protected environs. Well before their feathers break the skin, they spend a great deal of time "preening," their bills going through pre-

cise and stereotyped motions, rif-
fling and nibbling feathers that
aren't yet there. I'm reminded of
watching my four-year-old son,
Liam, arranging his hair in the mirror. Not yet at the age of self-aware-

preening at
this tender age!

ness, he goes through the motions anyway. Not only are the nestlings naked but
they lie in the nest with their necks extended over its rim, hanging down like five
little Kilroys. When I blow on them or touch them, they chitter madly, waving
their heads wildly but never raising them. It's very difficult to feed a bird that begs
with its head hanging down. I realize that, in nature, an adult chimney swift drops
into the chimney, then swoops up and clings to the underside of the cantilevered
nest, feeding the young from below. I'm forced to hold each chick's head still, in
an upturned position, to be able to get a loaded forceps into its mouth.

Another peculiarity I discovered about chimney swifts is an absence of fecal sacs, those membranous coatings that constitute avian diapers. In most songbirds, adults feed a chick, then wait for it to produce a neatly contained fecal sac,
which is carried some distance from the nest and dropped. Swift droppings are
discharged in a loose splatter but with great fanfare. A chick feeling the need to
defecate wiggles its rump, backs up, clings tightly to the nest rim, and shoots the
liquid droppings as far out into space as it's able, just the way young raptors do.
You might imagine that this makes them a special joy to care for. But this behavior makes perfect sense in a chimney, where there are no predators that might locate the young birds by their droppings. Thanks to their energetically expensive
aerial foraging, adult chimney swifts visit the nest rather infrequently. Even if they
were agile enough to do so, they would never be able to keep up with removing
the young birds' copious droppings.

I'd always wondered at the construction of chimney swift nests. I have one before me on my desk as I write. How did it hold a brood of five young? It's tiny—only 3¾ inches across, with a cup only 1¼ inches deep. It's underslung, more a twiggy hammock than a nest, glued onto the bricks with the parent birds' sticky saliva. I've watched chimney swifts gather the twigs for their nests, swooping over the tops of giant maples and oaks, snapping dead twigs off in flight with their feet. I remember my jaw dropping as I realized what the birds were up to, fluttering among dead branches protruding from the leafy canopy, right there in

A 14-day old chimney swift, last to leave the nest. Its eyes have just opened. Now it will crawl, climb and exercise its wings for another 14 days, until its ready to leave the chimney for good.

The little hammock of a nest is shiny, lacquered with the adults' saliva—all that holds it together.

my Connecticut yard. They transfer the twig from foot to bill for the trip to the nest. The selected twigs are amazingly consistent, averaging 1¾ inches in length. Shorter, finer twig lengths—most around ½ inch—make up the inside base, and the twigs get longer and stouter—up to 2 inches—as the birds build the cantilevered nest outward, like a wall sconce.

It may take the swifts three to four weeks to finish building a single nest. The eggs are laid when the nest is only half-finished; the birds continue building it until the eggs hatch. A coating of dried saliva gives the nest a lacquerlike polish that allows any stray droppings to simply roll off. Debris, such as bits of feather sheath, simply drops through its open basket weave. Parasites, so common in swallow nests, have not been recorded in chimney swift nests. Holding it in my hand, with the experience of caring for messy chimney swift young under my belt, I suddenly understand that everything about this minuscule nest has to do with keeping the young birds clean, and away from their own accumulated droppings, just until they're strong enough to climb out of it. For broods of more than four, this happens around Day 14, when their eyes have just opened.

The sticky saliva, still flexible after four years, has the plastic texture of dried mucilage. It's got to be loaded with protein and collagen, but apparently its chemical composition hasn't been analyzed. Edible-nest swiftlets of Southeast Asia forgo the twigs and construct the entire nest of saliva. It looks like a cup made of rice noodles. When boiled, the gelatinous saliva is a binder for soups. As are many bizarre animal byproducts, it's highly valued in Asia for supposed medicinal and aphrodisiacal properties. I root around a little and find a scientific paper authored by Chao-Tan Guo, with nine Japanese coauthors, showing that edible bird's nest extract strongly inhibits infection with influenza viruses; they consider it a safe and valid natural source for protection against infection. Safe for the imbiber, perhaps, but the men who climb limber, impossibly tall bamboo ladders against cave walls in Malaysia to gather it might argue that point.

Predictably, edible-nest swiftlets are becoming scarce. Bird-nest merchants in Vietnam, Indonesia, and Thailand have started to build houselike structures in order to attract wild swiftlets. The most highly prized nests are white, made entirely of swift spit, free from feathers. Climbers destroy imperfect nests, along with the eggs inside. The theory is that this selection process favors birds that produce feather-free white nests for the trade. When I think about swift saliva, the last thing I think about is preventing flu, or aphrodisiacs. I think about baby swift droppings, about adaptations to life in odd places. It's a weird world.

Keeping the babies warm seems to help their vitality and appetite, which isn't at the level I'd like to see. But I worry that the heat lamp is causing them to get dehydrated. I decide to administer pediatric electrolyte with a dropper, and I'm amazed at the upturn in their condition. I follow every feeding of mealworms and crickets with an eyedropper shot of electrolyte. Their appetites pick up. I learn from another rehabilitator that dehydration is the main cause of anorexia in baby birds, and chimney swifts seem to need more water than any other bird. I guess flying insects must be high in water, just as they are low in calcium; I roll the baby swifts' crickets and mealworms in calcium before feeding them to the birds. I jettison the heat lamp and start sheltering the birds in a beer cooler with a jar of warm water beside them. It keeps them at a steady temperature without dehydrating them, and closing the lid gives them the darkness they seem to crave. Blindly feeling my way through my cave of ignorance, I'm hitting on the strategies I need to keep them alive. I've got only two left to learn on. I venture to name them: Sasha and Amelia.

June 30
Day 14-sibling. He has beautiful
eyelids today, and he peeks out,
then shuts his eyes.

Day 10. A spurt of growth. He's doing
really well. Primaries continue to
emerge, and upper tail coverts are
coming out.

Adult chimney swifts have a distensible throat area—the gular pouch—
which they cram with small flying insects, making a nickel-size bolus of protein
that is easily carried in the bulging throat. You wouldn't want a wad of insects
hanging out of your bill when you're ripping along at seventy miles an hour. I notice that the babies have strong tongues that they can use to lick out the corners
of their mouths—something I've seen no other small bird do. My macaw licks
the corners of his mouth and even the outside of his bill, but his tongue structure
is utterly different. It's a bent, fingerlike organ, not the flat ribbon that constitutes
most passerine tongues. It occurs to me that the adult swifts might use this strong
tongue to divvy up the bolus of food between as many as seven babies. By the
sixth day, a parent will disgorge the entire bolus to one nestling.

It's touch and go feeding the two remaining birds. They alternate, first one refusing food, and then the other. I'm consumed by worry that they'll die, too. I
consult on the telephone with Astrid MacLeod, an experienced bird rehabilitator, who advises me that the pediatric electrolyte I'm using to rehydrate the birds
might be robbing them of water because it's so high in sugar. She explains what's

going on at a cellular level and advises using plain water. I've concluded that flying insects must have a much higher water content than mealworms and that parent swifts must have some way of bringing water to their young that I know nothing about. I've never seen young birds need so much water; in fact, I've raised most birds without any more water than is in their moist formula. If only I'd known about their water requirements, I'd be raising five. It bothers me to think that simple dehydration was killing them.

Next to Astrid I feel like such a piker, more of a witch doctor than a scientist. I look around at my house, ankle-deep in the kids' toys. I haven't had time to pick them up, to go to the grocery store, to do any of the things I do to keep the house running and livable. I'm mixing sloppy batches of bird formula, grinding kitten chow, adding pinches of calcium and vitamins, washing eyedroppers, feeding the birds every forty minutes from predawn dark to bedtime. It is all-consuming, and it's depressing to teeter on the brink of failure, to wonder what I'm doing wrong. Yet, I've gotten them to the point of feathering out.

By July 2, things have settled down. With copious supplemental water, Sasha and Amelia are begging and chittering for food. I learn to look at their droppings to see if they're getting enough water, and I notice that drier droppings tend to go with anorexia. I relax and begin to enjoy my role as chimney swift mother, even as I chafe at the enforced confinement of having to drop everything once an hour. The fun part is about to begin, and this odd job I've taken on will get much more demanding before it gets easier. I'll have to provide proper housing for these birds, and it's not going to be a strawberry box or a parakeet cage. These birds are aerialists, and I'm going to need a big cage. Not only that but I'm going to need something that approximates a chimney for them to roost in when they're not flying. I'm going to have to add a sixth star to their difficulty rating.

By July 7, I've had my two swifts for fourteen days. The phone rings in the morning, and the caller has five baby chimney swifts that have fallen down a high and inaccessible flue. They've kept the birds alive for three days with small balls of raw hamburger, fed five times a day. When the caller arrives with her eleven-year-old daughter, I learn that the young girl shouldered the chore of feeding them. Only two would gape readily; she hit upon the trick of roaring at them, which caused them to open their mouths and shrill in fear. This call, a harsh, incredibly loud *reaaah! reaah! reeeaahh!* is given when the nestlings are startled and only, as far as I know, by nestlings. It's doubtless effective in frightening small mammalian predators away from an occupied nest; I've heard young titmice give a snakelike hiss in the same situations. When the swifts' mouths opened wide in the fright call, the girl would pop in a hamburger ball, and she kept them alive that way. I praised her innovation, this budding animal person, hugged her, and promised her I'd do my best to raise them all.

These birds are a little older than my two, and though they're a bit underweight and dehydrated, they're bright-eyed and beautiful, having been raised by their parents until they met with misfortune. My two look a bit scruffier, but they seem thrilled to have an instant family. When I put them all in a rattan wastebasket, Sasha and Amelia scuttle into the middle of a pile of soft, soot brown chimney swift feathers and look up at me, their eyes twinkling.

I mix up my latest avian culinary offering, suggested by Astrid—a scrambled egg, its shell crushed to powder and stirred back in, with two tablespoons of dried insects added for extra protein. Fried up, the bug omelet smells nauseating and looks even worse, a gray mess of bug bits and egg. But they eat it with gusto, and it should have everything they need to grow and thrive. I order $36.00 worth of dried flies and one thousand live crickets online for $16.50. Raising chimney swifts is neither easy nor cheap, but it pays richly in intangibles.

The newcomers are frightened and still, in contrast to my raucous foundlings.

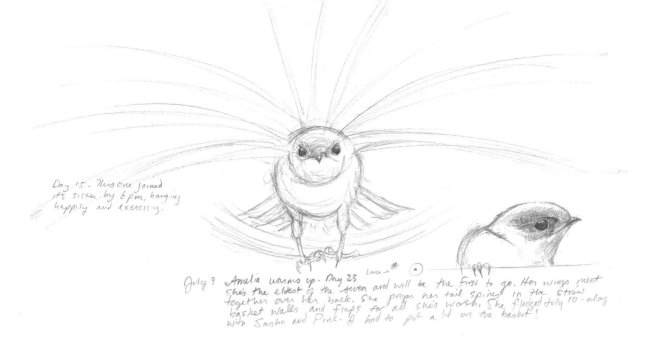

Day 15 - This one joined its sister by 6 pm, hanging happily and exercising.

July 9 Amelia warms up. Day 23 Louie→ She's the eldest of the seven and will be the first to go. Her wings meet together over her back. She preps her tail spines in the straw basket walls and flaps for all she's worth. She fledged July 10 - along with Sasha and Pink - & had to put a lid on the basket!

They sit with bills clamped shut, watching me warily. I can't blame them — they've been a bit intimidated by their foster mother's technique. When they see Sasha and Amelia begging lustily, they join in, immediately at ease. Now my problem is remembering which of the seven have been fed in a session. Bill suggests that I color-code them, so I dab a dot of acrylic paint on each bird's forehead: pink, green, red, blue, white, and yellow. I run out of colors, but I don't need to mark scruffy little Sasha anyway, any more than a mother needs to mark her child on the first day of preschool. He's still in pinfeathers and looks reptilian next to Amelia and these smooth, paint-dotted newcomers.

From two to seven — it's a bit more work, but as long as I'm dropping everything on the hour, I might as well feed five more birds. My little flock feels like a quorum now. The bug omelet agrees with them. I supplement with live mealworms. They're old enough to handle the smooth, chitinous coating on the larvae, which is a good thing, since I can't find enough tender, freshly molted mealworms to keep seven hungry birds fed.

July 8, 2004. It's fledging day (Day 21) for Amelia, the older of the two original orphans. She's impossible to corral in the berry box and refuses to sit for her daily portrait, fluttering to my chest and clinging there. Once, she flutters down and manages to land on my smooth calf, so sharp are her nails and strong are her toes. Oh, that smarts. I paint one more portrait of Sasha, who's eighteen days old and finally free from sheaths on his head and body. He's gone from a porcupine to a sleek, beautiful bird. He watches every stroke of the pencil with minute turns of his snakelike head. But for the shape of his eyes I'd never have known it was Sasha. I feel a flush of accomplishment, washing away the apprehension that's dogged me for the past two weeks. Somehow he's survived my ineptitude, and now there are five more chimney swifts for him to socialize with. With my two-week crash course in nurturing swifts behind me, I feel confident they're all going to make it.

I'm keeping all seven in the rattan wastebasket, lined with paper towels at the bottom. They cling handily to its weave, and it's easy to feed them, then change the paper toweling every hour. When I need to wash the basket, I simply remove the nestlings and hook them like living brooches onto the front of my shirt; they'll hang wherever I put them. Amelia and Sasha immediately scuttle up to nes-

July 8
Sasha - Day 18- It's hard to believe this is the same bird in the first paintings. Amelia would not sit for her portrait today. She flew to my chest and clung there — very endearing. Sasha is watching me draw his picture here, head moving with each movement of the pencil.

tle under my chin; these birds have never known any other mother, and it's revealed in behavior like this. I keep everything as clean as possible, but I occasionally must put a bird under the warm-water tap and wash it after it ends up at the bottom of the basket. I start covering the basket with a towel in between feedings, lest one of the birds make an unscheduled flight in the house. I keep them on the kitchen table, the better to reach them for feeding and cleaning. They chitter and preen in their darkened basket, and they rasp rhythmically like an engine burning up when I raise the blanket.

After one feeding, I forget to cover the basket, and one bird makes an escape. I'm not aware of it until an hour later, when I find only six gaping mouths on going to feed them. My son, Liam's voice comes from the adjoining living room. "Mommy, there's a bird in the chimney!" And there is Sasha, up inside our big stone chimney, clinging quietly. This bird was brought to our home at perhaps four days of age, a blind pink blob of protoplasm. He's never seen a chimney. And yet he knows where to go; he's following an instinctive blueprint. Clearly, we owe him a chimney of his own.

I stuff Sasha back in the wastebasket, cover it, and go to the garage to rummage about among the lumber and garden tools, emerging with four stout, weathered boards. Bill revs up his circular saw and makes a narrow, four-foot-high box, a suitable substitute for a real chimney. I rough up the inside for clingability, and we mount it in the middle of a fifteen-by-seventeen-foot nylon-screen tent out in the yard. The swifts leave their basket, fly tentatively around the new space, and immediately drop into the box as if they've been doing it all their lives.

They throw their wings over each other's backs and sleep inside the makeshift chimney in one big, soft mass of feathers, studded with sparkling onyx eyes. After dark, I go into the tent, gently gather them into their old rattan wastebasket, and take them inside for the night. The nylon tent is anything but raccoon-proof, and I can't let these wonderful birds go to feed a bandit.

By July 14, all seven are careening around wildly inside their soft net tent. It's an ideal way to let them fly without damaging themselves. They pester each other, landing on each other's backs and chasing. When I go in the tent, they land on my chest and head. Amelia seems to delight in landing on my eyebrows, even my lips. It is excruciatingly painful to have a swift hanging on one's face from needle-sharp claws. Tears start in my eyes and roll down my cheeks even as I shake with suppressed laughter at being suddenly turned into a perch. I inhale the fusty, warm bird scent of her belly against my nose and marvel that she'd choose to cling to my face. It would feel like a hug if it weren't so painful.

There is a spark in these birds, a mischievousness and intelligence that I'd never had the luxury of noticing before I stood in as their mother. It's easy to assume that a bird that spends most of its life on the wing must not be very interesting or intelligent. And yet I perceive predictable differences among all of the seven fledglings. Some are adventurous, like the aptly named Amelia; some more timid; some are assertive and reckless; some, like Sasha, just sweeter, for lack of a better word. Amelia has figured out where the door is on the flight tent, and she's clearly

*Fledging day! for Amelia – at noon she fluttered up out of the berry box and climbed the side of the box – so I put her in a wicker wastebasket where she fluttered madly, and clung the rest of the day. She loves to cling to my shoulder and clatter in my ear.*

hoping to make a break for it. It's accessed by a floor-to-ceiling zipper. Because of her insight, I'm forced to unzip it at the bottom, just enough to insert my foot, and block the opening with my body, literally zipping my way into the tent. Amelia will land on my thigh as I'm trying to get inside. These swifts are not slow in any sense of the word.

Just as we're poised on the brink of release, it gets tricky again. I learn from other rehabilitators that I must wait until the flight feathers have completely emerged from their sheaths before releasing the birds. Every day, I watch them circling their tent, and I check their flight feathers as they cling to its screened sides, watching the sky. To my consternation, they begin refusing all food. Every time I think I have them figured out, they throw me another curve. I dive into the literature to see what might be going on. They're healthy, flying strongly, bright-eyed, preening. They just seem to be fasting. The *Birds of North America* account states that body mass of fledglings that first leave the nest and begin exercising their wings is three grams less than peak mass on Days 18 to 22. These birds are almost thirty days old, old enough to leave and not come back. I think they want to feed themselves now. Because I have no way of offering flying insects, I try throwing mealworms at them as they circle the tent. They feint but don't take the offering. I coax and cajole and manage to get a few crickets in them.

Once chimney swifts leave their nest sites for good, at twenty-eight to thirty days of age, their parents no longer feed them, even when they return to roost and beg. I know that these birds are equipped with the instinct to grab flying insects, but it seems like an abrupt transition to go from total subsidy to none. Because some of them still sport sheaths on the bases of their flight feathers, I'm reluctant to just zip open the tent. I want to be sure their flight powers are as well developed as possible. Even though I sense that this anorexia is a natural prerequisite to fledging, I keep careful track of their food intake and occasionally take a recalcitrant fledgling's bill in my hand and stuff a calcium-dusted cricket down

its mouth. I'm not going to have devoted a month of intensive care to these birds only to lose them on the brink of independence. I'm consumed with worry again, slaloming down the steep slope of my learning curve.

JULY 19, 2004. There was something in the swifts' eyes this afternoon that made me realize it was over. They had to go today. They were wild, unruly, impatient, hungry, and keen. One by one, I hand-caught them as they clung briefly to the tent walls, and I put them in their little rattan wastebasket. I gathered the kids and Bill, and we drove into the old part of Marietta, Ohio, and walked out onto a railroad trestle over the Muskingum River.

Ironically, we had to take these birds eighteen miles into town to release them, for chimney swifts need chimneys for roosting and nesting. Marietta is swift heaven, full of old buildings and uncapped brick chimneys, and situated on the confluence of two rivers, with associated hordes of aquatic insects overhead. Clouds of swifts swirled over us; there was a huge caddis fly hatch on the rivers this July evening. There couldn't be a better time or place to release these birds than here, on this quiet river beside this lovely old riverboat town, beneath a peach-colored sky.

My daughter, Phoebe, who had so faithfully helped me feed these seven foundlings, uncovered the rattan basket. Pink was the first to leap into space, flying with verve and vigor high over the smooth, peach-hued Muskingum. Then came Red, Blue, Green, and Willa. Sasha and Amelia, the ones we'd hand-raised from tiny squirmers, stayed at the bottom of the basket, their heads tracing little arcs as they followed birds high overhead. A squadron of wild swifts came down to meet and flank each new flier, and I laughed out loud to see the fledglings dive, circle, cut side to side, feint, and especially glide—none of which they had been able to do in the cramped confines of their fledging tent. My fears that the human-acclimated swifts might land on passersby evaporated when I saw how high, fast,

As each fandling is released, wild swifts
swoop down to flank it, following its every move.
I never expected that! July 19, 2004

and freely they flew. They took such obvious joy in pushing the sky's envelope, these avian DeLoreans, these high-maintenance, high-performance aeronauts, who would now be taking care of themselves.

The air was charged with joy, liberation. Finally Amelia sprang from the basket, and Sasha soon followed. The wild swifts made them welcome, swooping down as a body to fly alongside them. I tracked their flight as long as I could through binoculars, their eyepieces muddled with tears. I looked at Phoebe and Liam, who, like me, had known from the start that our strange little orphans would have to leave someday but had gotten hopelessly attached anyway. Tears dripped from their chins. And I decided at that moment that it was time to get these kids a puppy.

On the way home, we passed streetlights swimming with caddis flies. I sighed happily, knowing that I could sleep in tomorrow, that I could take the big tent down and finally mow the lawn, knowing I'd done my best by them, these seven birds who would have died without us. A small voice came from the back seat, four-year-old Liam: "Will those birds be okay in the night?" I assured him that the wild flock had most certainly shown them to a big chimney where they could all roost together; that they were probably snuggled under a blanket of new companions, and happier than they'd ever been.

Looking down at
three swifts sleeping
Red and Willa have each
thrown a wing
over Yellow.

# Rose-breasted Grosbeak

## Close Encounters of the Bird Kind

JUNE 22, 1988. The call came from Connecticut Audubon's nature center in Fairfield. A nestling rose-breasted grosbeak had been brought in, and it was doing poorly. Would I take it off their hands? I pondered the eighty-mile drive from my home to the state's western coast and thought about the possibility that the bird had been misidentified. What if I made the drive all the way down only to find a look-alike brown-headed cowbird nestling waiting in a shoe box? "Are there any feathers on its head?" I asked, hoping to smoke out a cowbird impostor, for they stay bald until well after their bodies sprout feathers. "Yes, the head is feathered, and we're sure it's a grosbeak," the caller replied. "He's not doing too well, and we're afraid we're going to lose him." I reshuffled my schedule, gathered some feeding supplies, and got in the car. The chance to raise a rose-breast was worth the slight inconvenience, worth the months of care, the worry and work.

The tiny bird looked bad, all right, his left leg sprawled out from lack of support and a calcium deficiency. He'd been trying to stand on smooth newspaper when he needed the support of a nest. His droppings were runny, and his appetite was nil. But his eyes were bright, and he was a nine-day-old rose-breasted grosbeak all right, and my heart fluttered and landed over him, clucking and brooding, gathering him in. First, the spraddled leg: I cut white artist's tape into a narrow strip, taped his sprawled leg to the good one, bringing them together in a natural pose, and installed him in a tissue-paper nest in a small strawberry box for support. I mixed up a diet of mealworms and ground puppy chow, parrot chow, lactobacillus, and vitamins, and fed him from a syringe. He was brighter by nightfall, chirping for food the next morning. That night, I untaped his leg, and it held in a normal pose. We were on our way. I named him Jeff, guessing at his sex, for all rose-breasted grosbeaks are striped brown at the start. By Day 22, salmon pink feathers were emerging in his wing linings. My guess at his sex had been correct.

June 25, 1988
Jeffy, Day 12, struggles to stay on my wrist. I will have to tape his tarso-metatarsi together to correct his spraddled legs. He doesn't look like much right now, but what a fine bird he'd become!

If chimney swifts are the extreme slope in the ski course of wild bird rehabilitation, rose-breasted grosbeaks must be the bunny slope. Jeff's transition from syringe feeding to picking up his own food was seamless and painless. His natural curiosity about inanimate objects that might be food caused him to pick up and taste anything small enough to fit in his bill. By Day 28, his syringe-fed diet was supplemented with fresh garden peas, diced fruit, parakeet pellets, and ground dry puppy chow, which he picked at himself. On Day 30, I was called away for the day, and the young rose-breast fed himself.

From then on, he refused hand feeding. That was easy—such a contrast to other songbirds I'd raised, which seemed to need real deprivation to try picking up their own fare. Jeff processed live mealworms by flipping them against his perch before masticating and swallowing them down. He bathed daily in a shallow dish and slept in a homemade cage, a two-foot cube of hardware cloth and wood. I left the top open most of the time so he could come in to feed and rest as much as he wished. Jeff was a "trusty": a clean, quiet bird who stayed out of trouble and kept to predictable perches, refraining from bashing himself against the windows or whitewashing my home. He began his day by leaving his cage, hopping across the bedclothes from my toes up to my head, and gently pecking my nose until I opened my eyes with a chuckle. A rose-breast reveille was a fine way to wake up.

Because I lived on a Nature Conservancy preserve in Salem, Connecticut, surrounded by approximately one thousand acres of woods and field, releasing such hand-raised, human-acclimated birds rarely presented a problem. It was the ideal environment for soft release, whereby a hand-raised bird gradually becomes used to being outdoors.

Jeffy Day 22
7/05/88

Day 28
July 9 '88
He likes Rob better than me,
lands on him all the time
Where's the justice?

Training them to come when called, rewarding them with food from a brightly colored plastic dish, I could ease their transition to the wild over a period of weeks.

Short outings transitioned to several hours outside, and finally to entire days. On Day 32, I hung Jeff's cage outside, his food bowls in place. I opened the cage, and he flew to the top of an apple tree, where he remained through the afternoon. He descended to eat mealworms from my palm at 8:00 P.M. and spent an uneventful night outside. Though one might expect a hand-raised bird to simply vanish upon first being released outside, my foundlings showed a strong bond to me and to the place where they were raised. The first overnight outdoors is a watershed moment, probably more for me than for the bird.

The next morning, I heard Jeff's juvenile contact call, a soft, whistled *teeawee*, at first light. I emerged from the house with a dish of mealworms, chopped peaches, and cherries, to an enthusiastic reception. By his fourth day out on his own, at thirty-five days of age, his natural wildness was kicking in, and he'd come with increasing reluctance to my hand to be fed.

One of the largest obstacles in releasing hand-raised birds is their lack of vigilance behavior. For Jeff's bene-fit, I imitated sharp, sibilant avian alarm calls and acted frightened when a blue jay, crow, hawk, or mammalian predator (my landlords' galumphing Labrador retriever) happened by. But it was exposure to other birds, some of them hand-raised, at my yard and feeders that probably most helped my foundlings learn appropriate vigilance behavior. These hand-raised birds occasionally presented a problem as well, since they associated my call with food. One catbird, raised and released the summer before, made a specialty of pilfering each new recruit's food, no matter where I'd hide its special dish. It was hard to be annoyed at such a clever and personable bird, especially since I was his foster mother.

Throughout the waning days of July, Jeff hung around, his soft *teeawee* contact call sounding in the trees around my house whenever I emerged. To thwart the

Jeffrey Day 26
July 9 1988
He's getting weary of being hand-fed and picks up worms, cherry & blueberry by himself
Bathes a lot since day 23.

crafty catbird, I rigged up a portable metal stand with a food cup wired to it. I'd carry it and set it nearby as I worked in the yard, and the young grosbeak would land and feed unmolested by the somewhat shier catbird. But Jeff's visits dwindled in frequency and duration. On Day 38, he came in with his dusky pink bill covered in wild cherry pulp, took three mealworms, and left.

By Day 41, he was showing up at my bedroom window each morning at six. I'd obligingly pop out with a dish of mealworms and fruit. It was a routine I could get used to. I liked having daily contact with this lovely little brown-striped bird, liked knowing that he remembered where I slept and knew to call in the window, just as he had once pecked at my nose.

I was called away on Day 44, and Jeff disappeared. Four days later, he showed up, landing on my arm, and accepted a feeding of mealworms. He showed up regularly for the next four days, though he was now fifty-two days old and well able to fend for himself. He left for a week, then returned, called, and swooped low over my head as I gardened. It was August 9. I was pretty sure that was a grosbeak's way of saying goodbye.

I knew I'd miss Jeff when he left for good. He'd been so companionable in his quiet way. Almost a month later, I was weeding the garden in the clear September air when a bird circled high over my head, spiraling lower with each pass. From the pinwheel white in its whirring wings, I could tell it was a rose-breasted grosbeak, and the bright salmon pink underwing feathers told me it was a young male. *"Jeffy!"* I called, and the bird swooped lower, circled a few more times, and lined out for the western border of the preserve. How good of him to stop by! It was one of the priceless rewards of raising orphaned songbirds—the check-in by a free-living, wholly wild foundling that confirms that you've done the soft release right. Migrating, wintering, finding a mate next spring if all went well—it was up to Jeff now, and that's as it should be.

September 1988 – Jeffrey
checks in. To look up and know
I raised this bird – that is a fine thing.

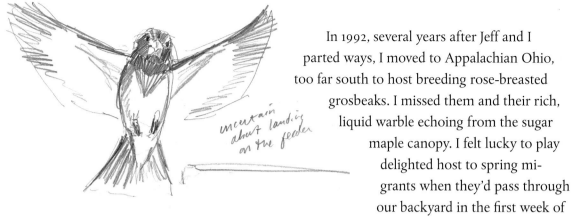

uncertain about landing on the feeder

In 1992, several years after Jeff and I parted ways, I moved to Appalachian Ohio, too far south to host breeding rose-breasted grosbeaks. I missed them and their rich, liquid warble echoing from the sugar maple canopy. I felt lucky to play delighted host to spring migrants when they'd pass through our backyard in the first week of May. I'd look out and spy something at the feeder that was large, black and white, and wasn't a woodpecker. The bird would turn its head, and the stunning cravat of carmine would give him away as a male rose-breasted grosbeak. Sometimes there were three or more, and a brown-striped female, too. Oh, how I longed for them to stay, but two weeks later they'd all be gone to more northerly latitudes. Though they breed about one hundred miles north of us in Canton, Ohio, and in West Virginia's mountains (even adorning that state's enviable license plate), I was out of their range, too far south and too low in elevation. Or so I thought.

In the waning days of May 2007, I was startled to see an adult male rose-breasted grosbeak clinging to a cylindrical mesh peanut feeder on our front porch. What on earth was a rose-breast doing here in the last week of May, eating peanuts? He should have been a hundred miles north at least, and nesting. The oddity didn't stop there. He was missing half his tail, and his cravat, instead of being deep carmine, was the pale pink of a Carolina rose. More than that, he was ridiculously tame.

My mental wheels started turning. Poor plumage and soft part coloration generally indicate an inadequate diet. Tameness can mean a lot of things. Sometimes it means illness or injury, and sometimes it means that a bird has prior association with people. Sometimes it just means that a bird is unafraid, for reasons we can't divine. I began to wonder if this bird had been hand-raised. When a deep-forest bird hangs around your front door, perching freely on man-made objects, you have to wonder. When I popped out of the front door to refill the feeders, he flew to a tubular metal hammock stand, perched on the slippery, shiny surface, and sang a sweet melody. If someone really pressed me, I'd say this bird had been captive-raised and be pretty sure I was telling them the truth. But he'd have to have been captive-raised a year ago, as a nestling, to behave like this. Well, stranger things have happened. I didn't think for an instant that Jeff had somehow found me in southern Ohio; that was eighteen years ago. I was simply delighted that another rose-breast had chosen Hotel Zickefoose for a stay.

He came to the feeder every morning for four days, parking on it, threatening the cardinals and woodpeckers who stared at the colorful new visitor hogging their peanuts. He drank and bathed in the bubbling bird spa, and he bossed the resident birds around. He didn't seem ill, just odd and much too tame.

Messing around in my gardens, I was startled when all the mourning doves spooked from the feeders with a roar of wings. Urgent *seet* calls from the tufted titmice indicated a hawk was nearby. At almost the same moment, there was a hollow *bonk* on the studio windows, and I cringed, wondering which bird had hit. Crumpled in the flowers beneath the window was the grosbeak. Of all the birds to hit the window . . . He lay stunned in the cardinal flowers for a half-hour while I kept watch over him from the studio.

Finally, he flew up, made a rocky landing on a low limb, and sat there for a while, gathering his scattered wits. I had to leave then, to take the kids to a softball game. When we came back, the grosbeak was perched attractively on the trunk of one of my potted bonsai trees, right by the front door. Oh, poor thing. Are you feeling shaky? Do you need help?

I put some peanut bits and suet dough in front of him. He considered those for a few minutes, then launched in flight—straight into the foyer window. He didn't hit hard, having flown only a couple of feet. I came to his rescue as he lay on the ground, and he hopped up on my finger like a tame parakeet. I froze, memories of Jeffy flooding back and filling the crevices in my heart. And then he was gone, flying strongly over the roof of the house.

He stayed through June 4, eating peanuts, somehow avoiding further trouble, past the "safe date" for suspected breeding in Ohio. I doubted that there was a female rose-breasted grosbeak for one hundred miles around. I hoped he headed north, away from windows and houses, when he finally left. He was a gift, that's all, and I still shiver with the remembrance of his strong, slate blue toes, clutching my fingers.

A month passed with the heavy hum of summer on the land. On the morning of July 6, while watching a dozen barn swallows trundling happily out on the garage roof—where we strew baked eggshells for their calcium-boosting pleasure—I saw a newly fledged rose-breasted grosbeak hopping among them. Small tufts of down waved atop its head; it was a rank baby, right out of the nest. I must have looked like a wolf in a Tex Avery cartoon, my eyes briefly leaving their sockets to ogle this unaccustomed sight. For fifteen years I'd been watching everything that happened in and around these eighty acres, and I'd never seen a just-fledged rose-breasted grosbeak, in July or any other month.

My mind flew back to my little spring gift—the pale male rose-breast who ate peanuts on the front porch for almost a week, past the rose-breast's safe date of June 4, after which you can suspect the bird is a breeder in Ohio. I had convinced myself he was just a late migrant in questionable condition. He'd smacked himself hard on the studio window, shown up on the bonsai bench that afternoon, perched on my hand for a few golden moments, and I really lost hope that this peculiar little bird might be a viable breeder. I just hoped he'd live through it all.

Later that morning, I heard the thin, sharp *EEK!* of a rose-breasted grosbeak. A pale, streaky brown bird flew over, white wing patches contrasting weakly against the sky. The juvenile grosbeak was still around. I leapt up and trotted around the corner of the house, following it, hoping for a snapshot to document the occurrence. I stared at the quiet line of trees bordering our meadow. Two cardinals, a white-eyed vireo . . . and a parti-colored bird flew out of the thick cherry leaves and teed up for a moment in a dead ash. Binoculars locked on him — and I thought I knew this bird. It was an adult male rose-breast, with a little dash of white behind each eye. If he's got a pink breast, it's too pale to see in profile. He's a bit messy. Yes. Maybe my little spring gift never left. And perhaps he had a mate hidden away, or where would that baby have come from?

I trotted down the orchard after him when he flew. I stopped in the clearing, where I stood a chance of seeing him again. And then he sang, just one phrase of his liquid song, from the sugar maples. Thank you.

I still don't know for sure whether it was the same bird who visited my peanut feeders in the first week of June. Chances are that it wasn't. But it was an adult rose-breast keeping company with a freshly fledged juvenile in early July, and that's good enough for me. This is what is so compelling about bird watching; this is what keeps my nerve endings firing, my ears perked for the slightest *eek!* or *teeawee.* One

*Rose-breast in the orchard*

of my favorite birds of all, and a well-marked, distinctive individual at that, never before (to my knowledge) recorded breeding in my county, comes to my yard, perches briefly on my finger, then raises a baby practically on my doorstep, and it takes until mid-July for me to find out about it. You never know the whole story about a bird. Not even close.

I hum a little Appalachian tune, a secret smile spreading over my face.

> *Where'd you come from?*
> *Where'd you go?*
> *Where'd you come from, Rose-breasted Joe?*

# Scarlet Tanager

## A Voice in the Canopy

"YOU HEAR THAT?" my sister Micky asked urgently. "It's saying, *Chip-BANG! Chip-BANG!*" And dimly, over her cordless phone, held up to the tall pines and hornbeams in her Connecticut backyard, I did. "It's a scarlet tanager! Try to see it! Grab your binocs and get out there!" I urged. But the bird remained hidden, chip-banging its alarm call in the canopy. I desperately wanted Micky to be able to see such a lovely bird in her own backyard. So many encounters with scarlet tanagers are like that—auditory only. In a given spring, I generally count myself lucky to see a handful of males, vivid blots of vermilion, so bright in the rusty haze of buds, on a spring migration. After the leaves emerge, they're back to being disembodied voices in the treetops. I don't catch up with them again until fall, when the olive-drab, immature birds flood through southern Ohio, chasing each other in gleeful loops through our old orchard.

I don't know by what provenance we in the United States came by our four species of *Piranga* tanagers. We almost missed them completely. Tanagers are otherwise solely Neotropical and are among the most recently evolved taxa of songbirds (hence their position near the back of the field guide). In the New World tropics, tanagers' adaptive radiation has resulted in a dazzling array of genera and

A tanager sang in
our pin oak by the
mailbox all
summer long.
I loved to try to
spot him in the
canopy.

August 14 2010

species: hooded, spangled, streaked, daubed, and painted with every shade from gold to violet, scarlet, acid green, seafoam, silver, yellow, black, and red. One, the paradise tanager, is called *sete cores* (seven colors) by Brazilians, and it's got them all. When our scarlet tanager overwinters in northern South America, it tends to flock and feed in fruiting trees with paradise tanagers. I would, too, just for the pleasure of gazing at them.

Our scarlet tanager sneaks down to South America wearing olive drab, changing back into radiant red beginning in January. By March, he's glistening scarlet and ebony, and ready to head north again. Doubtless these winter weeds he wears help keep him safe from sharp-shinned hawks on the fall trip and from forest falcons on the wintering grounds.

There are other adaptations to the scarlet tanager's tropical time-share. That heavy, toothed bill works well to subdue fast food—katydids, grasshoppers, cicadas, and other orthopterans—which are generally supersized in tropic climes. Back on the breeding grounds in North America's moist forests, almost any insect that crawls or flies is game for the scarlet tanager. Tanagers hover, glean, hawk, and even root for insects on the ground. Even bees and wasps are beaten and eaten. Spittlebugs, aphids, cicadas, and dragonflies find themselves in the tanager's firm clutches. But lepidopteran larvae are the tanager's favorite. In gypsy moth infestation years in New England, I picked up a number of road-killed scarlet tanagers—hit while they were bashing the hair off gypsy moth caterpillars on the asphalt surface. Wide-scale spraying for gypsy moths, which kills most nontargeted lepidopteran larvae as well, forces scarlet tanagers to scrounge for fruit, beetles, spiders, and whatever insects survive the spraying.

Late-summer fruits and fall berries, even the waxy white fruits of poison ivy, help sustain tanagers on their southward flight. They pass through surprisingly late—sometimes well after the first frosts of October—with fruit as fuel. They're night migrants, and the first warmth of fall mornings finds our orchard loaded with refueling tanagers, bickering and cartwheeling against a quiet backdrop of dewy leaves.

In our heavily agricultural part of southeast Ohio, we find scarlet tanagers breeding rather sparsely. The woodlands are too fragmented, the pressure from predators and brown-headed cowbirds too great. We have to go to large contiguous patches of national forest to hear the tanager's burry song with any frequency. Ten to twelve hectares (twenty-five to thirty acres), in fact, is the minimum size forest patch that can support breeding scarlet tanagers. With so much forest fragmentation, it is a pleasant surprise to find national Breeding Bird Survey data since 1966 showing fairly stable populations of scarlet tanagers. Declines are occurring mostly in heavily agricultural areas, which do not produce enough young birds to replace the loss of breeding adults. Ornithologists believe that fragmented woodlands actually draw birds from more productive areas, acting as population sinks. Clearly, the species depends on the preservation of contiguous forest tracts for its survival. In Michigan, selective logging—an innocuous term for a practice that can foster wholesale destruction of breeding habitat for many forest songbirds—eliminated scarlet tanagers from affected tracts.

Declines in tanager populations are in part due to the nest-parasitizing brown-headed cowbird, which ejects a tanager egg, replacing it with her own. The open-country cowbirds gain access to tanager nests along edges of fragmented forests.

Though most people assume that young cowbirds outcompete the remaining "host" young in the nest, this does not appear to be the case with scarlet tanagers. The presence or absence of a cowbird nestmate does not affect the fledging success of the scarlet tanagers remaining in the nest.

It is interesting that there are no subspecies of scarlet tanagers, nor is there appreciable geographic variation in the species throughout its range. There are some measurable differences in song type across the country but not in physiognomy. Does this perhaps mean that scarlet tanagers are relatively recent colonists of North America? Are the young birds long-distance dispersers, spreading their DNA far and wide, making for a homogenous gene pool? There is so much we don't yet know about scarlet tanagers.

Tanager lives — and their secrets — are shrouded, quite simply, in leaves for most of the season. By the time they arrive in southern Ohio, it's the end of April and we have a narrow window of time in which we can enjoy them before the leaves are bigger than they are. Males arrive a week or so ahead of females on spring migration. It's hard to believe they're North America's smallest tanager (well, we have only four *Pirangas* to choose from) when you pick a male out against a filmy spring sky.

He sits in the topmost twigs of an emergent tree, wings conspicuously drooped, rump feathers poufed, a startling blotch of brilliant red. Turning his head from side to side, he forces out his hurried, rasping song, which is often likened to that of a robin with a sore throat (and an appointment to keep). Approached by a female, he'll turn his back on her and stretch his neck, his ebony wings and tail making a frame for the brilliant scarlet rectangle of his back.

Tanager nests are slim affairs, shallow saucers of fine twigs, bark strips, and grasses that defy gravity, set atop forks, amidships on long, slender limbs. Flimsy nests and rather low clutch size, as well as single brooding, are characteristics many tropical birds share. The average number of eggs in the scarlet tanager's single clutch is only 3.8. Eggs are incubated solely by the female, which makes sense in a species with such marked sexual dimorphism. A male tanager motionless on a nest might as well be lit with neon for aerial predators like sharp-shinned and Cooper's hawks. The female's olive plumage, on the other hand, blends perfectly.

Young tanagers stay in the nest an eye-popping average of only ten days. They go from blind, almost-naked, pink squirmers to fully feathered youngsters capable of short flights in a mere week and a half! Thus do tanagers race through the most vulnerable time of their lives—the nestling period. Odd as it seems, they're far safer scrambling through the leaves, being fed by both parents, than huddled together in the nest.

Fall is my favorite time to watch tanagers, as they pour through our old orchard, eating poison ivy berries and sluggish katydids, chasing each other and the myriad red-eyed vireos, cedar waxwings, and warblers also passing through. They're abundant migrants, easy and fun to watch. Chasing seems to be a fall contact sport for them. There's a fair amount of it in late summer, too, when young birds are dispersing.

So it was that I walked out on an August afternoon in the late '80s to see a brilliant male tanager in hot pursuit of an olive-green youngster. The garden I tended on a Connecticut nature preserve was protected from marauding deer by nine feet of rusted stock fencing. It was nearly invisible against the greenery, a cruel steel net that claimed many a life, despite the streamers of white sheet I had tied all over it. The beautiful male tanager hit it and dropped like a stone, dying, while the juvenile passed on through, injured but alive. In a split-second bit of calculated triage, I pounced on the juvenile bird before it could cripple off into the underbrush. Sighing, I picked up the lifeless male in the other hand and headed into the house.

Sometimes the
only good look I
get at a
scarlet tanager is
right after they
arrive, around
April 24 in so. Ohio,
and I catch that
shock of vermilion
against a soft blue
sky. Then they disappear
in the leaves until
August 15, but by
then they're olive
drab. A lot
pass through here in fall.

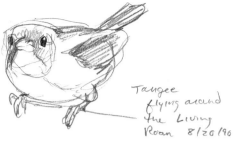

Tangee
flying around
the Living
Room 8/20/96

Examining the youngster, I found no broken bones, but it did have badly bruised breast muscles, which would rob it of flight for about a week. I set up a cage in the living room and went off to chop some fruit for it to eat. When I came back, the tanager was calmly eyeing me and the three other permanently injured birds then in my care. I liken these birds to bellwethers, who cue new arrivals that there is nothing to fear in my home. The tanager hopped down to its feed dish like any tame canary and helped itself to the food. Intrigued by its calm demeanor, I opened its cage door. It explored the carpet and the understruts of the couches and chairs. It was clear that this bird was calm enough to be given supervised liberty. I was glad, for I hate to cage any bird, unless it's frantic and likely to injure itself otherwise.

I couldn't resist naming the little green bird Tangee, after an orangish lipstick my father always said my mother wore when they were first dating. Needless to say, I became fond of the bird and thrilled to see it gain strength and flight powers each day. At last Tangee was flying strongly between the tops of open doors in the house, and I knew it was time to set the young thing free. It vanished into the treetops, with only its soft *cherwee* call to tell me where it had gone.

The next morning, I was at the drawing table when I was startled by the sound of bird toenails on the windowsill at my elbow. Clinging to the narrow sill was

Tangee comes
back, with a friend in tow,
to see where he once
lived. 8/21/90.

Tangee. And Tangee had brought a friend—another juvenile scarlet tanager. From the similarity in their stage of molt, I thought it might be a sibling. Together, they peered in at the cages, and at me, only inches away from them through a pane of glass. I forgot to breathe; my head buzzed with the thought that perhaps Tangee had been able to communicate something of his experience to a companion, sufficiently piquing its curiosity to make it fly down and land on a windowsill so breathtakingly close to me. They clung for several seconds, heads turning as they took in details of Tangee's former home, then flew together into the thick canopy of a sugar maple in the backyard.

Though this magic moment was more than twenty years ago, I will never forget the image of this free-living bird escorting another tanager to the place where it had been sheltered and healed. It was a thank-you note from the wild, a lightning bolt, illuminating my world with joy. It was tanagers being tanagers, in all their unfathomable beauty and grace.

# The Summer of Phoebes

FOR A NUMBER of years, I've been painting portraits of nestling birds as they come my way. I work with birds that nest in my boxes, as well as orphaned and injured birds that come to me each summer. As a licensed songbird rehabilitator, I never know what might be at the other end of the phone line: ruby-throated hummingbirds, chimney swifts, bluebirds, or waxwings; or perhaps another house sparrow, starling, or grackle.

I had started a series of paintings of eastern phoebe nestlings in 2005, hoping to capture their day-to-day development. I'd borrow a chick each day, paint its portrait, and return it to the nest to be raised by its parents. Carefully, I teased the new hatchling out of its nest. It was a bewitching shade of yellow—unlike any other nestling I'd ever seen, with a strange, pointed beak and

*A lot of mites in its ears. I got them out but fear for it. A haze of grey down!*

*7 AM - 7:25 AM June 27 2005 Day 1 or 2 Eastern Phoebe. There is one other sibling and an unhatched egg. These eggs (a clutch of 5) were laid the week of June 6. They're the second brood of the gutter Phoebes, who fledged 5 young on the . It's unexpectedly yellow! and so tiny my poor old eyes are straining to take in its details. Amazingly long bill. A strong cheep, just like its parents! This chick was dead the next day. Massive infestation of chicken mites. Bummer.*

copious gray down. As I painted a couple of studies, I noticed moving specks on its thin skin—mites. With a magnifying glass, I could see them, red with the chick's blood, clustered in its ears. Ugh! I dug them out with a toothpick, cleaned the chick as best I could, and returned it to its nest. I was afraid such an infestation would weaken or kill the chicks, and I didn't want that to happen to any bird, much less to such precious subjects for my study. What could I do? I couldn't use insecticides; the tiny birds' thin skins and high metabolisms would make them extremely vulnerable to poisoning.

I decided to remove the chicks when they were a little older and stronger, microwave and then cool the mud nest, and replace the whole, mite-free affair on the little plastic fuse box under our deck. I'd station my daughter (aptly named Phoebe) on a ladder next to the nest to keep the parent birds from flying close enough to find their nest missing while it was being purged of mites. It sounds crazy, but I knew it could work.

Full of anticipation and adrenaline for the experiment to come, I armed myself with Tupperware, spatula, and daughter, and climbed the ladder. I reached into the nest and found the chicks cold—dead. In just a day, the mites had killed them. A moving gray felt of the arachnids swarmed up my hand. These were probably chicken mites, brought into the nest by a feather picked up by one of the adults. What miserable creatures. Thus ended 2005's attempt to paint phoebes. Rats, rats, rats.

All winter, the phoebe nest stood empty, and the big sheet of watercolor paper I'd prepared for the phoebe series had but one small study in the lower left

12:30–1 pm Day 3 or 4
May 30 2006. What a funny little thing! This bird probably hatched May 27. Amazing amount of down, but its an open-cup nester, 'neath a caves and don't bridges. Bill quite wide at base. Legs and feet small and weak, esp. compared to a chickadee. I'm not used to seeing abdominal tracts of down. No mites!

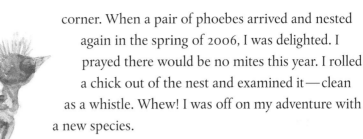

corner. When a pair of phoebes arrived and nested again in the spring of 2006, I was delighted. I prayed there would be no mites this year. I rolled a chick out of the nest and examined it—clean as a whistle. Whew! I was off on my adventure with a new species.

What funny little birds. They were covered with long, grayish yellow down, long-billed, and strange-looking. These would likely be the only baby flycatchers I'd ever have my hands on, and I was enjoying it thoroughly. Even at Day 1, the chicks' chip note was exactly like their parents' alarm call. Amazing. I'd never heard any passerine baby give a call that sounded anything like the adult's! But then, phoebes are wired differently from most oscine passerines. Experiments by Donald Kroodsma showed that the phoebe's song (and probably its call note) are hard-wired in its brain. A young phoebe, raised in soundproof isolation and deprived of any auditory contact with its singing father, develops a perfectly normal song, unlike most oscine passerines, for which imitative learning is a key component of song development.

Each day, I climbed the stepladder to borrow a chick for a few minutes and paint a new portrait. My dream was coming true, and I was not about to lose this brood of phoebes to mites or snakes. I watched carefully for signs of infestation. I had already baffled the nest, which sat alongside a drainpipe and atop a little plastic fuse box under our sheltering deck. I put sheets of plywood on the deck to create a snakeproof roof overhead, and two tempered glass shower doors beneath the nest to enclose the gutter in a shallow V so no snake could slither up it. I was pretty sure I had it covered. But one never knows.

JUNE 7, 2006. The chicks are ten days old, and I'm getting the materials together to paint my daily portrait. My six-year-old son, Liam, comes running to tell me there is a big black rat snake on the rocks by the fishpond. We run down and watch it drink, marveling at its just-shed perfection. As it turned out, the rat snake needed to wash down its meal of four phoebe chicks from the nest under the deck. Despite my ugly, painstakingly built glass-panel baffle, despite my fierce devotion to protecting the nest, I had inadvertently mounted one of the shower doors wrong-side out, and there was a small metal lever halfway up its length. That was all the big snake needed to give it a hitch the rest of the way up. I stared at the Goldbergian contraption, wondering how I could have overlooked that fatal flaw.

These weren't just any phoebes; they were the subjects of a number of paintings for my book. I felt the loss keenly, personally and professionally. They were just getting their feathers. Nothing should have to die that young.

Not one to stand around bawling, I got a small piece of wood, some long nails, a hammer, and my ladder. First, I removed the used phoebe nest and put rocks atop the relay box so no bird could nest there again. The spot is too hard to safeguard, and I'm not even sure that the shower door's metal handle was at fault. There were dozens of ways a snake could get to that nest. Then, I put up a shelf where the snake would have to grow wings to reach it—about ten feet away, with no climbable downspout beneath it.

Next, I put the old phoebe nest in the oven to kill any mites or other parasites lurking within it. I figured 250 degrees for a half hour would do the job. The odor of baking mud filled the kitchen. I dampened the mud in the well-cooked nest and stuck it securely to the new, safe shelf. As I was putting up the shelf, the male phoebe began to sing from just down the hill.

I mourned the lost phoebes all that afternoon. The next day felt empty without them to paint and watch. I wondered how many seasons it would take for me to complete the phoebe painting. The first brood I'd tried died of a mite infestation on Day 2. This second brood made it to Day 10, and, despite my efforts, got turned into snake food. The male phoebe sang intermittently around the yard. I didn't know if the pair would accept my new shelf, or if they'd even hang around. If my babies got eaten, I'd quit the place for good.

The phone rang around noon that same day, and a tentative voice asked if I was the bird person. I know now by the first couple of words when someone has a baby bird for me. They don't know whom they're calling or what to expect, and it takes them a while to stammer out what the problem is. I let the caller go a little bit, then asked, "What have you got for me?"

"I've got two baby birds. We were tearing down a shed in the backyard, and we found this nest."

My heart leapt. Carolina wren, barn swallow, house sparrow, starling, or impossible dream: eastern phoebe. It had to be one of those five.

"What color are they?"

"I dunno. Fuzzy. They've got pretty long beaks."

*Oh, yes. Long beaks are good.*

"What does the nest look like?"

"It's got grass and maybe a little bit of moss."

*Now we're down to wrens or phoebes. I'm thinking phoebes. I can't believe this.*

"Where was the nest?"

"On top of a little relay box."

*Yessss.*

"Where are you calling from?"

"I'm out Twenty-six, near Wingett Run."

*That couldn't be any closer to my home.*

"How did you get my number?"

"You're not gonna believe this, but I looked in the phone book under 'Bird' and didn't find anything. So I just figured there ought to be an 800 number. I dialed 1-800-WILDLIFE and got somebody who gave me your number."

Not knowing what to do, and hoping the parents would find their displaced brood, she had put the nest in a nearby tree for the night. It had rained all night. And somehow they had survived.

"I don't want them to die. Can you take them?"

"Absolutely!" I stammered, still reeling from the perfection of it all. *Hold on, Julie. They could still turn out to be house sparrows . . .*

I'd been doing bird rehabilitation since 1982, and I'd never even come close to getting phoebes. I tried to hold myself back, knowing that, even if they turned out to be phoebes, they could have pneumonia by now. I gave the caller directions, and her car pulled into my driveway not twenty minutes later.

The birds are still in their mud and moss nest. Phoebes. Two perfect little phoebes. And they are nine days old, a day younger than my brood of four was when they were eaten by the snake. I cradle the nest in my hands, seeing the rest of the phoebe painting rolling out in my mind's eye. Mites begin swarming up my arms. I take the phoebes out of their nest, swaddle them in a box with tissues, and put the nest in a slow oven to bake for an hour or two. The house fills, again, with the smell of baking mud.

I'm so thrilled I don't know where to begin. First, I feed them. I've made a bird omelet: scrambled egg mixed with dried insects and ground eggshell. They're debilitated, dehydrated, and scared, and I will have to force-feed them for several hours before they begin to gape for me. Each one voids an enormous fecal sac, accumulated since the evening before. It's 1:00 P.M., and I figure they've been without food for eighteen hours. That's pushing it for baby birds.

Kandy and her teenage daughter, Sandy, stand and watch, amazed that they have found someone to care for their birds so close to home. When the babies are fed, I dance into the studio and pull out my interrupted painting to show to my benefactors, explaining that it will be part of a book I've been working on for several years. Their eyes widen as they grasp the cosmic collision of it all, and see birds that look exactly like their foundlings, there on the page before them.

"I don't know if you're religious," Kandy says slowly. "But I think God did this."

"They talk about him working in mysterious ways. This has got to be one of them," I reply.

"They won't die, will they?"

"They are not going to die. I'll take good care of them, and I'll paint their portraits every day, and I'll release them right here on the farm."

"And we're gonna be in your next book?"

"You are definitely going to be in my book."

I take their picture, smiling shyly, glued together, holding the two nestling phoebes, a cosmic intervention, gift beyond price.

I am a bird-mother now. It's a familiar thing; I'm a bird-mother every summer to something or other. I should be able to handle a couple of phoebes. My nine-year-old daughter, Phoebe, names them, assigning sex arbitrarily: Luther for the smaller one, Avis for the larger. I concur on her guess as to their sexes, though I can't say why. I settle into the summer routine: a trip to the pet store for a thousand crickets; another order of five thousand mealworms; some messing about

*Avis (back) and Luther, Day 17.*

with kitten chow and the microwave, and, most important, setting my internal clock to go off every half hour, dawn to dusk. The phoebes let me know when it's time with a hungry *chip* note that sounds exactly like the alarm call of an adult. They huddle patiently in their Kleenex-lined box and wait to be fed. I paint their portraits each day, reveling in the luxury of having all the time I need to draw each new feather. All that changes on their seventeenth day, June 15.

The birds are fully feathered now, and they spend most of their waking hours preening, removing feather sheaths, and ruffling and exercising their wings. Their droppings are no longer voided in a fecal sac but are small and loose, and much more frequent. Even their voices have changed: they're giving a dry *chiddick!* I've never heard them make before. Like many other fledglings I've raised, they begin to refuse food. As many times as I've seen it, it still worries me. I tell myself that they're slimming down for flight, that they'll eat when they're really hungry. It's clear that they're bright and healthy; a sick bird doesn't preen its feathers.

I can feel in my bones that these birds will be flying by the next morning. It's time to put up the fledging tent. The best hundred dollars I ever spent: a fifteen-by-seventeen-foot nylon-screen tent, supported by jointed aluminum poles. It's meant to keep mosquitoes off the picnic table, but it's exactly what the bird doctor ordered for young songbirds trying their wings. It's the most spacious and gentlest of cages. The fine, soft mesh contains them but can't break their feathers. They can see the outdoors through the mesh sides, but a solid nylon roof protects them from the beating sun and rain. Best of all, the tent stores away in a box until I need it.

The next two weeks are a blur to me. I keep a log because I know I won't be able to remember the particulars of the birds' development from day to day. The phoebes are growing, flying, learning new things every day. We establish a routine: I take them out to their fledging tent at dawn, pop into the tent to feed them every hour until dusk, and bring them back inside, locked in a pet tote, for the night. I put them in a dark stairwell so they won't flutter and fuss; they hate to be put in the pet carrier. But raccoons and black rat snakes are relentless and ever vigilant, and as wonderful as the tent is, it offers no protection from predators. I caught a raccoon peering into the tent on June 21, in broad daylight. At night, after I remove the young birds, I leave the tent flaps wide open so the raccoons can come and go without tearing a hole through the mesh to gain access. It's an open-door policy that removes the mystery for the 'coons and saves me money in the long run.

On June 20, Day 22 of their short lives, they start to process their food, beating crickets against the perch. They get better at it every day. They aren't able to

Luther shows Avis how it's done, beating a cricket into submission. June 20, 2006 They're 22 days old, and this is a first.

knock the legs off the insects yet, but they will get there. On Day 23, Luther, the smaller, sweeter one, whirls out, grabs a housefly off the tent wall, brings it back to the perch, and releases it. Well, he's getting the idea, anyway! Witnessing this small event, my heart sings. They're acting like phoebes. They sit on high perches, bobbing their tails, sally out after nothing in particular or perhaps to peck at a moth, and then return to the perch. They're flycatchers at last.

Little things tell me their brains and neural connections are maturing. When a twenty-four-day-old bird grabs a moth from a forceps without gaping or needing to have it stuffed down its throat, that's progress. It's a developmental leap from being fed to feeding itself. Moths prove irresistible to these birds. They already know what they like. I mark each milestone like a mother charting her toddler's progress in words spoken and steps taken. *Like* a mother? I *am* their mother.

And I am confined like a prisoner to their schedule. Thank goodness they sleep all night, but they need to be fed every hour from dawn to dark. Because I have to take them everywhere with me in order to feed them, I try not to go anywhere. It's too hot to leave them in the car, so I have to carry them in and out of stores and businesses in a small pet carrier, feeding them every hour or so, reaching under my lawn chair at the kids' softball practices while managing the inevitable curious clutch of children and their questions. I have a week or more of hand-feeding them and taking them around with me until that magic day when they fly down and take their own crickets out of a dish. Until then, I do my grocery shopping while they're still asleep, in the predawn dark, so I can get home in time to put them in the tent and feed them at sunrise. Grocery stores are weird places just before dawn. I am a weird person when I'm feeding baby birds.

Each evening after I remove the birds, I set up a flood lamp in the tent, opening the flaps wide. Dozens of moths cling to the screen walls the next morning.

*Luther nails a moth in flight
June 22, 2006 - Day 24*

The phoebes must learn to catch natural food. On June 22, Luther's twenty-fourth day, he launches himself from his perch, grabs a little white miller moth off the tent wall, returns to his perch, masticates it, and swallows it. I cheer and whoop, and kiss Luther atop his head. He nips my nose. I can taste freedom, theirs and mine. Still, it will be four more days before they are reliably feeding themselves.

The young phoebes progress in stages. Moths are snapped up the minute they fly across the tent, but mealworms in a dish are of less interest to these birds, naturally hard-wired to take flying insects. On their twenty-sixth day, they fly down and take mealworms off our extended palms—a huge leap from having them stuffed in their bills with forceps. On their twenty-eighth day, I leave shallow dishes of mealworms all over the tent. The supplies dwindle, so I know they're being consumed, but Phoebe is the first to see Avis fly to a dish and gobble down a mealworm. We jump and cheer and slap high-fives.

Luther and Avis are learning, becoming independent, and undergoing an attitude change as well. They're uppity, quick, and flighty. Avis flares her crest and pecks my camera lens and my fingers if I get too close. Her tyrannid flycatcher tendencies are blossoming. By June 25, their twenty-seventh day, I can see that the time of separation is here. The young phoebes don't want anything to do with us. They bathe lustily in a shallow bowl, preen, and bathe again. The tent fills up with crane flies, moths, gnats, mosquitoes, and fireflies overnight. That's what they want. I tickle their bills with mealworms in the forceps, and they seem taken aback. "Why would I want that?" they seem to ask, then flash away on agile wings. They land, tails bobbing, and glare at me. This is the thanks I get, and it's exactly what I want. I'm a mother who can't wait to send her kids off to college. I'm dying for an empty nest.

And then the skies open, and it rains and rains. I can't let them out when it's pouring. Young birds, especially captive-raised ones, don't have good rain-coping skills. They get themselves soaked and don't know how to take shelter. It can be the death of them. I don't want to have come this far and worked this hard only to lose them to the incessant rain. The days roll by, and the phoebes grow and whirl and hit the sides of the tent. It's time. I have to let them go. I open the tent doors on the morning of June 27. The phoebes hang around the yard, basking in the un-accustomed sun, taking crickets from the forceps, mealworms from a Pyrex plate. They stay in the yard all day.

The morning of June 28 brings a pair of young phoebes, chipping to us as we groggily emerge from the house just after dawn. They are as glad to see us as we are to see them. Luther lands on my hand and gobbles down a good break-fast. Avis is happy to fly close and chat but won't eat. And therein begins a big problem.

A newly released bird should be ravenous and screaming for food, as was Luther. Birds I've raised and released go through a period of regres-sion when they figure out that they aren't on Easy Street anymore. From being aloof and flighty in the tent, refusing to be hand-fed, they turn back into begging juveniles. Just the sound of my voice brings them swoop-ing in. They shadow me around the yard, just as they would follow their parents. Needless to say, this is my favorite part of raising birds — having these free-living birds nearby playing, forag-ing, learning fancy flying techniques, yet still coming for reg-ular visits with me. I watch for them to catch their own food. As they get better at it, I cut back on the mealworms, and there comes a day when the bird comes in to chat but won't take any food. That's a beautiful thing, and it's what I work toward. But it should not happen the morning af-ter release.

I watch Avis closely that morning and am disturbed to see her looking increasingly lethargic. No amount of tickling her rictal bristles can induce her to snap at a mealworm. Along about noon, I find her back inside the tent, whose flaps I'd left open in case the phoebes felt a need to return. Smart move, Avis. Maybe you came in by accident, or maybe you knew you were in trouble. I zip the tent closed and sit back to observe her. Luther sits just outside in a birch, separated by thin netting, as close as he can get to Avis. They are both obviously upset to be separated, so I bring Luther in to keep Avis company.

I mix up some fresh kitten chow formula and begin to force-feed Avis. It is no fun having to capture this dear little bird, pry her bill open, and feed her the messy, loose formula, but I feel I have no choice. She continues to weaken, trembling as she tries to perch. How can we have come this far—thirty days old, apparently in the pink of health when she was released—only to fail?

All I know is that I am not going to let her die without a fight. In midafternoon, I catch her for the last time and put her in a pet carrier. I'll feed her formula every hour and see if I can turn her decline around. Poor Avis. She hates being force-fed (who wouldn't?); I hate having to do it. I e-mail the avian rehabilitator Astrid MacLeod, who has raised just about everything and is my first resort when I'm stumped. Astrid suggests that Avis might have eaten a lightning bug, which could have made her sick. I had seen her catch one in the tent a couple of days before her release, but she took it back to the perch and released it, doubtless because it tasted bad. It's a hypothesis. As she continues to decline, I decide to start Avis on an antibiotic, just in case she has something infectious that might be addressed. I figure it's better than wringing my hands and watching her go downhill.

Meanwhile, Luther is blazing new trails outside. The morning of June 29, I awaken to the sound of a phoebe singing in the lilac just outside our bedroom window. Three times Luther sings, a hurried, high-pitched, imperfect baby song.

I don't want to wake Bill, who is breathing deeply beside me, but I lie there listening, grinning from ear to ear. Phoebe had guessed Luther's sex right!

In the next three days, Luther does all the things a phoebe should do. He investigates the eaves and awnings, instinctively drawn to their cavelike structures. Perhaps most intriguingly, he figures out how to come back into the open tent for food and water. Tufted titmice have been raiding the dish I left outside for him, but they are leery of entering the fledging tent. He's hit on an ideal solution to the problem.

By Saturday, July 1, Avis is feeling well enough to be released from confinement in the pet carrier back out to the fledging tent. She is self-feeding again and looking brighter every day. I am happy and so relieved. I take her carrier out to the tent. Luther watches closely from a nearby birch. He chips excitedly, flies over to it, and hovers in front of its wire door, chittering and scolding. I take the carrier inside and zip the tent closed. When I open the carrier, Avis shoots out to the relative freedom of the tent. Luther throws himself against the mesh walls, trying to get back in. I open one tent flap just enough to let him dart inside. I am deeply moved by the strength of the phoebes' bond. They sit together all day, glued into one dusky lump of feathers on the same perch.

By the next morning, Luther is bored and hovering to get outside. I open the flap just a bit, and he zooms out. Avis stays put, not ready for the demands of the wild. Over the next few days, I leave the tent flaps open, and Avis takes longer and longer forays away from food and shelter. By the evening of July 4, both Avis and Luther are coming and going freely, taking mealworms, bathing and drinking inside the tent, then flying back outside. I see Luther attack a house sparrow that had sneaked in to steal some mealworms, giving it a wild, looping chase all around the yard. I begin to relax. It looks as though I've managed to pull Avis back from the brink yet again.

That evening, it rains, and the rain comes harder and harder. The fledging tent billows and bucks in the gale. Why now, on Avis's first night outside the tent? Luther tucks himself into his favorite lilac outside the bedroom window, where he is warm and dry despite the storm. Avis is wet, flying nervously from tree to tree. She is out of my hands now; I can't catch her, and I know I shouldn't. There will be storms in Avis's life, and I won't be there to shelter her. She sits low on a birch twig, wet, just out of reach as night falls. It pours all night and most of the next morning. I will never see her again.

Luther comes in at first light, dry and warm despite the downpour. Avis never appears. I search under all the trees she liked to perch in but find no trace. Well, one out of two isn't bad, I guess. I had to let Avis go, let go of the idea that I could save her no matter what. It hits me hard that, to survive, a wild bird has to be operating at 100 percent capacity. A rainy summer night shouldn't kill a healthy bird. She was doing so much better, but in the end doing better wasn't good enough. Not all of the lessons that songbird rehabilitation teaches are happy ones.

Those with no concept of the extended juvenile dependency period of songbirds might find all this feeding, intervention, and training incomprehensible. Why didn't I just kick them out the door and tell them farewell? Most people, even birders who should know better, seem to believe that, once a bird leaves the nest, it's on its own. On the contrary, most songbirds feed their young until their neural connections are all complete, until they are able to catch sufficient food on their own. The more complex the bird's foraging strategy, the longer the juvenile dependency period. American oystercatchers, which must learn to chisel shellfish off rocks and open bivalves by inserting their bills and cutting the adductor muscles, are dependent on their parents for at least sixty days! The adults open shellfish, feeding the edible parts to their young, as the juveniles watch and learn techniques.

Phoebes, pondering.

I don't know how old phoebes are when their parents no longer subsidize them. I doubt anyone does. I could only try to judge their competence in foraging and make sure that they knew where they could always find food. I've seen adult tree swallows still feeding juveniles in mass migration flocks in September. Having hand-fed these birds since June 8, I was not about to take the risk of starving them with a too-precipitous release. My last intention was to make pets of these birds. On the contrary, I wanted them out of my hair—badly.

Luther hung around another five days, suddenly disappearing on the afternoon of July 9. He was gone until the morning of July 11, Phoebe Linnea's tenth birthday. She walked out on the porch in her short pajamas and fed him from her palm. He perched lightly on her hand, grabbed a mealworm, dropped it, and caught it before it hit the ground, barely three feet below. Phoebe looked at me, her eyes aglow with wonder and pride. We both knew there could be no finer gift than a wild phoebe, 100 percent beautiful, healthy, and strong, perched on her hand. Happy birthday, little Phoebe. There's your phoebe. Not long after that, Luther was gone for good, but it felt right and natural, a *good* gone. Fall and winter 2006 came and went, and I thought about our phoebe summer and wondered how Luther was faring, wherever he was.

On March 13, 2007, a male phoebe showed up in the yard, singing and chipping. He sat on an ash branch that hangs low over our driveway, the same branch Luther fetched up on when he was hungry and wanted to attract our attention. I walked toward the bird, and he flew a short distance, not farther away but a little closer to me. He chipped and wagged his tail. From there, he lit in the birch tree next to the birdbath, the same spot where Luther liked to rest. All phoebes look alike, and I could never prove that this bird was really Luther. But my heart filled up, like a mother's does as she welcomes her child back from his first day at school, and I smiled like that, too.

# Piping Plover and Least Tern

## You Do What You Must

I WENT TO FIND THEM in March, as the first warm front was sweeping in, the small pale plovers with the plaintive whistle. I never managed to dress warmly enough for the wind along the shore, and I marveled at their hardiness as the wind would lift and turn the snowy feathers of the piping plovers' flanks. *Peep-lo!* The plover would stand erect, its button eye focused on me. Then it would duck its head and run ahead of me, orange legs a twinkling blur. Thus escorted, I'd walk the whole beach, noting the erosion after the overwashing waves of winter. I counted plovers, making notes on each one's distinctive black breast and brow bands, hoping to be able to identify them through the season.

For piping plovers, the more barren the beach, the better. Winter storms are their friends, but the same overwash that sweeps their nesting areas so alluringly clean is devastating in spring and summer, when eggs can be washed away. It would be enough to battle the elements in their habitat, but piping plovers and their frequent companions, least terns, have so much more with which to contend. They lay their eggs—four to a clutch for plovers, two or three for terns—in shallow, shell-lined scrapes right on the sand. Right underfoot.

I've never been a recreational beach goer. I like beaches best when there's no one around. The scent of cocoa butter, the sight of acres of prone bodies, and the noise of radios fighting with the lap of waves make me get up and walk into the clean offshore wind until the crowds fall away and my mind starts to work again. When I moved to Connecticut to work for The Nature Conservancy, in 1981, I was aghast to find the state's small and struggling populations of least terns and piping plovers nesting, unprotected and often unnoticed, on the beach sand right amid the throngs. Off-road vehicle tracks crisscrossed some nesting flats. Tern chicks crouched to hide in the depressions made by the tires and were crushed. Dogs ran freely, raising the terns in an angry cloud; people dragged coolers and beach chairs through the colonies. I couldn't know that and let it happen anymore. But I couldn't think of anyone else who would be willing to take on the problem. For four full-time summer seasons, I worked to protect these birds all along Connecticut's eighty-mile shoreline, doing whatever it took. For that, The Nature Conservancy allotted me mileage and a twelve-hundred-dollar stipend. I didn't need benefits. I was young and healthy, running on outrage and passion.

First, I'd have to tell people what the birds were and why they were there. I drew pictures of nesting terns and plovers, had them printed on heavy plastic, bought spruce firring in six-foot lengths, and nailed the signs together. I hadn't quite figured out how to get the signs out to the nesting areas, so I lashed together

*There is a young maiden who lives all alone she lives all alone on the shore. But to roam all alone on the shore. But to roam all alone on the... find far to comfort her mind But to roam all alone on the shore—o There is nothing she can...*

bundles of eight, threw them on my shoulder, and trudged miles through loose sand. I hammered the signs into the sand around the colonies, marking off areas that stretched well beyond the nearest nests to give them a wide berth from crowds. I strung twine between the signs, a technique referred to as "psychological fencing." Given a choice to comply with the signs' request that they keep clear of the nesting colonies, most people would. But there were those who wouldn't.

I realized that simply posting the areas and leaving it at that would be inadequate to protect the birds. I'd have to provide a consistent presence that reinforced the barriers. I'd also have to come equipped to replace signs torn down by vandals, to talk to surly fishermen intent on driving their trucks through tern colonies at high tide, to explain to dog owners why they must leash their pets, to deal

New Least terns

with nudists who sought out the privacy of bird-nesting areas for sunbathing. I discovered that the people who sunbathe nude in tern colonies are not the ones you'd necessarily want to see in dishabille.

I found out things about Connecticut residents that I hadn't known. There is a persistent tradition in urban Italian and Hispanic populations of gathering and eating birds' eggs. How convenient, that I'd marked the colonies and roped them off, letting the hunter-gatherers know just where to look. I found a family in New Haven sitting near a tern colony with a picnic basket and smiles on their faces. A cloud of least terns hovered overhead, screaming and diving. I asked to see what was in the picnic basket, and its dark interior hid three fluffy, frightened least tern chicks. "We found these and we're going to take them home and raise them. What do you feed them?" When I explained that the birds' parents were right overhead, diving and defecating on us, and that the chicks belonged here on the beach and not on their screened porch, the woman exclaimed, "How can there be birds nesting here? There aren't any trees!" Piping plover eggs kept disappearing from one small beach in Bridgeport, so I reluctantly took down the signs and string that marked the area. I gathered broken glass off the beach and scattered it near the nests, and the predation stopped. You do whatever works.

On Long Island, while training volunteer colony monitors, I found a private beach club that was unwilling host to a colony of least terns. The manager announced his intention to place scarecrows in the colony so their beach volleyball games could resume. Over and over, I was struck by beach goers' attitudes: that these beautiful and imperiled birds were nothing more than a nuisance to be shooed off. I heard enough references to the Hitchcock film *The Birds* to make me never want to see it again. People couldn't seem to connect that these birds had a good reason to be diving and screaming at them: their vulnerable eggs and chicks lay right underfoot. I developed a leaflet that I could hand out to anyone who'd take it, explaining the birds' predicament: that they were declining in numbers, highly vulnerable to disturbance and predation, and couldn't simply go somewhere else to nest. On the mainland beaches of Connecticut, there is precious little "somewhere else." In the modern world, where beaches are the most hotly contested real estate on the planet, a beach is a crazy place to try to lay one's eggs and raise young.

And it is never crazier on Connecticut's beaches than on the Fourth of July. Before starting my conservation program, I hadn't thought much about what it means to watch fireworks from the beach on the Fourth. Now, it became the low point of my season. I prayed for a week of rain but rarely got my wish. The nighttime fireworks shows coincided with the time when young least terns and piping plovers are running everywhere in the colonies (and often outside the string fencing). There are still plenty of eggs and young chicks in the nests as well. And there are thousands of people setting up lawn chairs right among them, and deafening explosions overhead for good measure. Tanning, fireworks displays, nude sunbathing: these mindless pleasures are forever tainted with anxiety for a tern and plover warden.

I checked with each municipality to see when their displays were planned, and I marshaled as many volunteers as I could to come out and help enforce the colony boundaries on the evenings of the fireworks shows. Unaffiliated with any state or federal law enforcement agency, I had not a shred of authority with which to do this. All I had was a fierce desire to protect the birds and the faith that we could do it. I found thirty like-minded souls and called each one to coordinate patrol shifts. I asked them to wear khaki, to attempt to look as official as possible, then bought and distributed toy tin sheriffs' badges to my volunteers. Each was to bring a flashlight and keep it shining toward the revelers' faces to distract them from our decidedly unofficial badges, rather small stature, and predominantly feminine gender. We used chairs and string to cordon off access to the nesting areas. "Sir, this section of the beach is closed. Endangered species nesting area. We're asking people to set up their lawn chairs over there." It was crazy and occasionally scary, but against all odds it worked.

After the first year of posting and patrolling, the education push eased up a bit, as people got used to the concept of respecting nesting areas. My volunteer phalanx grew, and one Bridgeport man stood out as a jewel among them. He'd always liked birds but had never had the opportunity to learn much about them or been around bird watchers. After one walk on the beach with me, one cradling of a plover chick in his palm, Tom Damiani latched on to birding and conservation with ferocious focus and endless energy, and within a couple of weeks he was not only patrolling area beaches but censusing the nests for me. I felt as if I had split like a hydra and gained another half, a huge benefit with a job that, day in and day out, pulled me in eight directions at once. Tom went on to be a preserve manager for The Nature Conservancy's Mashomack Preserve on Shelter Island, New York, to become an expert in bird vocalizations, and to make his living in natural history pursuits. Not bad for a wedding singer from Bridgeport who had always loved birds. I smile whenever I think of Tom, all aglow, a piping plover chick in his palm.

While patrolling, I censused individual colonies, trying to determine the various causes of nest failure and the birds' rate of success. I'd mark each nest with a numbered tongue depressor and note its contents with every visit. Because I knew when eggs were laid, I knew when to expect young chicks, which remain in the scrape for two days in the case of the semi-altricial least terns, and only a matter of hours for the precocial piping plovers. I learned to watch closely for tracks of mammalian and avian predators, to discern whether an eggshell fragment came from a naturally hatched egg or one that had been broken and eaten. I conducted regular counts of the mobile chicks, trying to determine how many made it to fledging. There was always an element of suspense in a colony visit, for there are few more vulnerable species than ground-nesting terns and plovers.

A single high tide, reaching a few feet above the wrack line, could devastate an entire colony with overwash. I became alert to the phases of the moon and the timing of the tides. A full-moon tide with an onshore wind could spell disaster. On several occasions, I rolled an old tire to a low-lying tern nest, removed the eggs and seashells lining the scrape and set them aside, filled the tire with sand, smoothed the surface, and made a new nest on the same spot, eight inches higher than the old one.

While I was working with terns and plovers, a Massachusetts graduate student named Eric Strauss hit upon the idea of erecting small enclosures around each of Cape Cod's piping plover nests. Stock fencing enclosures with openings large enough for piping plovers to slip through, but too small to admit mammalian predators, proved very effective. A "roof" of monofilament lines barred entry by avian predators as well. Because plovers invariably walk up to their nests, the adults could come and go freely, but gulls and grackles were deterred. At the time, it was an audacious idea, to expend that kind of money and effort on each plover nest, but the species's plight warranted a drastic approach. In 1986, after three years of steadily climbing plover numbers under my program, Connecticut's State Department of Environmental Protection began fencing individual plover nests. With a low of fifteen plover pairs in 1983, it was well worth the effort, and fencing individual nests had become common practice along the East Coast by the late 1980s. By the time I gave my program over to state management, in 1987, there were twenty-four nesting pairs in the state. In the summer of 2009, a record forty-one pairs of piping plovers fledged seventy-four young in Connecticut. I can't imagine where they all fit, but I'm delighted that persistent conservation efforts are paying off, and proud to have started them in Connecticut.

Walking in the colonies is not for the faint of heart. The fear of stepping on an egg or chick is ever-present. I learned to look carefully at each spot where I intended to plant my foot before moving. I found that amber sunglasses seemed to make the cryptic, speckled eggs jump out at me. Overhead, there was a constant din of screaming least terns, punctuated by spatters of warm fish emulsion. My broad-brimmed hat and faded, paper-thin denim shirt took the brunt of it. A gull feather tucked in the hat brim gave the terns a target for their strafing runs; they try to hit the tallest part of an intruder.

I often wondered if the piping plovers and least terns knew that I was working for their safety; that, but for my signs and string, they'd be driven over and stomped on. They recognized me, all right, but I'm afraid they recognized me as a major threat. After all, I was the one who breached the colony boundaries, marking nests, counting eggs and chicks, and checking for signs of predation. The birds didn't know I was working for their good; they knew only that, with my inordinate interest in their eggs and chicks, I was far more obtrusive than the average sun worshiper. Piping plovers would hurry out to escort me the moment they spotted me, leading me safely past their nests with distraction displays, dragging wings and spreading their tails as if suddenly crippled.

Often, a plover would settle into a depression in the sand just as if it were covering eggs, a distraction behavior called "false brooding." There was no

Distraction display by piping plover at nest

question in my mind that the plovers and terns focused such defensive measures more on me than on an ordinary passerby. Least terns went out of their way to anoint me with fish emulsion. There was one bird at Griswold Point who learned to hover low under my hat brim and shoot its droppings right into my face. That was the thanks I got. I have to admit I didn't much like least terns by the end of the third season of being bathed in their excrement.

Whatever happened in the colony, the sand told the story. I found the double, shuffling lines of striped skunks; the wobbly finger-stars of Virginia opossums; the neat single lines of red foxes and housecats; the bunched foursomes of long-tailed weasel feet. But the track I dreaded most was the large trident of the black-crowned night-heron.

Menunketesuck Island was a tiny spit of rock, sand, and cast-up bird bones that stretched straight out into Long Island Sound from Madison, Connecticut. I could wade out at low tide but had to work quickly or the water would be thigh-deep or deeper on the return wade. Least terns liked the island for its relative safety from land-based predators; I liked it because, thanks to the intimidating tidal channel between it and the mainland, I could be alone there, which is saying something on the summertime shore.

I'll never forget the first nest count on Menunketesuck after a

Kidee-kidee-kidee! A least tern brings home a butterfish. They always sound so joyful when they've got food.

black-crowned night-heron found the thriving colony. The sinister trident tracks wove from nest to nest, and nest after nest simply turned up empty. The herons liked chicks better than eggs, and they struck at peak hatch, taking each chick on the first night of its life. I stayed on the shore one evening, watching, to confirm what I knew was happening. Three black-crowned night-herons came winging in, giving their comical *QUOK!* call, ready to fill their gullets with tern chicks. The tern colony erupted in pandemonium, the adult birds helpless against the big nocturnal predators, reduced to circling and screaming, leaving eggs and chicks unattended and vulnerable to chilling and predation.

I knew it is natural for night-herons to eat tern chicks, but something about it just didn't seem right. Black-crowned night-heron populations were exploding at the time, their colonies radiating northward from a stronghold on Chimon Island off the southwest coast of the state. A single night-heron could eat thirty tern chicks in one walk through the colony and could easily eliminate the entire colony's reproduction in a season. How could the terns possibly survive such pressure from a long-lived, highly intelligent predator? Would the night-herons simply wipe the terns out? Could I do anything to stop it?

Thinking about it, I reasoned that eating least tern chicks was something not all night-herons did; it was a habit in a few individuals that lived near colonies. If I could eliminate those birds, the terns might have a fighting chance, at least until the next night-heron keyed in to the rich food resource. I've never been comfortable with guns, but I knew an ornithologist who was, and he offered to collect a night-heron under his permit. Staking Menunketesuck out, he managed to shoot one as night was falling. The predation continued unabated, and I knew the other two herons would keep decimating the colony unless I came up with something more effective.

That something was a poison called Avitrol. As with the "coyote getter" in a

Mingled fascination and dread as I watch two
black-crowned night herons plane into Menunketesuck Island
from a perch on a high seawall. Death angels for terns.
They'll start at the west end and eat every chick that hatched today.

collar on a sheep's neck that shoots poison into the predator's mouth when bitten, I could target the predator in the act of taking tern chicks. But how to deliver the dose? I emptied and cut a tea bag into tiny sachets, with a pinch of Avitrol in each one. Using thin strips of adhesive tape, I made tiny poison backpacks for a handful of newly hatched least tern chicks who lay at the start of the night route of the marauding herons.

I felt terrible about it, but I knew the chicks were destined for death in any event. If by chance they didn't get eaten, I could remove the poison backpacks. The next morning, I found the two night-herons, stiff and cold, lying right in the colony, each just a few steps beyond the place where it had swallowed its first sachet-wearing tern chick. Well, that worked better than expected. The predation stopped, and colony life went on. I couldn't rejoice at causing the death of these two beautiful, ruby-eyed night-herons, though I will admit a grim enjoyment in arriving at the complex strategy by which it was achieved. Seeing the terns settle back on their nests to fledge a few more chicks made my little war seem like a just one.

*Trojan tern chick, sachet in place. Should you ever need to bump off a marauding night-heron, this works.*

Weighing the survival of the vanishing terns against the death of three night-herons with a taste for threatened species, I'd probably do the same thing again, deaf to any charges of "playing God." These difficult choices face wildlife managers and conservationists wherever endangered seabirds nest. Unless wildlife managers controlled gulls, there would be no Atlantic puffins nesting in the Gulf of Maine. The same goes for the federally endangered roseate terns that nest on Bird Island in Buzzards Bay. Without vigilant gull control, the scarce and delicate terns wouldn't have a prayer. The estimated ten thousand pairs of common terns and one thousand pairs of roseate terns nesting on Great Gull Island owe their continued success to researchers, ever-vigilant against incursions by nesting gulls and a variety of predators eager to exploit this rich resource.

And why are there so many gulls? Because our fishing boats, lobster boats, shoreline shopping centers, Dumpsters, landfills, and fast-food joints feed them, encouraging a never-ending population explosion in the voracious predators. There are many who will be appalled at what they view as "playing God," but the truth is that we humans play God with every burger bun thrown out a car window and every new landfill or strip mall that creates fresh feeding fields for gulls.

The secondary, and vital, truth is that not all bird species are created equal. A gull is not a night-heron, is not a tern, is not a puffin. All are birds, but some will simply head for extinction without our help. There are some species—common, roseate, and least terns; black skimmers; piping plovers; American oystercatchers; and Atlantic puffins, to name a few—for which we must fight tooth and claw, and we will always have to fight to count them present on this altered earth. We fight the heedless, the ignorant, the hungry, the nasty. We carve out a place for them on our precious beaches. If you want terns and plovers, you do what you must.

I miss them so, the little strikers and pale plovers. Every so often as I travel I'll encounter them, and stop to watch the flashing white wings of a least tern as it streaks over, exulting with shrill calls about the sand lance in its bill. Or I'll see a pair of piping plovers with a brood of young, blowing like dust bunnies across the hot sand. And it all comes flooding back, the work and the worry of trying to ensure that they had a place to nest.

I think about the people I knew, the ingenious ways they came up with to protect these birds. I think about having nothing else to worry about but the nesting success of "my" precious terns and plovers, how they would fare in the next full-moon tide. They were my only dependents then. I remember walking the flesh

off my bones, 118 pounds of sheer determination, my hip joints loose and aching from trudging in deep sand. And I am thankful for those young women—and they are almost all women—who have come after me, who care enough to make sure I will always be able to see a least tern, wings flashing in the bright, bright sky, to hear the mellow note of a piping plover as it settles on porcelain eggs in the sand.

10:50   May 9 1988
                 ♀ on nest
         I didn't rise her as she
         slept
       The club is closed and I
       walked about ¼ mi in
       to find the signs posted 5/07
       still up and not a soul
       around. Plover heaven on
         this cool breezy bright
       Monday

         May 15 '88

# Autumnal Reflections

## PONDERING THE IMPONDERABLE

12-11-01
The Caywood road
redtail

# The Strange Case of the
# Companionable Grouse

I NEVER TOOK THEM for granted, even when they were here, and I encountered
at least one on every hike. The sudden kerfuffle, the heavy-bodied bird crashing
through the underbrush like a barely guided missile. *Grouse* was one of my daughter, Phoebe's first words, coming soon after *da* and *ma*. Still small enough to be
stuffed into a backpack carrier, she rode along on my afternoon hikes on the days
when she wouldn't nap. I carried a pocket mirror to look at her, sneaking peeks
at her pink cheeks, checking to see that her hat and pacifier were still in place. I
could tell the moment she fell asleep; I could feel her body suddenly relax into
the sweet heaviness of a dream. Thinking back, I was happiest when I could hike
and bring her along. It was as if I were stealing an hour for myself and sharing it
at the same time. It was a sad day when the backpack started to pinch her chunky
thighs, and she squirmed and braced her feet on my spine in her discomfort. I'd
have carried her forever.

On this January day, Phoebe was still awake as we picked our careful way
down the muddy slope I call the Chute. Falling flat on my back, as I've done so
many times here, would be contraindicated with my sweet backpack cargo to consider. There was usually a grouse on this slope in the late 1990s, sometimes two.

I'm sure he heard us coming for quite a while, but in grouse style, he waited to take wing until we were right on top of him. *BBBBRRRRRRRRRPPPPPTTH!!*

Phoebe jumped in surprise and whipped her head around to look.

"A grouse! That was a grouse, honey!"

Brief pause.

*"Gouse!"*

A huge, wet, not very toothy smile in the pocket mirror. My baby girl said "grouse!"

She's a lanky fifteen as I write, this limber, redheaded elf, and she loves to be told about her first encounter with a ruffed grouse. In the time it has taken to stretch my chubby baby into a graceful filly, ruffed grouse have vanished from our eighty-acre sanctuary. I don't know what happened, if the cause is any one thing or a combination. Perhaps the young brush has grown up too tall for their liking. The sumac, which made a vibrant, thick, fruit-heavy border on every path and meadow, is old, tall, and spindly now, fruiting sparsely. The flocks of hermit thrushes that used to winter here are gone, too, gone someplace with younger sumac and more smilax. Wild turkeys have moved in, aided by Ohio Division of Wildlife transplants and their own awe-inducing fecundity. The woods are laced with their meandering clearances, foot-wide traces scratched clean of litter. Other grouse limiters: coyotes have moved in, jiggling me awake with their high Martian chorus of weird yips and trills. The red and gray foxes I so loved to watch when we first moved here have vanished, most likely thanks to the depredations of their big, mean cousins. Great horned owls have come in this time, too, thinning our screech- and barred owls. Raccoons and opossums

are as numerous as ever; perhaps more so thanks to our bird-feeding efforts. There are many reasons the grouse might be gone.

We no longer thrill to the low *whump-whump-whump—brrrrrrrrrrrrrrp* of drumming males in spring. The males' whirring wings no longer beat out a love tattoo; the fallen logs they used for song perches have gone to moss and mushroom now. This low-frequency sound rolled through our spring woods, setting up a thrumming in my breast-bone, thrilling me to alertness before I even heard it.

Like many grouse, ruffed grouse are prone to population cycles—peaks and crashes in ten- to twelve-year intervals. There can be five times as many grouse in a single location in one decade than in the next. Alaskan and Canadian cycles have been linked, oddly enough, to population cycles of snowshoe hares. When hares are scarce, predators turn to grouse, causing crashes in their populations. Great Lakes grouse populations seem to decline when northern goshawks and great horned owls invade from farther north.

Many people in southern Ohio believe that turkeys eat the grouse's food out from under it. I can see how a bird that's four times a grouse's size but eats many of the same things *and* travels in large flocks could provide stiff competition. I suspect that that's what's going on here. I can hope that the turkeys, which seem to have population cycles of their own, might leave some room for grouse to rebound. It seems that between the active selective cutting our neighbors practice and the maturing, uncut forest we maintain, there should be ample habitat —young, old, and recovering—to provide for grouse.

There is so much here—there are whip-poor-wills and a dozen species of warblers, box turtles and seventy kinds of butterflies, but I still miss the grouse. Aldo Leopold said it best: "Everyone knows . . . that the autumn landscape in the north woods is the land, plus a red maple, plus a Ruffed Grouse. In terms of conventional physics, the grouse represents only a millionth of either the mass or the energy of an acre yet subtract the grouse and the whole thing is dead."

So I wait out the down cycle, if cycle it be, and remember the grouse in my past. There was the nest of eggs I stumbled upon in the Connecticut woods, when I lived in a tiny cottage and drew and painted by night. The hen was tending pipping eggs, and she crawled off the nest, flopping on her side and whining like a hurt animal, momentarily tempting me to follow. She left a drift of feathers and her precious eggs in the rain. I retreated as quickly as I could, knowing I'd intruded at the most delicate of moments. Late the next afternoon I crept back, fixing my binoculars on the spot, to see if all had gone well. There in the scrape on the ground at the base of a hemlock was a single egg. There was no sign of dis-

turbance. All the chicks had hatched and gone; tiny bits of pipped eggshell showed that the hen had carried the shells off as the chicks hatched. And when the chicks were able to walk, within a few hours, she had led them away, leaving this one behind.

I picked up the cold, roundish, buff white

egg and cradled it in my hand. I held it against a spot of sun in the hemlocks. It looked to have a chick inside. I hurried home, holding it against my stomach, and set up a heating pad, a thermometer, and a damp washcloth in a makeshift incubator. I didn't know if it would hatch; I didn't know what I'd do with the chick if it did. Maybe I'd walk with it until I found its family, put a tiny blindfold on it so it wouldn't imprint on me instead of its mother. I hadn't thought that far. But such is the magic of an unhatched egg, the potential and mystery of it, that I had to try.

The egg never peeped, never pipped. So, carefully, I made a nick in the shell and removed it piece by piece, an archaeologist uncovering the most precious of relics. Wet yellowish down, a curled pink foot. There was a full-term chick inside. I warmed it, dried it, couldn't believe it could be dead. It was so beautiful and new. Most amazing of all were its wings—not the downy stubs I'd expected but feathered with buff brown plumage, finely vermiculated with black scrawls. Seven of its ten primaries had burst the sheath; about half of the secondaries had emerged. I had never realized that a ruffed grouse chick hatches with feathered wings. How could that be? It was clear that the waxy sheaths had started growing while the chick was still in the egg. That an embryo could grow feathers within an egg, in only twenty-five days of incubation, still defies my understanding.

These minuscule feathers will hardly be able to support the bird's flight as it grows, so a ruffed grouse chick begins molting within a few hours of hatching. By the end of its first week of life, the chick's second set of flight feathers begins to emerge, starting from the innermost and working toward the outermost. At this age, the chick can fly, and it is disarming to have a downy fluff ball suddenly levitate, furiously beating tiny wings, and disappear into the upper branches of a tree.

The impression is more bumblebee than bird, but the net effect is escape. By Day 10, ruffed grouse chicks fly very well. They'll stay with their brood, following their mother, for twelve to fifteen weeks, dispersing in November, "the moon

A two-day old
ruffed grouse
teeters 15' up
in a balsam fir,
having flown there
under its own
power.

That this thumb-sized bird
can fly on Day TWO
astounds me.

when the grouse go crazy" according to Canadian naturalist Ernest Thompson Seton. It's then that people may be surprised to find a grouse crashing full-tilt through a living room window. Dispersing juveniles careen off in all directions, doing very strange things.

Speaking of strange, there is another aspect of ruffed grouse behavior that remains unexplained. I've experienced it three times in my life, and I have read and heard many anecdotal accounts that follow the form of my own.

When I lived in Hadlyme, Connecticut, we hauled our garbage to the town dump, New England style. The landfill was ringed by thick forest, attended by crows, turkey vultures, and one very assertive ruffed grouse. We learned to drive slowly down the dump lane, for when he heard a car, this wild male grouse would hurry out of the forest, shining black ruffs flared around his face, to meet it. He'd pace back and forth by the door, occasionally alighting on the hood, and rush us when we got out of the car. There was a gruff man we called the Dumpmeister, who kept us all honest about what we brought to the landfill. He had a soft spot for Dump Grouse. He named him, talked to him, but in the end he couldn't protect the bizarre and beautiful bird from running under the heedless wheels of a truck.

After we moved to our Appalachian Ohio home in 1992, a male ruffed grouse would burst out of the woods to meet Bill's car as he traveled the driveway. The bird would strut and display in the road, barely moving aside to let Bill pass.

People who witness such behavior in a ruffed grouse often assume that the bird was raised as a pet, but not many people have the ability to raise a grouse, and the behavior arises spontaneously and often in remote locales. Something else is going on, something odd inside the tiny grouse brain that causes it to substitute vehicles, machines, and people for more appropriate conspecific rivals or mates. Some have speculated that the rumble of automobile engines triggers a

Four Grass follows me at Dolbia Lane.

primitive response in the birds, which find in this sound some echo of their territorial wing drumming. How, then, to explain House Grouse?

She lived on a Nature Conservancy preserve in Connecticut, and so did I. Several thousand acres of unbroken forest surrounded my little cabin in the clearing. I was alone there much of the time and had no reason to speak much. When the telephone would ring and I'd answer it, a young female ruffed grouse would hurry out of the woods and pace beneath the window, peering up at me. If the conversation went on for a long time, as they often did, she'd fly up to a cedar branch closest to the window and settle in with her eyes half-closed and neck pulled in, as if soothed by the sound of my voice. If I walked with a friend, talking, she'd follow. Of course, I felt hopelessly flattered by her attention, even as I wondered why she gave it. There seems to be nothing adaptive in cozying up to a large omnivorous primate.

My landlords had a black Labrador at the time, and her mind-numbing behavioral repertoire included eating, begging, stealing, romping, and killing. I knew that only luck had kept House Grouse out of her teeth. I found a strew of the grouse's tail feathers, matted with dog slobber, in the lane she frequented, and knew that my endearing little companion wouldn't escape twice. Three days later, my little friend sought me out, ragged and half-tailed. How could I teach vigilance to a bird born innocent and seemingly without the sense to stay away?

Two more days, and here came Derry, roaring up the lane, huge-headed with her prize. I grabbed the dog's scruff, twisted, cut off her air, and extracted my dear friend from the Lab's hard mouth; Derry wasn't even a decent retriever. Grouse's left leg and right wing were broken; her ribs were crushed. I cleaned her wounds, applied antibiotic salve, fed her, and bedded her down on sweet hay. I measured her and sketched out splints for her leg and wing, hoping she'd live until the next morning. She whimpered as I wept over her. I left her in the cool barn for the night and read for three hours, unable to sleep, gripped in despair for my strange companion, for the cruelty of a world that keeps no place for a trusting game bird. I raised my head from the blurring lines, brought up like a fish to the surface, and knew Grouse had died. Her eyes were still closing when I reached her.

I carried her out to a rock in the meadow, an offering to the coyotes, an apology to the broken body of a strange bird. For a brief while, she'd brightened my life. I knew when we met that she wouldn't be here long; she was of another world, a better one; a peaceable kingdom where grouse bustle out of the forest to stroll with people.

# White-throated Sparrow

## The Song in My Heart

MOST PEOPLE KNOW white-throated sparrows as fall and winter migrants, kicking happily in the leaf litter beneath sheltering brambles, flocking to seed that's been cast on the ground. Their bright, sharp *queep! queep!* call, given as the birds go to a communal roost in the evening, was one of the first birdcalls I remember tracking down on a late-winter evening near my home in Richmond, Virginia. In the 1960s and '70s, there were still remnant patches of the old, horsy Virginia in the West End suburbs, and this little farm was one of them. I could walk up Academy Road and stroke velvet noses, inhale the good, sharp scent of horse sweat, even muck out stalls in return for the occasional harrowing bareback ride on a fat, ill-behaved paint mare named Apache.

There were horses and there were birds, and I spent many of my afternoons hanging around the place taking it all in. White-throated sparrows kicked and scratched all winter in the pine straw and oak leaves, picking up waste feed. Their quavering song, often represented as *Poor Sam Peabody*, occasionally arose from one of the flock, but that lusty roost call—*queep! queep!*—mystified me until the evening I decided to find out from whence it came. I could barely make out the crown stripes of the calling sparrows, but I still remember the thrill that shot through me when I was able to connect the odd call with a familiar bird. The horse farm is gone now, long since rolled under the parking lot of an enormous Baptist church, complete with its own broadcasting tower, which, on Sundays, replaced every one of our radio stations with the blustery tones of its preacher. With the woodland and pasture went the winter flocks of white-throated sparrows.

In the early 1980s, I spent six weeks in Newfoundland, and I hiked its cool, rocky paths on what passed for summer days—in the fifties, with a fine rain falling. The heady scent of balsam rose around me whenever the sun dared peer out. The wistful songs of white-throated sparrows—stronger now, not wavering, since the birds were on their breeding grounds—seemed the perfect aural embodiment of the aroma of fir: sweet, elusive, nostalgic, and intoxicating. Bright-eyed, they watched me as they carried spruce budworms and caterpillars to their young. I never hear a white-throat's song without returning, just for a moment, to the short, dark forests of the Rock.

Learning about birds is, for me, like piecing together a puzzle that lasts a lifetime. I chase down their songs, one by one, spurning audio recordings in favor of hearing that song coming from an open bill. I pick up and store random fragments of information: bits of songs and calls, foraging and breeding behavior, flight style, bathing behavior. I piece them together in memory until I begin to see the bird take form. I may never be granted an entire image, but occasionally I have an interaction with an individual that grants an unusual and unexpected insight, a glimpse into the imponderable. So it was with one white-throated sparrow.

A call came in on the evening of April 23, 1991, from a woman in Groton,

Sunshine
when he came to me
4/23/91
head twisted to the right
trembling
he cald hop in a circle,
fly in a spiral to the ground
It looked pretty hopeless
But when I fed him the first time
He took it so gratefully I decided to give him a chance
I force-fed him every two hours for the next 12 days
(That's seventy-two times) I rubbed his sore neck
And on the twelfth day he picked up a seed, then
another
Painfully bringing his head around right to eat
He gained strength and weight
And now it's May tenth
And I'm going to release him
His head high
His body strong
I'll miss his sweet song
He won't miss me—he's thinking of fir forests
and lady whitethroats
But he has been loved.

Connecticut. She'd picked up an adult white-throated sparrow in her backyard, seemingly uninjured but for its head, which was completely inverted. How odd. I wanted to see if I could help, so I met her to pick it up. The bird trembled and blinked, looking at the world upside down, its head twisted dramatically to the right, throat up, crown down. I asked the woman if it might have come into contact with any poisons. They had just fertilized their lawn. Perhaps the bird had picked up and been poisoned by some granular fertilizer, I mused, as I drove my new patient home.

On the advice of my veterinarian, I took the sparrow to a local practitioner who injected the forty-gram bird with atropine, an antidote for carbamines and organophosphates. Since the bird had been in this condition for at least twenty-four hours, we decided not to give activated carbon, which might have helped neutralize a more recently ingested poison.

Because it couldn't orient its head to pick up its own food, I force-fed the helpless sparrow with ground canary chow, fortified with nutritional supplements. It eagerly accepted live mealworms and bits of sunflower seed from my fingers. Its bright eyes and hearty appetite were at odds with the poisoning diagnosis, but its head remained inverted, and it was incapable of flying, hopping, perching, or feeding on its own. After two days of this, with no improvement, I decided to administer an antibiotic in hopes that the affliction might have a bacterial component. The bird was doomed anyway and would have died long ago had I not been feeding it. An antibiotic couldn't hurt, I reasoned. Its appetite remained hearty, and it calmly submitted to force feedings, accepting more and more tidbits directly from my fingers.

On April 27, I felt a clump of feathers on the sparrow's neck and parted the feathers to reveal a dime-size hole in the skin at the base of its skull. Oh! The matted feathers had concealed an injury, probably inflicted by a housecat, to the bird's neck muscles. I was floored, happy to have an explanation for the bird's bizarre head position and glad I'd decided to administer an antibiotic, since cat saliva teems with bacteria that can be lethal to birds. The injury was old enough that my veterinarian advised to let it heal naturally. I cleaned it up and began a new thrust in the bird's rehabilitation and a new, if temporary, job description: avian physical therapist.

*Midway through his recovery, when he was able to perch, he sat with his head to the side as though considering something weighty*

After every feeding, I massaged the twisted muscles of the sparrow's thin neck as I held it by the bill. With each session, I gently twisted the head closer to upright. Improvement was dramatic. The next day, the sparrow wriggled out of my grasp and flew through the kitchen into my living room, landing on the carpet. Its still-inverted head was a few degrees closer to vertical, and it blinked at me with a quizzical look as I laughed and scooped it up to return it to its glass tank home. I supplied it with a perch and was delighted to see it hop up and cling briefly, its head still twisted ninety degrees to the right, but no longer upside down. I gave it a dish of sunflower hearts, which it eyed but didn't attempt to eat.

Throughout the bird's therapy, I was struck by its calm demeanor and its willingness to eat what I offered it. It couldn't have been enjoying itself, but it was a willing and compliant patient, with a sunny attitude that matched the name the woman's preschool daughters had given it: Sunshine, for the brilliant yellow loral spot that shone against its bright white crown stripes. Children often name an injured or orphaned bird the moment they pick it up; wildlife rehabilitators refrain from such indulgences until it's clear that their charges will survive. Sunshine he would be.

By May 2, Sunshine was picking at the sunflower hearts in his dish, his strengthening neck allowing him enough coordination to hold it upright long enough to take a morsel before the muscles snapped sideways again. He trembled with the effort, but he was feeding himself, and his activity level increased. I gave him a larger cage and more perches, and moved him to a side room where he'd be less likely to panic at unfamiliar stimuli.

*he sang today 5/10/91*

By May 3, I had discontinued the antibiotic. Sunshine struggled free from my grasp and flew like a wild thing through the house, neatly avoiding the windows, negotiating the doorways. It was a good, if unexpected, test of his powers of flight. Another week ground by, and he picked up more food on his own with each passing day. It was a relief to know he could feed himself, and it gave me a little freedom. His head was still noticeably tilted to the right, so I kept up the frequent physical therapy that had gotten him this far along the path to recovery.

At dawn on May 9, I awoke to the quavering song of a white-throated sparrow — inside my little house. Sunshine was singing. I'd guessed his sex correctly, though the plumage of white-throated sparrows gives no hint of their sex. Some adults have bright white crown stripes and yellow loral spots; some have dull buff crowns and no loral spots, but the coloring is unrelated to sex; both adult males and females come in white- and buff-crowned morphs.

Sunshine had been feeding himself since the fourth of May and had laid on a good pad of fat in the V of his breastbone. He felt well enough to sing! During physical therapy that afternoon, he bit me. His head was now tilted just a few degrees to the right, giving him a rakish, inquisitive look. Oh yes, he was going to make it.

By May 11, I knew I'd done as much as I could for this

*Such a suspicious birdie! Always watching me*

sparrow, and he'd reached that delicate edge of wildness and vigor that can have only one outcome: release. I opened my hands in the balmy spring air, and Sunshine rocketed to a large mountain laurel shrub, where he dove into the tangled darkness like any good white-throated sparrow would. I scattered mixed seed all over the yard, left saucers of water on the ground, and said a prayer that he'd reach his Canadian breeding grounds before it was too late to find a mate and stake out a territory. Thinking about it, I scaled back my wish, hoping simply that he'd be able to survive, feed himself, and fly well enough to make it south come winter.

I didn't see Sunshine again until the next afternoon, when I saw him scratching at the mixed seed under the laurel. On the morning of May 14, I awoke to the song of a white-throated sparrow, and I knew it was Sunshine, because all the other white-throats had long since departed for Canada. I pulled on my clothes and walked out into the yard to listen to this small bird's hymn to the silence. Had the cat had its way, his song would have been forever stilled. I was changed, transformed by these three weeks of feeding, massaging, and hoping for a sparrow. Such work is its own reward. I knelt to pull some weeds from the neglected garden on the east side of the house, the May sun warming my back. Sunshine flew closer, to a maple just overhead, and sang. I smiled up at him, finished weeding, and moved to the iris bed in the front yard, happy to be in the company of a wild white-throated sparrow. He followed, perching in the top of a white pine just over a stone wall from where I was weeding. And he sang.

For the next two days, Sunshine would follow me around the yard, singing from the closest perch he could find. I don't know why he did it; whether, like a newly captured, hand-fed falcon, he'd imprinted on me in those three weeks of intensive feeding and therapy; whether he considered me a substitute mate, parent, or rival. I know far better than to make the anthropomorphic leap to say he was trying to thank me. What does a bird know of gratitude? Perhaps quite a lot more than we think. I can only say that he followed me, singing, and, in singing, touched an inarticulate place in my heart. By May 18, he was gone, headed north, I hoped, tracking his own course once again.

# Savannah Sparrow

## Forever Wild

ANY AVIAN rehabilitator can tell you that, when catching a bird, housecats almost always bite down hard on the right wing where it joins the bird's body, crushing the shoulder joint so that their prey is instantly and permanently disabled. Birds die by the hundreds of millions, and more than a billion small mammals die every year at the claws of some of our 90 million pet cats, tasty supplements to their bowls of dry cat chow, an anodyne for the boredom of house pets left to roam outdoors. An estimated 100 million additional stray cats add to the ranks of bird and small mammal predators. Some of these feral cats are romanticized by their admirers, housed and fed in colonies, left to range and hunt city parks and green spaces, clearing them of birds and small mammals. Whatever feral cat advocates and laissez-faire cat owners may rationalize about hunting as natural behavior for felines, this preventable carnage by an introduced predator is unnatural and unconscionable. Working in songbird rehabilitation gives me a close look at what cats do; talking to cat owners on the telephone helps me understand the denial and misplaced sentimentality that permit the killing to go on.

What becomes of a wild bird with a crushed shoulder joint, should it man-

age to escape a cat? It makes its way into dense cover, looks for food and shelter as best it can, and dies within a few days from trauma and infection. Its fate may play out quite differently if it is one of the very few found and taken in by people.

OCTOBER 9, 1989. The Hardings' cat caught a small, streaky, brown sparrow under their bird feeder in Old Lyme, Connecticut. Their neighbor Doreen Lammer took the injured bird and kept it in a cage in her kitchen for five weeks. It grew fat on parakeet seed but never became tame. Doreen, referred by a mutual friend, brought the bird to me on November 13. It was a Savannah sparrow, waylaid on its autumn migration, a bird I'd be happy to see through binoculars, now lying quietly in my hand. By that point, its right wing had healed, partially extended, with a crushed shoulder joint. No amount of surgery could have made this bird releasable, whether I'd been able to take it to a veterinarian minutes or months after the event.

What to do with this small, rather uncommon sparrow? I could euthanize it, knowing that it would never live like a Savannah sparrow again. I could look for a nature center that wanted an injured Savannah sparrow for display. Or I could keep it, cobble together a seminatural diet, use it as a model for sketches and paintings, and try to give it a decent life in my house. My foolish heart won out, and I entered unhesitatingly into another relationship with a sparrow. Little did I know that I'd be fixing this bird a hot breakfast, changing its cage papers, clipping its nails, and trimming the clumsy feathers on its injured wing for the next fourteen and a half years.

I removed millet from its diet and switched the sparrow over to a commercial pelleted food meant for canaries. I supplemented with live mealworms in moderation. Whenever I caught a spider in the house, I tossed it into the cage, where the bird pounced on my offering, seeming to savor its leggy spiciness. Fresh fruits and vegetables, natural millet sprays, and occasional treats of pasta, Cheddar cheese, scrambled eggs, and mashed sweet potato rounded out its fare. Vanna began to sing the next spring, a sweet, thin trill that started and ended with a sneezy stutter. By then, his feminine name, a corruption of Savannah, had stuck fast.

One might think that a bird kept in captivity for almost fifteen years would become tame, but Vanna never surrendered his wildness. When I approached the cage, as I did perhaps twenty-five thousand times over the years I kept and tended him, his reaction was always the same: drop to the floor and scuttle around like a mouse, looking for a corner where he could hide. I had no desire to tame him, but after a while I found his behavior a bit tiresome.

Vanna 3/05/93

*Vanna became very attached to an injured junco. It was a sad day for him when I let the junco go.*

To be fair to Vanna, I was the perpetrator of indignities, such as the twice-monthly toenail clip and the doubtless uncomfortable wing trim that kept the skewed feathers on his injured wing from impeding locomotion. But as the chef of what amounted to a gourmet bird restaurant, I felt I was owed something more than dread.

I felt sorry for Vanna, and I wished I could keep him outdoors in a grassy place. But a bird robbed of all powers of flight is immensely vulnerable to raccoons, weasels, chipmunks, opossums, even mice; it would be almost impossible to create a safe outdoor cage for him. As an imperfect solution, I would occasionally let Vanna explore the studio while I cleaned his cage. Ironic as it seems, a cage represents security to a captive bird, and visitors were amazed when I'd return with Vanna's freshly scrubbed cage, tip it up, and say, "Back to your cage. Chop, chop, Vanna!" This timid, wild bird would run directly toward me and scuttle back under the sheltering bars.

I had had Vanna for only ten days when my veterinarian gave me a dark-eyed junco to tend. Nothing was broken and his wings were fine, but he could get no lift when he tried to fly. Dr. Giddings suspected punctured air sacs, probably from a housecat's claws, and wanted to see if two weeks of rest and supportive care could restore his flight. Because both juncos and Savannah sparrows travel in flocks, I released the junco into Vanna's cage. At nightfall, the two birds were huddled into a single ball of soft feathers. My heart melted, and I wondered what would happen if and when the junco was ready for release.

After twelve days, the junco was healed and frantic for release. I curtained off the windows, closed the living room doors, and opened the cage door. Vanna hopped out and began inspecting the corners for spiders. The junco burst out and flew to the highest shelf in the room. Oh, sweet victory—he'd fly free again! I opened a window and wished him well as he arrowed out into a pearly December sky.

Vanna had been watching, too. He scuttled back into his cage, chipping frantically. He chipped all afternoon, calling to the junco, and became deeply depressed, refusing food and water. As a palliative, I put him in with two other long-term captives, a house finch and an orchard oriole. The oriole avoided Vanna; the finch pecked him whenever he drew near. For the next fourteen years, Vanna would be caged alone but for a mirror. He roosted next to it and pecked it gently, sang to it, and waited patiently while I washed it of the myriad small spots of his attempts to feed it.

What would Vanna have chosen, given a choice of dying quickly or living out his life in captivity? I try to divine this for each bird in my care. If it is frantic and miserable, dashing itself against the cage bars until it bleeds; if it panics and can't settle down in my presence; if it seems unhappy even after a few weeks of acclimation, I choose euthanasia. If it eats well, seems reasonably calm, sings, preens, and enjoys the company of other birds, I can't bring myself to end its life. It's clear to me that some birds are better suited to captivity than others, both on a species and on an individual level. One cardinal might calm down nicely, while another may remain insanely wild, ricocheting off the bars of its cage. In this, as in every other avenue, birds demonstrate their individuality. Vanna seemed reasonably content to stay with me, and so he stayed.

I never knew how old Vanna was when he was brought to me. He was in adult basic (winter) plumage. He could have been a few months or several years old. By the fourteenth winter of our lives together, Vanna had visibly aged. His eyes were a little sunken; the scutes on his legs and feet were thick and raised, like an old man's toenails. He fell from his perch with increasing regularity, lying on his back on the cage bottom, scrabbling feebly. I removed the high perches, laid soft paper towels down on the cage floor, and checked on him many times daily. On February 3, 2004, I found the small, still form in the cage corner, as I'd anticipated for several years. He'd lived longer than any Savannah sparrow known to man or science. Doreen, who'd brought him to me, had sent me a box of fruit in gratitude every Christmas for more than a decade, but Vanna outlasted even her considerable generosity.

I felt a curious detachment, born, perhaps, of Vanna's resolute wildness, his refusal to cozy up to his keeper. I dug a small hole beneath some emerging daffodils and placed his tiny body, wrapped in tissues, in the cold earth. My eyes blurred over, and I knew I'd miss his wheezy song, the patter of his feet on newspaper, the bright, mouselike gaze of his eyes. I still don't know if I did right by that sparrow, keeping him all those years. In living as long and as well as he did, he gave me a gift, a glimpse of what I may be getting into with each bird I take in. Remembering Vanna and knowing what lies ahead informs my decisions for the next time I'm presented with a shoe box, holes punched in the lid, a small, frantic scrabbling inside.

# Orchard Oriole

## I Know Why the Caged Bird Flutters

IN THE COUNTRY, when you leave the garage door open overnight, there's always hell to pay in the morning. Raccoons mine the garbage cans and sort through the recycling; they get into whatever might be gotten into. A lactating female raccoon is little more than a mini-bear. Recently, one tore a forty-pound sack of cracked corn into small shreds, and I was greeted with a golden pile to salvage and clean up. I straightened up from the task, and there in the rafters was an old cage, memories sifting through its brass bars. An orchard oriole had lived there for seventeen years, hopping with a pronking sound from branch to branch. That and her garbled, chattering song had been the soundtrack to my work, since her cage stood near at hand in my studio.

She had come to me as a juvenile, the victim of a free-roaming cat with a taste for exotica. The same cat owner—she had seven to clean up after—had also brought me a gray catbird and a wood thrush. The catbird was a lightly injured nestling; I raised and released it. I could see that the wood thrush was dying when the cat's owner brought it to me. Only a juvenile, it had a bad compound fracture of the left shoulder, the same injury suffered by the oriole. As many times as I've seen the injury, I get angrier every time at good birds gone to waste for a house-cat's play.

I looked at the woman as she cradled the little thrush, tears coursing down her cheeks. Having devoted weeks of care to the birds she'd already brought, I'd implored her to keep her bloodthirsty pets indoors. The thrush's shoulder break was inoperable, and sepsis from the teeming bacteria on the cat's teeth and claws had set in. There was nothing I could do to help now. Even if massive antibiotics could halt the infection, this thrush would never fly again. I had lost any desire to make it easy for the cat lover to relieve her conscience.

"Tell you what. Instead of giving this bird to me, you take it home, and you can make it comfortable while it dies, and maybe the consequences of letting your cats hunt will sink in on you. All this because you don't want to disappoint your pets by keeping them inside." She drove away with the dying thrush, and she never brought me another injured bird. I doubt that there was an epiphany or a reformation involved. If I owned seven cats, I'd probably want them outside, too.

In the meantime, I still had a gravely injured oriole to nurse. I had thought at first that she would die, too, lying in the bottom of a shoe box, pinkish orange lung tissue exposed by a long gash on her side. Her right wing was hanging, the humerus

broken just below the joint. I thought perhaps to have her euthanized, but in the car on
the way to the veterinarian's office, she crawled over to
her food dish and helped herself to some strawberries. I
watched the little bird masticating the fruit, her head high
and her eyes bright, and decided to have her broken
wing pinned instead. It didn't seem to be my place to
deny this bird a chance to live.

Dr. Giddings asked me to hold her still while he
pinned Ora Lee's humerus; it was that or amputate the wing. As I held the oriole,
watching in mingled fascination and revulsion, the room began to swim. The next
thing I remember is Giddings's voice. "Get her out of here." As I toppled sideways,
a helpful vet tech caught me and stretched me out on the operating room floor. I
came to in time to take my bandaged oriole home. This—and a vast ineptitude in
the harder sciences—is why I am a writer and not a veterinarian.

That was 1989. I moved several times, married Bill, bought land and a house,
bore two children; the millennium turned, and still the little green oriole with the
immobile wing hopped and sang in the cage in my studio, outliving every other
orchard oriole known to science. Seventeen years—who'd have thought I'd still
be whipping up sweet potato and butternut squash, three-cheese ravioli, and fresh
fruit for her every blessed morning? Granted, the longevity of captive birds in protected environs may be biologically irrelevant, but the wild bird closest in age was
recaptured in South Dakota, where it had been banded as an adult nine years and
seven months earlier.

Living with a bird close at hand, one can learn things about birds that elude
the casual bird watcher, and even the researcher. I named the juvenile oriole Ora
Lee, after one of my mother's bridge partners. Despite all she'd been through, Ora

Lee was unfazed by surgery and captivity. She moved with quick assertiveness, bouncing from perch to perch, banging on her mirror, chasing and pestering her cagemate, a male house finch who had to be removed after two batterings. She was dexterous and inventive, holding food in her toes, titmouse style, for processing. Given a mealworm, she'd behead it, then gingerly remove the coffee brown intestinal tract, flinging the nasty bit with a quick flick of her bill, painting the walls around her cage with impromptu oriole art. She liked to mess with thread and grasses, pulling and weaving them in a pantomime of nesting behavior. In spring, when the windows were open, a single *chuck* call from a wild orchard oriole outside sent her into a frenzy of calling and fluttering. It was painful to watch her strive to catch a glimpse of another oriole in the trees outside. I wished that she had even limited flight capacity, that she might be placed in an outdoor cage, but the cat had seen to that.

Wherever I've lived, from Connecticut to Ohio, there comes a time in late August when the haze blows away and the nights are clear and starry, with a chill that portends autumn. On such a night—August 24, 1989—Ora Lee began hopping and fluttering around her cage, looking for a way out, a way to anywhere. The next night was a repeat—as soon as darkness fell, she began to flutter. She was migrating, as much as a caged bird could migrate.

Unwilling to face another night diced to sleepless bits by her racket, I put her cage in the kitchen. After a few nights, her tail was battered and worn from contact with its bars, so I lined the bathtub with newspapers and released her to flutter harmlessly in its larger confines. I marveled at the pointless but powerful imperative that sent her to bash herself against the bars each night in a mock flight to Guatemala. She was still at it at Thanksgiving, flying for part of the night and sleeping much of the day. Living in a tiny cottage with a migratory oriole was asking more of me than I'd have foreseen.

Gradually, the Zugunruhe (migratory restlessness) died down, until spring —March 22. Her nocturnal madness started afresh; Ora Lee was on her imaginary way back for the spring. I sighed and reinstated our nightly bathtub routine, wondering if all the orchard orioles had awoken at precisely the same moment across Central America, hearing the call to fly north. It was a compelling thought, that this captive bird might be answering so ancient an imperative. I had no choice but to accommodate her as best I could.

I wasn't the only one having trouble adjusting to her captivity. Fall and winter and spring came, and Ora Lee never molted. She kept the same coat of feathers

*Ora Lee's morning bath,*
*sending spray everywhere.*
*She liked her water fresh.*

—her first basic plumage—for two and a half years. She still hadn't molted by the first of November, 1992. We moved from Maryland to Ohio, Bill driving a big rental van, I driving my old station wagon, remade into an ark of sorts, bursting with cages and houseplants.

In the fuss and furor of relocating, I ran out of the mealworms that had been Ora Lee's staple. The sudden loss of this protein-rich item seemed to trigger a catastrophic molt, and she dropped both fat and feathers. New pinfeathers burst through, and by the end of November 1992 she was reborn, a sleek, shiny yellow-green. From then on, I strictly limited her mealworm intake to six per day, saving them as treats, and kept her on a lean diet of commercial bird chow with mixed fresh fruits and vegetables. Scrambled eggs, Cheddar cheese, lasagna, cake, cinnamon toast, and bits of cookie were only a few of the infrequent snacks that delighted her. For the rest of her years, Ora Lee molted regularly in late summer, and she was as beautiful at seventeen as she had been at three. She started each morning with a bath in the fresh water of her drinking cup, soaking herself and then preening vigorously until she was dry. She bathed so regularly and enthusiastically that I was forced to cut Plexiglas sheets to fit her cage sides, lest everything within ten feet of the cage be sprinkled into ruin.

And so the years turned, and I wondered how long this little bird would grace my studio. Chestnut feathers painted her undertail and back, bits of malelike plumage, little tokens of the testosterone that elderly female birds sometimes secrete. She sang her chattery song in the spring and still looked and listened for other orioles out her big window.

But like a little clock, she slowly wound down. By December 2005 I knew that, if Ora Lee made it to spring, this, her seventeenth, would be her last. Her breathing had become labored, her appetite faded, and I had to come up with better

February 8, 2006 - Ora Lee finally managed to leave in the night.

and better menus to keep her interested. I could have dosed her with antibiotics, I suppose, but it seemed unfair to prolong her life. I had to let her go sometime.

On February 8, 2006, I got up from my chair and walked into the aviary, as I had almost every morning since 1989, and found her, silent and still, in the corner of the cage floor. This is how death comes to captive birds, in the wee hours of the night, just like birth. They slip away when no one is there to notice.

I wasn't good for much that day. My reaction to her loss took me by surprise. I thought I was ready to let her go. I wept a long time for this gallant little bird, who lived as good a life as I could give her, for so very long.

The caged oriole and I had much in common; we grew alike like old roommates. Bound by the welcome duties of a wife and mother, I could no more migrate in late August than could she with her crippled wing. I know I should be moving on in the fall, and yet I never seem to go. The certain slant of golden light, the songs of flocking starlings raise a lump in my throat. The quiet trill of a tree cricket in the coloring sumac makes me long for Martha's Vineyard in October, for cockleburs in my shoelaces, for loves lost but never forgotten. The only thing that makes me feel better is to walk, to come home with pants legs covered in beggar ticks. I should have a destination, but I don't; I walk a trail that makes a loop and ends up back home.

It's no different from the plink, plunk, hop, and flutter Ora Lee made around the perches in her brass cage, but it's enough to hold off cabin fever for a while. I think about her as I wear my woodland trails ever smoother, pacing the cage.

Two-spotted Tree Cricket
Neoxabea bipunctata on
Shining Sumac Rhus copallina.
September 2 2010

# Touched by a Redtail

THOUGH THEY PROBABLY know better, many local people assume that, in addition to publishing a magazine and booklets about birds, *Bird Watcher's Digest* is in the avian rehabilitation business. Sad to say, for several counties in southeast Ohio, there are no active avian rehabilitators, so the magazine is the only remotely bird-related place most callers can turn to. Each call presents a fresh dilemma. *BWD* is no more set up to take care of an injured bird than is the office of any other magazine. Yes, there are people here who know a lot about birds, but there are no flight cages or medical supplies, no X-ray machines. So the calls are routed to my house.

I did a lot of songbird rehabilitation when I lived in Connecticut, but I've been able to resist being sucked down the vortex of full-time bird rehabilitation since moving to Ohio. When I had no children, it was all right to drop everything at the ring of a phone. But fetching an injured hawk a half-hour away became much less alluring once the exercise required packing snacks, drinks, and diapers, and strapping two little ones into car seats in order to complete it. And once my toddler, Liam, figured out that he wasn't going to be able to get out to play when we went on a bird run, he'd squawk the whole way back, then fall asleep for ten minutes, effectively trading his customary three-hour afternoon nap for a very long, cranky afternoon.

So it was with immense relief that I punted the pickup to my bird-loving friend Leslie, who came to the door with a box full of red-tailed hawk. He'd been found at dawn by the road, lying on his keel, unable to walk or rise. Despite his odd posture, he looked absolutely terrific. He had smooth, buttery plumage, not a feather out of place; bright, clear eyes, both pupils expanding and contracting normally. He looked like a healthy but very mature bird, not a bar marring his deep russet tail feathers. A very lightly marked breast and heavy, craggy scales on his feet also spoke of advanced age. I turned the silent bird on his back and began my exam, gently palpating every bone in each wing, looking for breaks or shotgun pellets or the burned, clipped feather edges where they might have entered. Deer season had just ended, and I wanted to be sure this lovely bird hadn't been a target.

Finding nothing amiss in the wings, I turned to the breastbone, which was hidden under muscle and fat. I smiled to find him well padded. He had been down just a few hours and was in excellent condition. Next, the legs, extended and flexed. I was delighted to find a worn U.S. Fish and Wildlife Service band on his right leg. This hawk had a story, and before long we'd have one more piece of it.

Everything seemed to be in working order. I could only conclude that he'd taken a glancing blow from a car and was suffering a mild concussion. I fed him a mouse's worth of raw hamburger with a chaser of Ensure, which he swallowed grudgingly, as if he only wanted to clear his palate to be ready to bite someone if he had to. A typical buteo, though, he never tried to bite and was absolutely docile and motionless throughout his exam. I put him, still unable to rise, in a large cage in a corner of the basement. If he wasn't up and about by morning, he'd have to go to the Ohio Wildlife Center in Columbus, two and a half hours away.

Being a compulsive nurturer, I couldn't resist taking a peek at the crate only an hour later. I was astonished to hear the patter of talons on newspaper. The hawk was up and walking from one end of the crate to another, looking for a way out. His lovely head bobbed and weaved as he sized up the potential exit ports in the dog crate. He paused to nibble a loose thread hanging from the towel and resumed pacing. What a beautiful sight. Though happy endings usually take a lot more time and work, sometimes the stars align and things work out that way. Come morning, I'd take him out to our vegetable garden, which, thanks to the deer, has a nine-foot nylon-mesh fence around it. If he could get out of that, he'd have no need of my services. He'd find his way home in short order. Morning came, and I spent several hours with the hawk, sketching him. My drawings are all defensive poses—head-on, feathers raised—but they clearly show that I was in the presence of a living bird, and a magnificent one at that. Finally I could stand seeing him confined no longer. It was time for his flight test.

The hawk failed his test miserably. Released in the large garden, he hunkered on the ground.

*Dec 11 01*
*The [illegible] Rd*
*Redtail*

Leslie and I withdrew and watched through binoculars. Finally I held him as high as I could and gave him a boost into the air. Five weak flaps, and the hawk crash-landed in the long grass. Oh, dear. It was time to call in the experts. Leslie dropped everything, we packed the hawk in a towel-lined box, and she started the long drive to Columbus.

Ten days later, a Christmas card arrived from the Ohio Wildlife Center. The hawk was "recovering nicely and should be ready for release soon!" The clinic manager, Sylvan Campbell, and the veterinarian Donald Burton never found anything wrong, save a healthy crop of bloodsucking louse flies that may have weakened the hawk temporarily. A creepy thing, the louse fly looks like a flattened cross between a big tick and a housefly, and it scuttles through hawk feathers like quicksilver, occasionally landing on a handler's arms and neck. I couldn't see how parasites could ground a fat, healthy hawk, so I stuck to my concussion theory. After all, he was found by a roadside.

The important thing was that he was going to get to come home.

In the same batch of mail there was a certificate from the U.S. Geological Survey, indicating that the redtail had been banded as a juvenile near Ashfield, Pennsylvania, by Mr. R. F. Frock Jr., of Upper Black Eddy, Pennsylvania, on October 9, 1991. Ten years and perhaps eight months old! The unmarked tail and craggy feet had been good clues. He was an old bird, and with the help of a team of dedicated people, he'd have a chance to grow even older in his Ohio home.

I wrote a letter to Mr. Frock, enclosing a sheaf of copies of my sketches. I wanted him to know that, though he would receive a certificate stating that the bird's band number had been recovered, the hawk was far from dead. I was delighted to receive a lengthy e-mail from Roy Frock, in which he revealed that he'd been banding hawks since the 1960s. His banding station is at Lehigh Furnace Gap, on the Kittatinny Ridge about 15 miles east of Hawk Mountain. It's about

131 miles west of Manhattan. Of seventy-three redtail recoveries, this was his first from Ohio, and he measured it as 315 miles west-southwest of the banding site. He advised that I couldn't be sure of the sex of the bird I'd guessed to be a male by its smallish size; that he'd handled redtails ranging in weight from twenty-five to fifty-eight ounces. No other raptor, Mr. Frock added, varies so much in size. He went on, "Another bird you might be interested in was a redtail I banded on 10-20-73. It was found dead in a trap set for a coyote in Benson, Vermont in May of 1998! It was an adult when I banded it, and it is the oldest wild redtail that has been documented. The banding office aged it at twenty-five years, eleven months!"

Mr. Frock, it turned out, is a longtime subscriber to *Bird Watcher's Digest* and was familiar with my work. He closed his letter: "You know, Edwin Way Teale is my favorite natural history writer. I have every book he ever wrote (first editions of all except two). But in all the years I read his books, I never took the time to write and tell him how much I enjoyed them. So I am happy to have the opportunity to tell you how much I enjoy your work."

Already, the redtail had repaid me in spades for helping him out. Roy Frock's letter was a gem. I wanted to honor him by getting the bird back home, but it was hard to find the time to put both kids in the car for a five-hour round trip. Luckily, a consultant to *Bird Watcher's Digest* was planning a flight into Columbus and a drive to Marietta on Jan-

Dec 11 '01
Gaywood Rd redtail

uary 3. With a few e-mails and phone calls, I arranged to have the slightly apprehensive consultant serve as a hawk taxi. The hawk arrived with the consultant and cooled his talons in a cardboard box under a desk until I could get to the magazine's office at four that afternoon. Leslie met us at the office, and we drove out to Caywood Road, where he had been found on December 11.

Oak- and pine-studded ridges stretched around a patchwork plain of pastures and farms. It was perfect redtail habitat, with views stretching for miles. We opened the box, and the redtail crouched, breathing hard. We stepped back, and he stayed still. I moved forward to bend a carton flap back, and he sprang from the box, wings out, head feathers flared, talons forward, perfectly conjuring Garuda, the Indonesian hawk-god.

Seeing his chance, he gave a twisting leap and beat his great wings, gaining altitude and lining out for the valley. I couldn't suppress an involuntary whoop of joy as his wings cut the air, beating faster than I'd ever seen a redtail flap. He turned his head as he flew, taking in the familiar contours of home, and wisely made a hard right turn toward a thick stand of white pines. He landed deep in the middle. The harrying crows would be less likely to find him there while he gathered his wits.

That was it. He was gone, and all was as it should be. There wasnothing in the air but joy. Leslie and I hugged each other, beyond words. Then a large redtail, followed by a second, smaller individual, appeared out of nowhere, flying purposefully over the valley to land near the pines where our bird had taken cover. His release had not gone unnoticed. Was this a neighboring pair, or had his mate replaced him in his absence? With the power of redtail eyes, she could easily have recognized him as he sprang from the box. They'd have to sort it out together now.

There were so many mysteries, past and present, encapsulated in this bird. The

band had given us a couple of answers we'd never have had otherwise. We knew approximately where the bird had hatched, and when. How he had traveled 315 miles west-southwest; what had happened in the nearly eleven years since he'd last been held in human hands; how he had been grounded; and what would happen to him now would remain a mystery. But opening the door into his life, if only for a little peek, brought home to me that almost everything in nature is so much more awe-inspiring than it first appears. That redtail sitting stolidly by the highway—to you, just a blur of white hung up in the bare branches—might be older and better-traveled than you are. I thought about those who would question whether one middle-aged redtail was worth all the fossil fuel and frozen mice, man-hours, phone minutes, medical expertise, and X-ray film expended on his behalf. I'd argue that he was worth all that and more. Though it would not matter to him, in the Ohio countryside beneath his outstretched wings, he'd left a handful of human hearts, connected in joy.

# Ivory-billed Woodpecker

## Not Saying Goodbye

IN THE WINTER of 1999, my husband, Bill, asked me to paint a rose-breasted grosbeak for the cover of his family's magazine. I thought about it for a day or two and replied, "I can't. I have to paint ivory-billed woodpeckers. And I have to write about them, too."

"But we need grosbeaks. Do we really want to put an extinct bird on the cover of the magazine?"

"I'm not so sure they're extinct. I have to do this. Ivory-bills are what's on my mind right now."

Bill knew better than to argue, wheedle, or strong-arm. I can't say why I was moved to write this piece that long, gray winter of 1999. Nothing fresh had been heard from the supposedly extinct woodpecker for many years. David Kulivan's sighting of a pair while turkey hunting in Louisiana wouldn't come to light for another six months. Tim Gallagher and Bobby Harrison wouldn't fix astonished eyes on the white-paneled wings of an Arkansas bird for another six years.

But I'd been thinking about ivory-bills since I was eight, trying to find a way to connect with the unattainable, and this is what came out. Oddly, all that has been done and written about ivory-bills—the countless human hours of bayou slogging in the Big Woods of Arkansas and the panhandle of Florida; the mysterious and equivocal Luneau video; the blurred and indistinguishable bits of photographic evidence; the miles of often vituperous online commentary about whether or not this bird still exists—have not changed my feelings about it by a molecule.

I think the ivory-bill is still out there. At least, I hope so. Here's the 1999 piece.

You can think about heat like this from the comfort of an air-conditioned home or nestled in the remove of winter. But until you're out in it, it isn't real. This is the kind of heat that makes you sprint for your car and turn on the blowers to full, gasping and soaked through to the skin. Admittedly, I'm a tenderfoot; at home in Ohio, we'll have a week or two of high nineties and be done with it. Here, in deepest backwoods Florida, I am amazed to see people going about their business, even being cheery, occasionally pulling out handkerchiefs to wipe their brows, but otherwise hardly acknowledging what to me is a crushing, all-defeating overlord. Add to that the hordes of mosquitoes that have evolved with the image of a minivan in their tiny brains, knowing instinctively that within lies exposed human flesh. They ping and bing off the windows, probing with their fine needles around the weatherstripping, waiting for the window to roll down so they can flood in. I am here to watch birds in the pine-ringed cypress swamps, and so I spray myself one last time with repellent, roll down my sleeves, button up my collar, and launch myself once again into the barrage. The scope is heavy, and it cuts into my shoulder as I alternately walk and wade to the place where I heard something yesterday, something I had never heard before.

Dusk falls faster down here. It almost feels like the tropics, the way the sun kind of lazes, then crashes down to the horizon, going from twilight to pure dark in a short period. I was sloshing down the ghost of a trail, listening to the insect chorus swelling, when I heard a high, nasal *ank*. It was distant, but I could tell it was given with some volume. It was the call of a big bird. Turkey? I wondered. That's it, the yelp of a turkey. Again! That's no turkey, I muttered. Really, it sounded like a giant nuthatch. I didn't let myself think what it might have been. I waited until insects and nightfall forced me back to the car. Later, in the hotel room, with the clarity that comes only with time, I admitted to myself what I had heard. I would be out at first light, waiting, tomorrow.

If it went to roost here, giving a couple of calls just before going to sleep, it would be here at first light. Hurriedly, I pick my way back up the trail, a tiny headlamp beam bouncing along the ground. Moths spiral and hit the lens, to be replaced by mosquitoes as the light continues to grow. It's already oppressively hot and damp. Finally, I reach the spot where, last night, I'd impaled a tissue on a twig, and switch off the light. There's no way it has left its roost, if roost it is, yet. I wait, and the sky brightens to gray, then to rose, then yellow-white. The sun's up! Should I stay another hour? Two? And then, a sound to stop my heart. *HENK!* And again. And the calls are punctuated with the lusty whack of a strong bill hitting wood. *Ba-bam!* An ivory-colored bill.

A silent scream rises in my throat, and I quell it with difficulty. I will the bird to stay near its roost hole. The irregular whacking and chipping continue. I can't believe my luck. I've tracked pileated woodpeckers countless times, following the sound of their working. It's far easier to zero in on than a call. Warily, I slip into the underbrush, spider webs draping across my face. It's farther away than I thought, but I should be seeing some motion soon. It's not very high off the ground, by the sound of it. There's a huge hackberry ahead missing tea-tray-size pieces of its bark, riddled with round holes. It's a mess. I close in on it. I'm too close, and the chipping suddenly stops.

Claws scritch on bark as the bird heaves itself up for a look at me. Its head pops around the warty gray trunk of the hackberry. Oh, I am too close, but I say a prayer that it will stay, if only for a moment. I've had my binoculars at chin level as I crept forward. They're foggy from my breath as I ease them to my eyes. His eye meets mine through the lenses. It is palest yellow, almost white, and it stands out in his velvety black face like a topaz. The pupil is tiny, a pinpoint. His crest is standing straight up, flared in surprise. It is backlit by the dawn, afire around the edge. His bill, horn white and huge, juts from his head like the primitive chisel that it is. In my mind's eye, I have searched for him, seen him in dreams, but even in dreams I have never seen anything like this. The white line running from his eye down his neck is immaculate, shining. And, almost casually, he hitches around the trunk and begins a long spiral up the tree, giving me a look at the lavish white rectangle of his folded wings over his back.

The motion of his legs and body is so fluid I can't tell how it is he's hitching upward; it just seems to happen. He thrusts back with his legs, and his body is effortlessly propelled up, his long crest flopping with the motion. His claws are like grappling hooks, slaty semicircles that seem just to prick the bark. I can see daylight under the soles of his feet as he spirals around the side of the tree. A couple of calls, brassy and explosive at this close range, a nervous toss of his head, and he launches himself, wings closed, off the trunk toward the rising sun. I gasp as they open, catching his fall—a fanfare of white, so brilliant and unexpected in the gloomy understory. He lines out just below the canopy, weaving through the great trunks of the bottomland giants, and is gone. I roll backward from the aching crouch I'd held the whole time and start to laugh as an ant picks its way through the tears streaming down into my ears. I had never given up hope that they were still here, still anywhere, not lost forever, but forever found.

Who to tell? Who, perhaps more important, not to tell? How to tell it? I don't have a photograph; I don't have a recording. I am an idiot. Why couldn't I have packed my hand-held video camcorder, which lies safe in its foam-padded case in Ohio? Why didn't I bring even a disposable camera? I could have bought one at any filling station on the way here. Well, I think, who expects to stumble on an extinct bird? I decide to stop chastising myself and get busy. I can draw, so I reach around for the sketchbook and pencils I keep in my backpack. Oh, to have him back, even for a second. I do my best, conjuring the exquisite angles of his head and bill, the long, spiky taper of his central tail feathers, even the color of his toes and the bristly white feathers covering his nostrils. These will have to do. Lord knows, these details aren't in any field guide I've ever seen!

When I start thinking about ivory-billed woodpeckers, I find it hard to stop. They hitch and flap and peck around in my head; they make me think about large issues—like extinction—and small things—like the look in their eyes, the gloss of their feathers.

You will, I hope, forgive me my flight of fancy. I don't wish to be ornithology's Orson Welles. It's all fiction, up to this paragraph, made out of whole cloth and a wild and deep longing to have been one of the chosen, to have seen this bird before it was gone.

With few exceptions, I write what I know about, what I have done or seen, and I draw that way, too, usually with the creature, fruit, leaf, or landscape right in front of me. That works best. I can draw, but I can't cartoon. Put me at a table with paper and pencil, but nothing to look at, and I'm almost helpless to produce a believable drawing. I can write, but I find fiction a terrible stretch. But the ivory-bills won't leave me alone. I think and stew and mutter about this piece, how to write about something I only wish I had known. Finally, I decide to look outward for help, to talk to those few who made the effort to know the great woodpecker.

Any study of the ivory-billed woodpecker has to start with James Tanner's elegant treatise, written as his Ph.D. thesis at Cornell and published by the National Audubon Society in 1942, while a few birds still hung on in the cypress and bottomland forest of Louisiana, Florida, and South Carolina. As a college student, I painstakingly photocopied each page of this book and bound it and every article I could uncover in an old leather binder. Not long out of college, I was invited one summer afternoon to meet Dr. Tanner and his wife, Nancy, at the home of a friend in Lyme, Connecticut. He was an affable, quiet man, who willingly signed my makeshift copy of his book. I felt completely helpless to tell him how much his work meant to me, and I fretted as the conversation in our afternoon tea party turned away from ivory-bills and on to topics of greater interest to the group. What I wanted to do was touch him, this man who knew the ivory-bill better than anyone who had ever lived, to soak up some of that magic. But you don't go touching people you barely know, nor do you drag them off to ask questions about their Ph.D. theses, forty years in the past, when they're having a nice get-

together with friends. A year and a half later, James Tanner died. Nancy Tanner's warm voice on the telephone was a balm to my regret. Between natural history travel and lectures to universities and ornithological societies, she shared her reminiscences of ivory-bills:

"Jim had written his book based on his studies of the Singer Tract [Louisiana] population in the late '30s. We went back down at Christmastime of 1941 because he wanted to see what was happening there. There were still five ivory-bills, and we spent two weeks down there. The bark [from their workings] peels off and falls on the ground, and that's how you find where they are. You could hear them [calling] a mile away, it seemed. They were extremely loud. Very loud. The pounding was pretty darn loud, too. They are a very, very conspicuous bird. They impressed me as being extremely large and gorgeous—so much white is showing. We had located one roost hole, so we were relatively close, sitting quietly on a log in the dark, soaking wet in the swamp. The bird is the last of the woodpeckers to come out [in the morning]. He climbed to the top, pounded, and then called; pounded and then called, and the female flew over next to him, and with a great racket they flew off. Jim went cantering after them, leaping over logs, slashing through briar. They fly extremely fast, and when they fly high, they're going to be gone for a while.

"The Singer Tract was being cut quite heavily when we went down. After Jim wrote his report, he and [the Audubon Society] both went to Congress and tried to get it preserved. But the war was coming on; Pearl Harbor had just come along, and Jim went off in the service in a few months. To lose such great beauty . . . there was something about that bird that's attracted everybody."

About a week after our conversation, a package arrived in the mail from Mrs. Tanner. With shaking hands, I removed a neat stack of photographs and two typewritten stories. They were unpublished reminiscences by James Tanner, which weave a haunting spell of the primeval forest and the flashy, regal woodpeckers that once dwelt there:

> *We, the woodpeckers, Kuhn [his assistant], and I, lived in the forest, and I came to know it well. It was a bottomland forest of oaks, sweet gum, wild pecan, hackberry, and several other kinds of trees covering over a hundred square miles . . . All the animals that had ever lived there in the memory of man, excepting the [Carolina] paroquet and passenger pigeon, still lived there . . .*
>
> *Finding and following the ivorybills was a fascinating game, and when the chase was successful it had a fitting reward, for ivory-billed woodpeckers were not only very rare birds—they looked like rare birds. Their plumage, in bold pattern, glistened, their big bills shone white, and their piercing yellow eyes held the look of a king. I never tired of watching them.*

In these words, James Tanner's awe of and respect for ivory-bills come through, loud as a double rap. His writing is too good simply to excerpt; it deserves a forum of its own.

I fervently want to talk to more people who've seen an ivory-bill. My next call is to Thomas R. Murray of Owen Sound, Ontario. An avid birder since the age of twelve, Mr. Murray was nineteen years old when he accompanied three friends on a birding expedition to South Carolina in 1936. Mr. Murray's good friend, Rich-

ard M. Saunders, wrote of their trip in his 1951 book, *Carolina Quest*. They'd traveled by rail from Toronto to New York, and by ship to Charleston, South Carolina. Seeing the ivory-bill was not, initially, a goal of this group. While staying at McClellanville, South Carolina, they heard a rumor that a group of bird watchers had seen ivory-bills less than a month earlier, along a branch of the Santee River:

> *We didn't know the ivorybill had been seen there at all, until we got there. There were rumors around that they had been seen. We didn't believe it, hardly, you know, but we found the guide who had taken the people in. We weren't there too long looking for them, actually, because the guide was able to take us to the immediate area where they had been seen. It was a long trip up the river, in a dugout canoe with an outboard motor. We split the guide's pay four ways.*
>
> *There were two of them, a pair. We had a good look at them. There was absolutely no question; we were familiar with pileated woodpeckers. I don't recall how close we were, but it was fairly close to them. Flaming red crest, and all that white on them. But it was for less than a minute, I would say. They both flew off, of course, as soon as they realized we were there. There was a tremendous amount of white in the wing. Once they started flying they disappeared almost immediately; it was in heavy bush. I've done a lot of birding: Argentina, Kenya, Costa Rica, Australia and New Zealand twice, New Guinea, Java . . . My world list is around 2,800. But that's most certainly the crown jewel.*

I try to imagine stumbling on a rumor of ivory-bills, being lucky enough to follow it up, and seeing them on the first try. That was a neat trick, even in 1936, but I can't quite imagine it happening today. I want to hear from someone who went after the ivory-bill, on a quest to see the bird, so I call Don Eckelberry, ornithologist and peerless painter of birds, at his home on Long Island.

My imagining
of Don Eckelberry's
lone female
ivory-bill

"I may be the last ornithologist to have seen them in the States. As far as I know, it is the last absolutely authenticated sighting. It was in April 1944. This is northeast Louisiana, the Tensas River bottom. Dick Pough had gone down there, and he'd seen it. He was the ornithologist for [the National] Audubon [Society], and I was in New York, working for the magazine. When he came back and said he'd seen it, I was in a lather to go see it, and I convinced John Baker, the president, to let me go down and see it.

"I never saw a male; this was a female. I went back and would follow her through the woods when I'd hear the double rap. And I saw it several times after that. We knew then it was on its way out. There were several in that area, and that was the last one seen. Pough had been down there for quite a while searching all over, and that's all he came up with, this one female.

"It isn't really a woodpecker; it's a bark peeler. When she was peeling bark, her head was turned back to the side and went under the bark. Down at the base of the tree you'd find big strips of bark, not little chips. She'd start and hitch down and keep peeling it down and eating the grubs in the cambium layer, between the bark and the wood.

"The voice is like a loud *HENK*, like a red-breasted nuthatch, only louder. But it was not nearly as loud as the double rap. It had a double rap like *ba-BOOM ba-BOOM*, and that was very loud and would carry a long way. And once you'd heard that double rap, you could locate the bird. When it flew, it flew like a pintail duck, not like a woodpecker that goes down and up, down and up—it went straight. And it wasn't easy to locate; it went straight away.

"The German prisoners of war [World War II] were helping lumber the Singer Tract. Not too far away you could hear the little donkey engine, and the cutting. I don't know how much is left today. I never went back. I went in on the train, the donkey engine, and there were all these German prisoners who would rather be out in the fresh air than sitting in a camp. It was an interesting experience."

Don Eckelberry has brought the meaning of extinction home to me as no one else could. Extinction, to me, is powerlessness, inexorability, rage, and despair. Extinction is the buzzing saw that drowns out even the double rap of a powerful woodpecker. Suddenly, I have to get some air, and I turn out the lights, put on my boots and coat, and walk deep into our woods. On this late January afternoon, the sky is oyster gray, and not a breath of air stirs the bare branches. I climb partway up a steep hill and sit to catch my breath and retie my shoes. I lean back on my arms and listen. A brown creeper calls, three, four times, then falls silent. Overhead, a jet roars and thunders, but soon it fades from hearing. A shot sounds from the east, a chain saw from the north. Over it all, I can hear traffic on the interstate highway, eight miles to the west.

There are pileated woodpeckers in our woods. I've found four nests over the years. The woods are being cut on three sides of our eighty-acre property, and the two pair we have been watching since 1992 are seen ever more frequently on our land. I can't take a walk without hearing their high, wild yelps, or seeing the sweep of pied wings. I think about a world without pileated woodpeckers, as James Tanner and Don Eckelberry, I'm sure, thought about a world without ivory-bills. I listen again. Not a note from any bird. But I, too, can hear the saws.

In the mail, a week later, a package arrives from Don Eckelberry, the same day I received Nancy Tanner's. I hope none of my neighbors sees me and wonders

7/20/93 On our land behind
the pines She had no idea I was
there as she swung and clambered after
Smilax berries I heard two drum today— the
first I've ever been sure it was a Pileated— A sharp,
commanding roll, softer at start and finish— lasts about 1¼ seconds.

why I am suddenly down on my knees by the mailbox. He's made a tracing paper overlay on one of my color studies of an ivory-bill, moving its leg to a more believable position. Thank you, Don. He's included a reproduction of his painting of a pair of ivory-bills, muscular, bold, impeccably constructed, as are all his birds. My eyes bug out as a little sheaf of original field notes and sketches from his 1944 expedition falls out. The life sketches he'd described to me as "nothing, really," leap off the page: living, preening, flying ivory-bills. There's an essay, too, that had appeared in John Terres's *Discovery: Great Moments in the Lives of Outstanding Naturalists*. In it, the artist paints his encounter with what was perhaps the Singer Tract's last ivory-bill, but this time with words:

> She came trumpeting in to the roost, her big wings cleaving the air in strong, direct flight, and she alighted with one magnificent upward swoop. Looking about wildly with her hysterical pale eyes, tossing her head from side to side, her black crest erect to the point of leaning forward, she hitched up the tree at a gallop, trumpeting all the way. Near the top she became suddenly quiet and began preening herself. With a few disordered feathers properly and vigorously rearranged, she gave her distinctive double rap, the second blow following so closely on the first that it was almost like an echo — an astonishingly loud, hollow, drumlike Bam-am! Then she hitched down the tree and sidled around to the roost hole, looked in, looked around, hitched down beneath the entrance, double-rapped, and went in.
>
> At 7:20, after I had finished all my notes and we were about to leave, she popped out and raced up the trunk to its broken top where, bathed in rich orange light of the setting sun, she alternately preened and jerked her head about in a peculiar, angular way, quite unlike the motions of any other woodpecker I knew. I was tremendously impressed by the majestic and wild personality of this bird, its vigor, its almost frantic aliveness.

*. . . One day on my way in I investigated some desultory hammering expecting to find a pileated woodpecker, but it was the ivorybill working on a broken stub not fifteen feet above the ground. I watched her for a good ten minutes. I hope I am not dispelling belief in what I have said about the regal qualities of the bird to add that there was something comical about it too. That big pale bill sometimes looked almost like an ice-cream cone jammed into her black mouth, and then the expression of her eyes seemed the natural one at such an occurrence. Call that anthropomorphism if you like, but it is just such impressions which give the bird painter the key to that "rightness" of expression, for which he is always striving.*

The ivory-bill, in life, so vividly described by Tanner and Eckelberry: how can it be gone from the earth? Could the birds somehow still survive in the southern United States? Could enough bottomland forest have been left for a small breeding population to hang on? Pileated woodpeckers have undergone a resurgence, as once-cleared land has been allowed to grow over to forest. Why couldn't the ivory-bill, too?

Extinction is, as a rule, unkind to specialists, creatures that make their living in unique and rather narrow niches. Think of the snail kite, which depends almost entirely on apple snails for food. Drain the apple snail's marsh, lose the kite. While the ivory-bill was more flexible, taking a variety of wild fruits and poison ivy berries, for example, it relied most heavily on the great, thumb-size larvae of cerambycid (long-horned) beetles, which tunnel just beneath the bark of dead trees.

These larvae inhabit not just any dead trees but very large dead trees that have been dead only two years. A stand of mature trees killed by fire, wind damage, or flooding was a bonanza to the birds, which were, by some accounts, seminomadic, traveling widely to exploit such stands. Tanner referred to them as "dead-

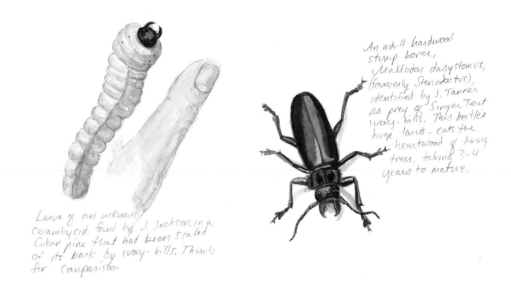

An adult hardwood stump borer, *Mallodon dasystomus*, (formerly *Stenodontus*), identified by J. Tanner as prey of Singer Tract ivory-bills. This beetle's huge larva eats the heartwood of living trees, taking 3-4 years to mature.

Larva of an unknown cerambycid, found by J. Jackson in a Cuban pine that had been scaled of its bark by ivory-bills. Thumb for comparison.

enings," and he watched ivory-bills peel loosened bark from the trees to reach the grubs. Enter modern forestry practices. Clifford Shackelford, a biologist with Texas Partners in Flight/Texas Parks and Wildlife, explained:

"[Mankind] removed fire and flooding by creating dikes and channels. Those kinds of things have shut down the disturbance [that the ivory-bill depended on]. You can see how quick we are to respond to beetle outbreaks and fire—we go in and fell the trees so it doesn't spread. Pine plantations and the lack of flooding in the bottomlands: I don't know which is worse. Loblolly is the pine of the bottoms in the coastal plain. They were always sparse, but now we've mass-produced them in rows. The management of trees is to make sure they are harvested before they die of natural causes. To somebody who's looking at a tree as a dollar, a snag is a sign of mismanagement! You didn't make your dollar off that tree. And you can't blame them when there's a tremendous demand for paper products. That's why all this is going on. If an ivory-bill were worth one hundred dollars a sighting, we'd have a lot more ivory-bills."

It's clearer to me now that the chances of these big-tree peelers hanging on in the face of full-scale forest exploitation are slim. While ivory-bills could use their great chisels to advantage in digging nest cavities, they were not, by nature, true excavators, as are pileated woodpeckers. The smaller birds do peel bark, but they also dig deeply into wood, from living to decades-dead, finding a great variety of insect food along the way. Pileated woodpeckers inhabit a wider niche; they're closer to being generalists in their food requirements and foraging strategies. Even in the Singer Tract, Tanner estimated a density of thirty-six pileateds inhabiting the foraging territory of a single ivory-bill!

What of the "unsubstantiated" records since Eckelberry's sighting in 1944? I want to hear from someone who's seen an ivory-bill more recently. The ornithologist John V. Dennis of Princess Anne, Maryland, has had three more recent encounters with this will-o'-the-wisp. In April 1948, he and Davis Crompton found an active nest site, three adult birds, and a skull in Oriente, the easternmost province of Cuba. On April 5, 1951, he heard an ivory-bill call five times in the Chipola River swamp of northwestern Florida. Not until December 3, 1966, did Dennis hear the call again—but this time, he was following up, by request of the World Wildlife Fund, on an excellent description of a female ivory-bill given by Mrs. Olga Hooks Lloyd, in the Neches River Valley of East Texas. On December 10, he finally saw the bird:

"It flew up from the ground and lit in a big cypress tree. It had a large amount of white on the rear of the wing. It flew off in a straight line. I'd read in Tanner that once the bird flies it goes in the same direction for quite a while. I was so excited. It was a pretty cold day in December, but I took my clothes off and waded into this bayou. The water came up almost to my chin. I was holding my clothes over my head. I climbed out on the other side and I didn't have an opportunity to dry myself, and I was pretty cold. I got my clothes back on as best I could, and headed in the same direction. The woods opened up a little bit. In front of me was a stump, and the ivory-bill was on the stump, wings outspread. A pileated woodpecker pair was in the neighborhood. I got the impression that the ivory-bill was directing a threat display at the pileateds. The ivory-bill flew off again. It disappeared over the Neches River.

"I spent a lot of time in the Big Thicket. Across the river there was a big area owned by the Army Corps of Engineers that hadn't been lumbered for a long time. It was pretty good habitat, so I spent a lot of time searching over there as well as on the same side where I saw the bird. I found places where the bark of trees had been knocked off and scaled. I couldn't always be sure whether it was ivory-bill or pileated work. My wife and I later practically moved to the Big Thicket. There were some generous people who loaned us their cabin, and a couple of people joined us and we made that our headquarters. We got quite a bit of publicity, and people would call in, but 90 percent of the time they hadn't really seen the bird. We went out every day looking and listening. We got the Cornell recording and played it out in the woods, and hoped that it would attract the live ivory-bill. We never heard any response. When I went searching for it in South Carolina's Congaree Swamp, we never got any response, either.

"My feeling is that the ivory-bill is extinct. There just haven't been any reports coming in. I don't want to be the last one to see it. I'm hoping and have been hoping all along that the birds are still around."

Given the aura of secrecy that surrounds later ivory-bill sightings, I wonder if the lack of reports might be because of unwillingness on the part of observers to reveal the birds' exact location. After all, if ever there were a Holy Grail of North American bird watching, the ivory-bill is it. I try to imagine the stampede that would ensue if an authenticated sighting were to hit a rare bird alert hotline. I picture helicopters and satellite television trucks as the media and throngs of camera-toting birders swarm whatever quiet backwater might still shelter the reclusive log gods. I wonder what I would do if the stars aligned and an ivory-bill appeared before me. What was the most recent sighting out there? An Internet contact leads me to Dr. Dennis G. Garratt, a Canadian chemist who's made an amateur study of ornithology for many years. In 1985, he made a month-long trip to study birds in Florida. His story:

"I wasn't looking for them at the time. It [the bird] was on a dead palm tree, and it was pecking away. The hammering sounded like an ordinary pileated. It was a large woodpecker, with a great deal of white on its back. I did get good views of its back and underwings. The pattern is very different from a pileated's. The pileated will tuck its wings and look like a torpedo, and I don't recall [this bird] doing that.

"It certainly did not care to be watched. I froze, and it froze. It was tapping when I first saw it. It gave a call totally unlike a pileated, a single note. It was considerably larger than the Florida subspecies of the pileated. It had a red crest, which would make it a male. I had a camera, and I didn't think to pick it up and aim at it—I was so stunned, I just stood there looking at it. It took off through the swamp, and I took off through the swamp. It was perhaps fifteen minutes from my first sighting to the last; I saw it one more time after the initial sighting. I lost it in some mangroves and then it flew across a river—I didn't cross the river myself because there were a number of alligators in it.

"When I came out of the swampy area I had been in, I tried finding some forestry workers, but they had all closed up shop for the day. I sat in my car trying to cool off for a while—it had been a very warm day. When I got back I typed all of this up. I sent the report directly to a person with the American Ornithologists' Union. I sent notes out to all the state authorities. I wrote to *American Birds*, and that's when we got into the question of should we publish it at all, and we decided no.

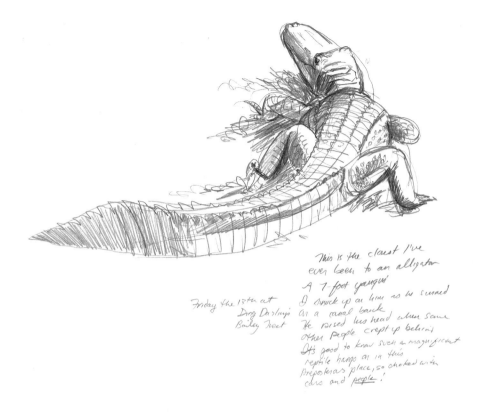

*This is the closest I've ever been to an alligator. A 7-foot youngun'. I snuck up on him as he sunned on a canal bank. He raised his head when some other people crept up behind. It's good to know such a magnificent reptile hangs on in this preposterous place, so choked with cars and* ~~people~~ *!*

*Friday the 13th at Ding Darling's Bailey Tract*

"I did a lot of research back in the libraries, and the first chance I had to get to a museum where they might have a specimen, I went to look at it. That just reinforced my feeling that I had indeed seen it, and not some aberrant pileated with partial albinism.

"I did look for a number of years thereafter in the same spot without any success. The last time I looked was in 1991. The area was protected, but there hadn't been any reports in many decades. As far as I know, that area is still protected, but I don't know if any of the surrounding area has been gobbled up since I was last there. It was a cypress swamp with a lot of mangroves along the river.

"I was awestruck at the time, and I still feel that way today. I could still find the tree it was on, if it hasn't fallen down."

His mention of the year 1985 has an immediacy that stops me cold. Although no one knows what the life expectancy of the ivory-bill might be, Ken Parkes, curator emeritus of ornithology at the Carnegie Museum of Natural History, estimated that it might be around twenty years. And yet, parrots of similar body size have made it into their seventies. How sad, to think of a handful of survivors somehow hanging on, with no others to answer their high, strange calls. Better, I suppose, than to think of the earth without ivory-bills at all.

It has been an absorbing and strangely sad exercise, this phoning and interviewing the last people to see ivory-billed woodpeckers. I want someone to assure me that the great birds are still out there, but no one does. Some dismiss the idea outright, almost as if wanting to be the last to have seen it. Others seem wistful, yet dubious that new sightings are yet to be made. Clifford Shackelford has compiled recent published sightings of the species in Texas. To this day, hundreds of purported ivory-bill sightings come in to his office each year. He tells me, "There are a lot of people who claim to see it. I think people are just getting out more, and probably none of them who call in are competent bird watchers. The majority of the people are interested, but really don't realize there are two by-gods [colloquial name for pileated woodpeckers]. Everybody wants to see a ghost. I throw it in there with UFOs and Sasquatch and the Loch Ness Monster. I think people can convince themselves that they see it. I wish I could convince myself."

I think about how modern endangered species management practices might handle the discovery of a relict population. The birds captured, one by one, with giant mist nets strung near their roost holes. Taken into huge enclosures. Artificially inseminated. Their eggs placed in incubators in some humming laboratory; their chicks fed by lifelike puppets until they are ready to join their parents in the enclosures. Would the populations be built up until a precious few were deemed ready for release? Would there be any place to release them? Given a choice between such intervention and certain extinction, and the intellect to consider it, what would an ivory-bill choose? I imagine it flying away in a long, straight line, wingbeats steady, putting miles of swamp between it and the further workings of humanity.

Almost as elusive as the bird itself is Jerome Jackson, a Mississippi State University biology professor [now at Florida Gulf State University] widely considered the foremost living authority on the ivory-billed woodpecker. He keeps a punishing schedule that includes teaching, writing a book on the species for Smithsonian Books, and searching for ivory-bills both in Cuba and in the last tracts of bottomland forest in the southern United States. We communicate via e-mail for a long time before I actually pin him down by telephone. Jackson was appointed in 1986 by the U.S. Fish and Wildlife Service to an ivory-billed woodpecker advisory committee that also included his fellow woodpecker experts Lester Short and James Tanner.

Jackson tells me, "We had a meeting in Baton Rouge, Louisiana, and the pur-

pose of the meeting, we found out after we got there, was to put the stamp of approval on declaring the species extinct. I said I wasn't willing to go along with it. I said, 'How can you declare a species extinct when you haven't even looked for it?' The habitat has improved dramatically since [the 1940s], because there were still fifty thousand acres of the Singer Tract that were still relatively virgin forest. As a result of my complaints and refusal to go along, they decided to give me a grant in 1987 for one year to look for it. I had to be on sabbatical to do it. There was no money for help, or a boat. I did spend that time searching the swamps of the Southeast. I bought a boat and canoes on my own money, and I took student volunteers. When you're in the Atchafalaya Basin, and it's over one hundred square miles, it's like looking for a needle in a haystack.

"In '87, Malcolm Hodges, a student of mine, and I were in an area north of Vicksburg, Mississippi. We'd play a forty-five-minute segment of tape, walk for fifteen minutes, and take transects. We got to a point where I said, 'Malcolm, this is the best habitat I've seen anywhere!' He said, 'There it is, there it is! Listen!' I couldn't hear anything. 'It's coming, it's coming, it's coming!' he said. It was repeating exactly the call on the tape. It got to within a hundred yards of us and then stopped, wouldn't come any closer, and it called for eighteen minutes. Finally I said, 'Malcolm, we've got to see it; we've got to get a picture or at least a sight record.' On the count of three, we rushed toward it. Nothing, no more sound, no

Up and over the muddy baya it goes,
in a fanfare of black and white.

more bird. We never saw it. This is within forty miles of the Singer Tract. If they left the Singer Tract, they could have easily ended up there. We went back in, and the next day we met a forester in the area, cruising timber, and he informed us that they were going to take a million dollars' worth of timber out of there. And the next year they did.

"They [the ivory-bills] had to have old-growth forest with lots of dead and dying trees, no question. They were feeding on large cerambycid beetles. You had to have big trees for big insects, and big roost cavities. The humidity of the forest was important because it provided the fungi that would rot the wood that would allow the beetles to exist. It had to be humid, as in the tropics. They wouldn't have occurred farther north, except right along river bottoms. The beetles are still out there, but some of them are quite rare. The ivory-bill is the tip of the iceberg. What else have we lost along with it that wasn't so glamorous?

"I saw an ivory-bill, and we heard them on eight different days, in Cuba in March of 1988. No one was able to find them after that. I continue to follow up on leads, and the F and WS continues to send me leads. I followed up on a lead in Florida, where a woman had one in her backyard. She described it perfectly; she described the call perfectly. But everyone reads the books. The habitat around her house was not at all appropriate, but there was appropriate habitat within five miles."

If all the stars aligned and a population of ivory-bills were ever discovered, what would be the best course of action? I put the question to Jackson. "The best thing that would happen would be to secure the property, not one thousand acres, but thirty thousand acres, and keep it from the public. The fortunate thing for the ivory-bill is that any population that could be found would be in the most inaccessible of places."

Jerry Jackson, by virtue of his unique combination of ornithological expertise, woodsman's smarts, and unalloyed faith, refuses to close the book on the ivory-billed woodpecker. Alone among all those I've spoken with, he continues to search. He truly believes that, somewhere on the planet, ivory-bills still hitch and rap and toss their fluffy topknots, pound their great white bills into bark, fly in long, straight lines over a sea of treetops. As much as I would like to see an ivory-billed woodpecker, I wish more that Jerry would see one.

As I read over my writing, I can't decide whether to use past or present tense when referring to ivory-bills. I go back and forth between the two, tense in either camp. Ambivalence permeates my every thought about the great woodpeckers. I can't look at the old photographs of ivory-bills and believe they're gone; it's like holding a still-warm bird in the hand, one that's just struck a window. Its eyes are wide, its feet soft and pliable; its wings snap back when they're extended. Surely it will regain its senses and spring into the air. It's too beautiful to be dead.

The ivory-bill was an extravagant creature by all accounts, a vision in ebony and white. It had a big bill and a big appetite for oversize beetle larvae. It needed a lot of timber, with many old, dying trees, and it was willing to travel to make its specialized living. We cut its habitat right out from under it, and we continue to cut it. We've sent it countless messages with our saws and our columns of smoke. Leave or die out. Find somewhere else to live. This land is our land now. And it just doesn't listen to us; it goes on, somewhere, I have to believe it; not dead but missing in action; alive, defiantly, desperately, joyously, alive. No one can tell me I'm wrong, and, it seems, no one can tell me I'm right. There are those of us who cannot let it go.

# Winter Musings

## BIRDS WE FEED,
## BIRDS THAT FEED US

A cardinal robs a robin of its grasshopper prize

# Love and Death Among the Cranes

NOVEMBER, FOR ME, will always be associated with sandhill cranes, with their purling rattle and the easy beat of slate wings overhead. Two recent Novembers have found Bill and me at New Mexico's Bosque del Apache National Wildlife Reserve, working the Festival of the Cranes. We take Phoebe and Liam along, and, at fourteen and eleven years, respectively, they settle well into the rhythm of predawn wake-ups and evening banquets, just glad to be included. Thoroughly plugged in at home, when they're in the wild they revert to a primal state, playing with rocks, sticks, and water as their parents line up the next interesting animal or bird to be viewed in the spotting scope. They're lucky to be in New Mexican sunshine in November, and they know it, beg for it as the Ohio skies go leaden and start their winter weeping.

It's hard to find a written piece about sandhill cranes that does not invoke the word *ancient*. Their sonorous voices and gangly form in flight are unarguably primeval. You can imagine them gliding over a group of mastodons, imagine a giant ground sloth craning its thick neck to see them land. In fact, the fragmentary fossil record suggests that *Grus canadensis* has survived virtually unchanged for at least 2.5 million years, and, if a single Nebraska fossil is factored in, perhaps almost 10 million years. The sandhill crane is a Pliocene relic, the oldest known surviving North American bird species. No wonder it inspires such reverence in those of us who came late to the party.

Sandhill cranes come to Bosque del Apache to spend the winter, flooding in from the northern plains and Canada. The cranes walk along the roads atop the dikes at Bosque, heads high, and they stare over their stone gray shoulders and stand down vehicles, in no hurry to clear the way. It's good to see them at ease, and I will them to stay here on the refuge. Only a few hundred yards outside its boundary, hunters in blinds wait to shoot them.

I remember where I was standing when I found out that midcontinental sandhill cranes are considered game birds and could be shot in every state where they occur except Nebraska. It was here, at Bosque del Apache, on hearing shots near one of the reserve's borders, that I asked around among refuge personnel. Yes, they're hunted in New Mexico, right outside the refuge boundary. Wait a minute. We're here celebrating the Festival of the Cranes while they're being killed just over the refuge border? Knowing that the millions of snow geese were being hunted was one thing, but learning that cranes are on the list of hunted species was another. Seeing men with blinds and decoys waiting for the cranes as they skeined over, trying to reach the refuge, took the realization to yet another level. It has taken years for me to think about this in any but the most primal of ways.

The next spring, as I watched cranes drop to their Platte River roost against a vivid Nebraska sunset, I couldn't hold it in any longer. The observation platform was crowded with people: young, old, and middle-aged, most from the area, some from as far away as Seattle and Ohio, all come to see the birds, to watch them settle peacefully onto the braided waters of this river. "And to think," I said not too quietly, "that these birds are shot everywhere else they go." There was a murmur from the assembled birders.

I didn't get any direct response from the birders on the platform, nor did I expect one. They had come to enjoy the cranes and doubtless would rather not think about people who shoot them. I just wanted to plant the concept, to ask them to think about this consumptive use of a species they are content simply to watch. Upon returning home, I decided to learn more about crane hunters. I visited website after website and read article after article, all devoted to the pleasures of killing sandhill cranes. The topper? A Texas outfitter that bills sandhill cranes as "Ribeye in the Sky." Only in Texas, I thought, could a sandhill crane be so gleefully described as steak on the wing. I looked at the outfitter's gallery images. All men, all dressed in camouflage, each with a dead crane at his feet or a brace of them dangling by their necks from his fists. They were the kinds of photos you might see in an old book, blurred and black-and-white, except that these were brand-new digital images, in vivid color.

Now I understood why sandhill cranes in the Central Flyway won't let you park within gunshot range, why they raise their beautiful heads at the slightest shuffle or scrape in the blind. Why viewing them is best through a powerful spotting scope. They think that we are coming to kill them. It's brought home to them nearly everywhere they go and gather.

In the United States, sandhill cranes are legally hunted in Alaska, Arizona, Colorado, Kansas, Minnesota, Montana, New Mexico, North Dakota, Oklahoma, South Dakota, Texas, Utah, and Wyoming. In Canada, cranes are hunted in Saskatchewan and Manitoba, and in Mexico, they're hunted in nine northern and central states. Kansas implemented its season as recently as 1993, Minnesota in 2010. Bag limits vary, but most states have daily limits of three birds per hunter, or a total of six in the hunter's possession. To be in the presence of these birds, to know that they may have kept the same mate for decades, to know that each one can find its relatives in the throng of birds by voice alone . . . and then to think that in every Central Flyway state where they occur except Nebraska there are hunters setting out decoys, waiting in blinds to shoot them . . . the jagged edges of these thoughts rubbed like broken bones in my mind.

I couldn't imagine wanting to shoot sandhill cranes. I suppose I have been so thoroughly inculcated by my experiences huddled in observation blinds with other quietly reverent bird watchers that the notion that someone might wait in a similar blind aiming to kill them had never entered my mind. Clearly, I had to step back from the brink, calm down, and find out how this could be happening.

So I started to ask questions, things I'd come up with as I tried to wrap my mind around sandhill crane hunting. First was the sustainability of crane hunting—are there enough of the birds to support it, and, more important, is their reproductive rate sufficient to replace harvests? Answering this required some digging, and the Nebraska ornithologist and prolific author Dr. Paul Johnsgard gave me a tremendous amount of information to digest. My concerns, which admittedly had very basic aesthetic and emotional roots, grew.

From the start, it seemed odd to me to hunt a bird that, if it's extremely lucky, can raise only two young per year. The vast majority of lesser sandhill cranes with successful nests are able to raise only one "colt" per year. And in fact, the sandhill crane has the lowest recruitment rate of any bird now hunted in North America. Recruitment rate is the percentage of any population that is replaced with new young birds in a given year. Historic recruitment rates of all documented migratory sandhill crane populations have ranged from 7.5 percent to a high of 11.0 percent.

Over the two decades from 1975 to 1994, the average estimated hunting mortality on the Central Flyway was 21,250 birds annually. By 2010–11, the harvest of midcontinental cranes, including crippling losses, was 38,561 birds, which is a 5

Sandhill cranes
with their colt — a
high-investment baby.

percent increase from the previous year's estimate.

Long-term trends (1982–2008) for the midcontinental population indicate that the harvest has been increasing at a higher rate than population growth. With a three-year average population count of 600,892 cranes, this harvest represents a 6.4 percent take. Texas hunters take the lion's share (65 percent), followed by North Dakotans. These two states account for 88 percent of the total kill.

Given the projected recruitment rate, that seemed to me to be cutting it pretty close to the edge. What about all the birds that die from inexperience, disease, natural predation, and accidents? Time will tell whether midcontinental sandhill crane populations can hold up to this harvest.

Other questions arose, ones that I couldn't answer by paging through U.S. Fish and Wildlife Service documents. Does anybody eat these things? Who has an oven big enough to roast a crane?

Luckily, I have a forum where such questions can be posed and discussed in a respectful and informative way—my blog. A post on the subject in November 2007 caught the attention of some readers who see things differently—people who hunt in order to eat, not necessarily for subsistence but as a way to preserve a connection with wild things and the places where they live.

In the post and subsequent comments, I pondered the irony that until George Bird Grinnell sounded the alarm, in 1886, millions of birds, including terns, herons, and egrets, were slaughtered for their plumes, which went to decorate women's hats. Herons and egrets have escaped persecution in ensuing years. Why should cranes come under fire?

Simply put, they taste good. The writer, falconer, and hunter Matt

Mullenix responded: "Sandhill cranes eat grain (at least in winter on the western plains) and their breast meat is dark and rich and tasty as premium beef or elk. I've eaten it grilled, which one would expect to dry out any wild bird meat, and yet found it to be juicy and flavorful and indistinguishable in texture from beef."

Of all the adjectives I've used to describe cranes—*intelligent, monogamous, family-oriented, social, prehistoric,* and *wary* among them—one word I'd never considered employing is *flavorful*. Is it that simple? What if red-tailed hawks—our most abundant raptor—were tasty, too? Would we have seasons and bag limits on them? Mourning doves are said to be delicious, and mourning dove hunting is a hot-button topic in many states. Some call them "songbirds" (which they technically are not) and believe them worthy of protection, while others take pleasure in shooting them as game on the wing. So which is it? Which should it be?

Let's say American robins are tasty. They look like they might be (so plump) . . . lots of Europeans eat thrushes. Why shouldn't we establish a hunting season on robins? They've got a great recruitment rate; it's estimated that there are one hundred newly fledged robins for every ninety-three adults by November 1 each year. In Iceland, Atlantic puffins are sold in the grocery store, wrapped and packed in Styrofoam. They're probably hard up for protein in Iceland, and they do have a lot more puffins, but as I looked at my "adoption certificate" for a puffin on Eastern Egg Rock hanging on the wall, I had to shudder at the thought of harvesting a sea bird that might still be trying to breed into its thirties. Suddenly, every human judgment about which birds we kill and which we cherish seemed hopelessly arbitrary. I was walking in a minefield, a mental corridor lined with species both hunted and protected, passing in and out of the light of reason, trying not to hit the tripwires of anger and emotion.

And then other hunters and conservationists joined the polite fray in my blog comments section, and my thoughts about hunting took a turn. They pointed out

the direct link between hunting and habitat acquisition, a link that has yet to be firmly established with recreational birding.

Here's the system: a hunter who wishes to shoot sandhill cranes must first purchase a hunting license in his or her state—at a cost of anywhere from thirteen to thirty-two dollars. A Federal Migratory Bird Hunting and Conservation Stamp, commonly known as a Duck Stamp (fifteen dollars), is currently not required to hunt cranes. A free Harvest Information Program (HIP) certification is required. This makes it possible for hunters to report just what they've killed, in part to help state game agencies set bag limits in coming seasons. Some states require additional permits to hunt cranes; North Dakota, for example, charges five dollars. So someone who wants to hunt cranes (or ducks, for that matter) might pay in the neighborhood of thirteen to thirty-eight dollars yearly for the privilege.

What would you be willing to pay if you needed permits to watch birds? Of course, anyone can watch birds; it's free, and it should be free. Or should it?

The Duck Stamp is a license to hunt wetland waterfowl. It is also the single most direct conversion of money to wetland acquisition going. It is these hunting licenses, plus a tax placed on guns, ammunition, and other gear by the 1937 Pittman-Robertson Act, that have purchased and protected more than 5.2 million acres of wetland habitat, not only for ducks but for sandhill cranes, turtles, muskrats, yellowthroats, and dragonflies, too.

And it is here that hunters hold the economic, if not the aesthetic, high ground (though Matthew Mullenix, Stephen Bodio, and others write so eloquently of the beauty of feeding oneself with a gun or hunting falcon that that point could be argued, too). Hunter contribution to habitat acquisition is not only mandatory but also voluntary. Ducks Unlimited, a private organization, has raised $162 million, 80 percent of that going to the protection of 82 million acres in three countries.

Where does that leave bird watchers, notorious for our quest for free entertainment, other than in the dust? Well, I'm not sure. How many of us join Ducks Unlimited? Or is that organization just for hunters? And how many of us buy Duck Stamps each year and proudly paste them right on our binoculars? Or is that just for hunters, too? Is habitat acquisition just too much for us to bother with, because we know that somebody else will worry about it? Isn't it time we stepped up to the plate, too? Whether we admit it or not, birders benefit greatly from the conservation dollars contributed by hunters. We watch the birds they've saved, standing on habitat they've bought.

The economic contribution of passive wildlife watchers to habitat acquisition and maintenance is difficult to track, since there is as yet no tax on birding and photographic equipment such as was imposed on hunting gear by the Pittman-Robertson Act. Bird watchers are not required to purchase Duck Stamps in order to pursue their quarry, though an increasing number are doing just that. Though my husband and I buy Duck Stamps each year and display them on our binoculars, for all intents and purposes the credit for our yearly investment goes to hunters.

And yet bird watchers, wildlife photographers, and passive wildlife watchers are growing in number even as hunting license sales decline. The explosion in digital photography, making it possible for even pikers like me to take and distribute acceptable bird images, allows many more people to stalk wildlife without harming it. Some figures place expenditures by wildlife watchers outpacing those by hunters six to one.

The U.S. Fish and Wildlife Service estimates that thirty-three states saw declines in hunting license sales over the past two decades. Massachusetts alone has seen a 50 percent falloff in hunting license sales in that period.

With mounting interest in nonconsumptive wildlife watching outpacing recruitment of new hunters, it is a particularly sensitive time for Eastern Flyway states to propose new hunting seasons on sandhill cranes, but Tennessee, Kentucky, and Wisconsin are doing just that. Tennessee was the first, proposing its season in the winter of 2010. This, after having planted crops that feed the cranes and holding a festival celebrating them on its Hiwassee Wildlife Refuge for seventeen years. Around fourteen to twenty thousand of the big gray birds flock there each year, and about that many people come each year just to watch them fly over, to hear their calls, to see them go to roost and rise again in the morning.

Word was slow getting out to the birding community about Tennessee's proposed hunt, but when it did, thousands of letters and e-mails protesting the hunt deluged Tennessee's Wildlife Resources Commission offices. The public packed TWRC's meeting in January 2011, voicing opposition. The notion of once again opening season on a bird that had been hunted nearly to extinction in the East did not sit well with bird watchers, or with a good number of hunters. Opponents of the hunt pointed out weaknesses in data gathering (winter counts are all done by volunteers, and loosely coordinated) and the hazy overall picture of the population status of Eastern Flyway birds, along with voicing their concern over potential collateral kill of endangered whooping cranes, which travel in sandhill crane flocks. Tennessee responded to the outcry by tabling its crane hunting proposal until 2012, citing a need for more data.

Hoping to make Kentucky the first Eastern Flyway state to open season on cranes, that state's Department of Fish and Wildlife announced its proposed season in December 2010. Once again, a storm of protest ensued, prompting Kentucky to put forward a reduced season, allowing four hundred permit holders up to two cranes each and carefully timing the season to avoid migration periods for whooping cranes. The season was approved by the U.S. Fish and Wildlife Service in August 2011.

Sandhill cranes are a touchstone species for many, stirring something primeval in the souls of those who watch them gather, swirl overhead, and dance. The proposal to hunt them in the East, when they are just becoming common enough to gather in good numbers and be seen on migration, has caused many to question the sovereignty of their state wildlife departments. How can it be that, as in Kentucky, a nine-member commission, elected solely by holders of hunting and fishing licenses, is given the power to declare the sandhill crane a game bird and propose seasons and bag limits? How can it be that Kentucky birders and wildlife enthusiasts, who by a 2006 National Survey of Fishing, Hunting, and Wildlife-Associated Recreation, now outnumber hunters 1.5 million to 820,000, have no say over the birds' fate other than to write and call the KDFW in protest? Three hundred and thirty-seven people wrote USFWS in protest. Petitions with 3,000 signatures demanding the hunt proposal be withdrawn also arrived at USFWS offices. No letters supporting the Kentucky hunt were received. There is something very odd about this picture.

There are enough cranes around now to hunt some, run the states' arguments. Hunters should be given the opportunity to bag a new species if there are enough of the birds to support hunting. Wildlife managers state that crane populations will not be adversely affected; in Tennessee, state officials assured bird watchers that crane-viewing opportunities would be enhanced by hunting, since it would drive wintering birds from private land onto the already densely populated Hiwassee Refuge. But would such concentration be good for the cranes? And would bird watchers be happy to see bigger flocks of cranes, knowing that the birds they enjoy were fleeing hunters just outside the refuge? Does the simple fact that there are enough to shoot some mean they must be shot?

The struggle over crane hunting in the eastern states has cast into sharp light the division between consumptive and nonconsumptive wildlife enthusiasts. It seems odd and deliberately divisive to push hunting of a charismatic species like a crane at a time when wildlife watchers outnumber consumptive wildlife enthusiasts and are actively seeking ways to contribute to habitat acquisition and conservation. Try as I might, I can't cram the lanky four-foot length of a sandhill crane into the slot in my brain marked "Game Species." They're huge, slow-flying, and vulnerable; they reproduce very slowly, with only one-third of breeding pairs managing to produce one colt per year. That youngster is still heavily dependent on its parents for guidance in its first winter of life, yet states are proposing to let hunters shoot into and shatter those family units. For sport, for fun. For food, if they have enough strong marinade.

Should we be marinating the meat of sandhill cranes? Or should we be looking up at them alive and flying, our heads thrown back in wonder, gratitude, and awe? Shouldn't we be searching their cloud gray numbers for the big white cranes who travel with them, and are at risk of being shot, their precious genes squandered in the mud of a cornfield?

People who believe strongly in their perceived right to hunt whatever they wish can be persuasive in characterizing birders and wildlife watchers as sentimental and silly for having an emotional connection to birds and animals, for being guided by heart and not head. I believe that it is desirable to hold some species sacred. I feel that way about sandhill cranes because I have observed, from Nebraska to New Mexico, from Michigan to Ohio, that to the many thousands of people who are moved by them, they are potent ambassadors for wild things and wild places. These are not necessarily birders, just ordinary people who are stirred by the sight and sound of cranes. Is a crane worth more alive than dead? Just ask the director of the Lillian Annette Rowe Sanctuary on Nebraska's Platte River, where crane tourism draws fifteen thousand visitors from all fifty states and forty-six foreign countries, bringing more than $10 million into the local economy every year. All without firing a single shot. Alive and flying wingtip to wingtip with their families, purring sonorously, cranes awaken the untamed places in our hearts.

Despite an aggressive Internet information campaign, very few of the birders with whom I've spoken personally since I found out the truth about sandhill cranes were aware that they are a hunted species, and that they are now a game species in the East. Perhaps I've had a skewed sample, but I've been surprised at our collective ignorance. Crane hunting has been a hard thing for me to grasp, an even harder thing to accept, as if something sacred is being violated when such a long-lived, truly prehistoric bird is killed. And yet dedicated hunters feel that there is something sacred in their pursuit of and ultimate primal connection with—nourishing their bodies—their prey, something just as ancient and stirring as the rolling purr of a crane overhead. I can't deny them that just because it offends my sensibilities. And in a time when sustainability and animal cruelty are coming to the forefront of many people's thoughts about the food industry, Matt Mullenix's views resonate with me. "There is hardly a more humane 'ranching technique' than letting animals alone to do as they please, feeding and breeding in good habitat until the very last second of their lives. No suffering from confinement or poor husbandry. What could make better meat than that?"

As nonconsumptive admirers of cranes, I'm afraid we bird watchers will have to share them, until we come up with the resources and the resolve to save them—and their habitat—all for ourselves. Are we ready to do that? Yes, there are a lot of cranes now. Will there always be great flocks settling on the Platte? Will the Eastern Flyway ring with their calls; will we in the East one day be able to look up and see cranes migrating as a matter of course? It's a good thing to wonder; to question accepted management practices; to challenge the conceit that state game agencies, in opening seasons on sandhill cranes, have an adequate grasp of crane population dynamics. It's worth it, I think, to bring up the topic; to suffer the disapproving glances of nature lovers who've come only to worship at the crane mass; to challenge ourselves to look beyond the primeval beauty before us, toward the horizon beyond.

# Mourning Dove

## The Meatiest Songbird

THEY'RE MORE A HERD than a flock, these nineteen mourning doves that work my feeders. Every time I open the front door, I'm startled by a great winnowing roar of wings as they explode from the ground like a case of bottle rockets. Nineteen buffalo could make a quieter exit.

Depending on how you look at them, mourning doves are elegant, subtly colored, graceful beings; songbirds; walking birdseed vacuums; or tempting targets. They have their detractors, their passionate defenders, and even a place on some dinner tables. Some of us feed them; some of us feed on them. No wonder they seem a little paranoid, a wee bit too quick to flee. "You're not just being paranoid," I tell them. "We really *are* out to get you!"

Though they'd doubtless take issue if they could with their status as game birds in most states, the way we've changed the natural landscape apparently suits mourning doves well. They avoid heavily forested areas, preferring a patchwork of suburban and agricultural areas for feeding and nesting. Patchworks, we humans do very well. Mourning doves have expanded their range north and west just as settlers did. By 1900 they had moved from the southern half of the United States into New England, and they now breed across the southern tier of Canada.

Many observers are touched by the apparent devotion of the male mourning dove to his mate. Watch a pair for a while in April, and see if you don't find that devotion bordering on obsession. A male dove guards his mate jealously, always a half step behind her as she tries to forage. He inflates his crop with air, flashing an evanescent rose pink and amber iridescence along the sides of his neck. He sometimes resorts to a comical crabbed hop as he strives to keep up with her. He'll stop, lean forward, inflate his crop even fuller, and voice the sad coo that gives this bird its name: *oooah, ooh, ooh, ooh.* Odd that no one in the old ornithological literature seems to have put words to it; the song begs for a lyric. To me, it is a song of the South, of tall pines and dirt roads and long evenings heavy with honeysuckle.

*A mourning dove steps to puff up and coo as he: herds his harried mate around the yard. May 13, 2010*

To most human ears, it speaks of longing and loss. It's probably more a hopeful come-on for the doves.

Sex is never far from a mourning dove's mind, nor should it be for a species that's been recorded nesting successfully in every month of the year. I remember trying to focus my binoculars on a female gathering nesting material in a blowing snowstorm. It was late January in Connecticut. I've picked up freshly pipped mourning dove eggshells in April and September.

There's a slapdash quality to the doves' whole reproductive scheme that might seem maladaptive. Sloppiness is a hallmark of mourning dove nesting; an inexperienced hen may find one of her two eggs falling through the nest's see-through bottom. But burgeoning dove populations indicate that the birds are doing something right. The researcher David Blockstein outlined a suite of adaptations to high reproductive output in mourning doves. Small, flimsy, quickly built nests, often reused, house two small eggs per clutch. Males produce greater quantities of crop milk, a nutritious secretion of the crop lining that nourishes the young, than do their mates. Females put their energy into the next clutch. Nestlings grow phenomenally quickly; they're feathered and starting to fly at fifteen days. By the time the two young fledge, the female may well be incubating a second clutch. While she's thus occupied, the male is feeding the fledglings from the first. Blockstein found that mourning dove nesting cycles are 22 percent shorter than would be predicted for birds of their body mass. These smooth, tawny birds are geared to high production. According to the 1989 North American Breeding Bird Survey, the species ranked second only to the red-winged blackbird in the number of survey routes in which it was encountered.

In any conversation about mourning doves, at least in my family, the subject of their IQ invariably comes up. I caught my own mother recently calling doves "notoriously dumb," and my eldest sister, an avid bird feeder, refers to them as "dippies," a nickname applied when she'd find them milling about in her Plexi-topped windowsill feeder, bumping their heads on the clear ceiling as they strove to find their way back out. The size of a mourning dove's head relative to its body does little to bolster my case for its intellect. I think, though, that this nasty rumor arises in part from the mourning doves' escape strategy. They crouch until the last second, then, with a rush and rattle of wings, startle the predator into abandoning its pursuit. This happens to be a highly effective plan when employed on mammalian and avian predators, but it does seem a bit outdated when used in defense against speeding automobiles. Still . . . ever hit a mourning dove? Me neither. Rest assured that, while they're sitting there looking stupid, the doves are busy assessing the approaching threat and choosing the best moment to employ their startle defense.

As an ombudsman for mourning doves, I feel especially qualified. I've raised and released three orphans. The first came to me as a naked nestling, barely the size of a fifty-cent piece, when I was eighteen. My father, who had raised a few pigeons as a boy, helped me concoct a slurry of half-and-half, hard-boiled egg yolk, ground oatmeal, and ground sunflower hearts, which I administered through a bulb syringe. It worked fabulously. The nestling slept on a curtain rod or, more typically, on my chest under my chin; grew and flew; made the Sunday *Richmond Times-Dispatch*'s front page; and even came back to visit on July 4, two weeks after I'd last seen it fly off. It was a bird-teenager bonding experience to remember.

The second one blew from her nest in 1999 in a sudden May squall, and I watched her wandering sulkily around the patio for a day, pecking about but finding no food, until she lay down, too weak to rise. I sighed, picked her up, let my then-three-year-old daughter name her (Cookie), and fed her with a syringe until she was ready to pick up millet and chick scratch. Released, she became a delightful addition to our sanctuary. She spent much of the day sheltering in a roofed

A just-fledged mourning dove pecks at anything remotely seedlike, picking up and flinging pebbles and grit. How do they find enough to survive on? Some don't. I've brought a few back from starvation, skin and bones.

wooden bird feeder we put out for her, pecking savagely at any other mourning dove that dared to intrude in her retreat. With each day, she flew higher, faster, and harder, trying her newfound freedom and her strong young wings, but she sat still for little Phoebe's friendly approach, preening companionably as they sat together on the deck.

The 2010 dove came to me through a phone call, having fallen from its nest fifteen feet up on the tip of a pine bough into a yard with seven free-roaming cats. Since replacing it in the nest was impossible, I had to raise it. The dove traveled with us to a West Virginia birding festival, where I was busy dawn to dusk. Phoebe, then thirteen, syringe-fed Libby Lou through all my commitments. Back home, the foundling became a pleasant fixture in the studio, sitting on the arm of my lamp or on my shoulder as I painted. I strewed seed on the ground just outside the studio window, bringing in a small flock of mourning doves that cooed and courted in the spring sun. I painted them from life with Libby sitting warm on my shoulder, gently fussing with strands of my hair and nibbling my ear. As a bird artist, I have to say it doesn't get any better than that.

Mourning doves are easy to raise; commercial parrot hand-rearing formulas, mixed up with warm water to the consistency of yogurt and fed through a plastic syringe, work fine. You can load a baby dove up, filling its crop with food, and go about your business for a couple of hours. It's a nice contrast to raising insectivorous birds, which need food every half-hour. I offer millet-based seed mix and a little fine grit in shallow dishes. Mourning doves instinctively pick up their own food starting around seventeen days of age and are reliably self-feeding by about Day 30. Affectionate and even petlike as squabs, they nevertheless transition well to the wild, making longer and longer forays from home on their own. Rather than break it suddenly, Libby and I stretched our bond. I stopped supplemental syringe feeding at Day 32, then moved the orphan outdoors to a nylon flight tent at Day 36. I zipped the tent walls open at Day 40. Libby flew out, perched in the birches for a few hours, then took off like an arrow, heading east, around noon. She was gone until 8:00 P.M., when she came down, famished and trembling, to eat and drink. Crop filled, she flew back into her tent for the night.

For the next week, she'd take a different compass direction each day, seemingly exploring the surrounding area. She'd drop into the yard before dusk, to the relative safety of the fledging tent. Not about to donate my month of hard work to a screech-owl, I brought her inside the studio for seven nights. I enjoyed those last sweet evenings of contact with my wild foundling. Yes, we'd made a pet of her, but I knew her nature would triumph in the end. She spent her first night outside on Day 51 and ceased to come in at dusk from then on. On June 1, Day 52, she began seeking out the company of other doves and found one she liked—a juvenile the same age. This is just what wild mourning doves do—form small flocks of juveniles that learn about independence together.

Watching Libby sitting shoulder to shoulder with another juvenile, preening companionably and occasionally touching bills, was a full-circle moment. As much as we'd fussed over her and walked around with her balancing on our shoulders or heads; as much as we loved to bury our noses in her warm, seedy-smelling back feathers; we had always known she'd go back to the wild, for it was where she belonged. Still, I laughed to see her learning vigilance behavior from the wild doves. I'd walk out onto the deck to refill the feeders, and they'd all take off in a cacophony of whistling wings. Only one would remain: Libby, her small head jerking back and forth, looking for the threat. "What? What? Oh . . . *that*? That's just Mom!"

Though I have my pick of birds to paint, birds that are more colorful or impressive, I am drawn to mourning doves. I've watched them grow up in my hands, and I've exulted when they have left me, to whistle through the air with their own kind. Drawing them from life, choosing which of their graceful poses to paint, is pure pleasure. Yes, they're common, even abundant, but part of my coming of age as a bird watcher and a painter is learning to settle down and appreciate what is wonderful in the familiar. Mourning doves have a dancer's poise and unconscious grace. Their rounded contours and soft colors, I think, make them beautiful from any angle. More than this, they've taken this altered landscape and made it their own.

It's that adaptability and abundance, in part, that gets mourning doves on the wrong end of a gun in many states. They're the only "game" birds to nest in all forty-eight contiguous states. They're members of a family, the Columbidae, that, being outside the taxonomic pale of songbirds, find themselves among the hunted. The language of lobbyists on both sides of the dove-hunting question is a semantic minefield. "Don't shoot them! They're songbirds!" the antihunting faction cries. However fervently they protest, doves aren't passerines, or songbirds. Yes, they have a mellow song, but the structure of their feet, the number of their tail feathers (fourteen rather than twelve), and certain properties of their spermatozoa put them in a more primitive order. Woodpeckers and whip-poor-wills aren't songbirds, either, but nobody's shooting at them.

So what is it that makes us call mourning doves game birds? Well, they're edible, if you can get enough of them. They're brown; they look like game birds. (I've always wondered if we would think about shooting them if they were blue or bright red. But remember that its slate blue and peach beauty did nothing to save the passenger pigeon from extermination.) Most important, it seems, they're fast — from thirty up to fifty-five miles per hour in timed flights. They're hard to hit, and, by extrapolation, they must be fun to try to hit.

If I sound like someone who doesn't hunt, well, I am. In fact, I once was asked by the Marietta League of Women Voters to speak on a local cable TV channel about why I thought it would be a bad idea to reinstate mourning dove hunting in Ohio. It had been banned in 1917, voted back in 1975, then banned again from 1976 until 1994, when the sportsmen's shooting lobby got a season passed by one vote in a lame-duck senate. It seems the Ohio populace at large had a certain amount of ambivalence about the practice as well. In 1998, Ohio citizens gathered over three hundred thousand signatures to attempt to repeal the dove-hunting season with a ballot proposal. And I was thinking the issue through, trying to come up with a good argument to support my gut feeling about shooting doves.

This was an unexpectedly educational experience. First, I had to examine why I object to dove hunting. I knew the populations have been proven to sustain their numbers in spite of hunting. In 2003, the yearly harvest was 20 million nation-

wide, of a fall population that's estimated from 350 to 475 million birds. They're hunted in thirty-eight of the forty-eight contiguous states, and they're still abundant. But for parts of the West, where slight declines are being registered, the birds' reproductive strategies more than keep up with the harvest. When I really thought about it, I decided that I had two defensible concerns: the incidental kill of other species that might be mistaken for mourning doves and the question of whether mourning doves were being consumed by the hunters who shot them.

Examining the ballot arguments for and against continuing the doves' protected status, I learned some things I hadn't known about mourning doves. From my work skinning window-killed doves while preparing museum specimens, I knew that a mourning dove is twelve inches long, and six of those twelve inches are made up of tail feathers. An average adult weighs four and a half ounces. Since the dove's drumstick hardly merits the name, measuring less than an inch long, the breast meat is all that's used. Each breast fillet is about as long as my thumb and weighs one ounce or less before cooking. These already cracker-size hors d'oeuvres lose further weight and volume in the process.

I stared at the pro-hunting ballot issue. It stated: "One dove equals ten large shrimp, one chicken leg, two chicken wings, 2½ wieners, three sausage patties or one bratwurst." Wow, I thought. Either they're comparing dove fillets to Vienna sausages or the legs and wings of newly hatched chickens, or there's something I have to learn about mourning doves. Since chicken parts vary a lot in size, and I didn't know how big those sausage patties or bratwursts were, I decided to go weigh a wiener. I dug one out of the refrigerator. Fifty-six grams, or 1.97 ounces. Two and a half wieners weighed 4.92 ounces. Hmm. That's more than a whole dove weighs. A whole mourning dove breast weighs 2 ounces, or about a wiener's worth of meat. As far as I could tell, the ballot literature overstated the dove's edible meatiness by 250 percent. Unless, I concluded, you were to eat the *whole* dove, wings, feet, tail, feathers, and all.

A few days later, armed with my wiener-weighing data, I sat, quietly sweating in a gray pinstriped pantsuit, notes in hand, under blinding television lights. The cameraperson asked me to look straight into the lights and relax as I made my case. Right. I took some comfort in the fact that the opposition speaker had actual rivulets of sweat running down his face. I made my points one by one, starting with incidental kill. I stated that, although I study birds for a living, I misidentify flying mourning doves on a nearly daily basis. At fifty miles per hour or more, it takes a second, and sometimes third, look through my binoculars to identify them. The autumn dove shoot takes place as hawks, falcons, blue jays, robins, and flickers are all migrating. If I can't tell right off whether I'm looking at a kestrel or a mourning dove, could an excited hunter using only his naked eye make a correct identification?

I moved on to the meatiness factor, citing a recipe in *The Joy of Cooking* that calls for four to eight birds to serve a single person. A shooter would have to down two dozen birds to feed a family of four. I suggested that, given the bird's demonstrably small food value and famously swift flight, mourning dove hunting might have more to do with shooting than with eating.

On to the useful bird argument. Mourning doves eat weed seeds and waste

1-02-94
14 at the
cheap mixed
feed we bought
by mistake

grain in cultivated fields, competing with rodents for these food sources. One dove's stomach was found to contain 7,500 yellow wood sorrel seeds, and another had 6,400 foxtail grass seeds. They're beneficial, or at the very least harmless to agriculture. I wound up my talk encouraging Ohio voters to restore the protected status mourning doves had enjoyed for all but two of the past eighty years.

My opponent spoke next. I learned that people who opposed dove hunting were members of the organized animal-rights movement, which opposes using animals for farming, medical research, even fishing, circuses, and zoos! Oh. I'd thought I was just a bird watcher. Worse, he said, we were vegetarians, determined to take meat from all American tables. I couldn't suppress a small snort, as I thought of myself extracting, then weighing a wiener from my own refrigerator.

In certain seasons, there might have been venison, a gift from hunter friends, in that same refrigerator. Ah, well. I'd done my best. We'd see what happened when the issue hit the polls.

We lost. By "we," I mean the mourning doves, and those of us who enjoy watching and feeding them. There's now a season on mourning doves in Ohio, as there is in most of the rest of the country. I watch the smooth brown birds moving across the lawn under my feeders, stuffing their crops with millet, sunflower, and corn. They pause now and then to jet their heads upward, as if making room for a little more seed. It's an odd feeling to know that, alone among the twenty-odd species at my feeder, mourning doves may find themselves under fire just the next field over. If any of them do find themselves topping a cracker, I guess I'll have done my part to make sure they taste good.

I have to admire mourning doves. They're not nearly as dumb as they look. My foundlings proved themselves able to take the best parts of captivity—the unlimited food and the safe shelter—and use their association with me to their advantage as they slowly gained independence. Wild doves accept our handouts of grain and seed even as they dodge sudden blasts of birdshot in once-quiet fields. This uncomfortable dichotomy in humanity's relationship with mourning doves doubtless bothers me more than it does them. They fill their bellies where they can, make more mourning doves when they can, and leave it to us down below to decide whether we'll take aim or let them be.

# Northern Cardinal

## Stoking the Red Fire

IT IS SEPTEMBER. I look out the studio window and see seven northern cardinals in various stages of undress, festooning my feeder. There is an adult male, who's lacking a crest; a juvenile male, painted in shabby shades of dull red and brown; a juvenile female, her bill still nestling black. The juveniles keep up a noisy pippering even as they shell their own seeds. They are only a couple of weeks out of the nest and already on the sunflower dole, my welfare subsidy for their little population explosion. Every one is molting. Every one looks terrible. I look at them with mixed feelings, wondering if they're as healthy as they ought to be. Perhaps it's moot to fret about their health and reproductive success. There are too many in my yard to worry whether they'll prevail. They've already taken the place over.

I've been thinking lately about bird feeding, about what happens when I pump several hundred pounds of prime cardinal food into my backyard habitat each year. And then what it means to multiply that effort by tens of millions of backyards, and millions of cardinals. Cardinals aren't the only beneficiaries of this largess, of course; there are titmice and doves, nuthatches and jays, sparrows of every stripe, finches of every color, woodpeckers who've laid off their honest carpentry for an easy handout; all of them stuffing themselves with sunflower seeds.

Any way you look at them, northern cardinals are something of an amazement. European birders visiting the States gasp in astonishment on first spotting them, these brilliant daubs of carmine that most Americans so thoroughly take for granted. The male is a solid scarlet bird with a huge orange bill, black mask, and expressive crest. Females are suffused with red over tawny fawn. The cardinal is a stunner, at least when it's not molting. And it is almost ridiculously common, thanks in part to our providing it a continuous supply of artificial food throughout its range.

Cardinals seem to have unlimited reproductive capability, fashioning their shallow twig nests in low bowers of bramble hung with honeysuckle or grapevine. Clutch size varies from one to five eggs, with an average of three in most nests. I'd always wondered why cardinals seem to have small broods, usually seeing two or three young in the nests I'd peeked into. And I'd wondered about their long nesting season. The only other birds still feeding nestlings in our yard in September are American goldfinches, which nest late in order to exploit the flush of weed seeds in late summer and early fall; and mourning doves, which, being pigeons, come by their fecundity naturally and will nest in every month of the year, feeders or no feeders.

Was the persistent late nesting in cardinals a response to the intensive bird-feeding efforts in which I'd always indulged, or something that cardinals brought when they expanded their range into New England? Apparently, cardinals have always maximized their reproductive potential by nesting often and late into the season. A. C. Bent's elegant *Life Histories of North American Cardinals, Grosbeaks, Buntings, Towhees, Finches, Sparrows, and Allies* cites this pattern in the 1930s, '40s, and '50s, when bird feeding consisted of throwing a few bread and meat scraps out on the lawn, not the orchestrated barrage of cardinal-perfect seed that we deploy today.

I'd always suspected cardinals are heeding a call to reproduce that may have less to do with their natural history than it does with the unnatural abundance we lay before them year-round. But Bent's and other early accounts of their long nesting season, marked by multiple nest attempts, argue against that suspicion. Besides, cardinals feed their young protein-rich insects, not seed. It's likely that smallish clutches and multiple nesting attempts have more to do with intense predation pressure on cardinal nests than with supplemental winter feeding. If your nest is likely to be wiped out by a predator, you probably shouldn't lay six eggs.

However, the abundance of cardinals has to have something to do with the

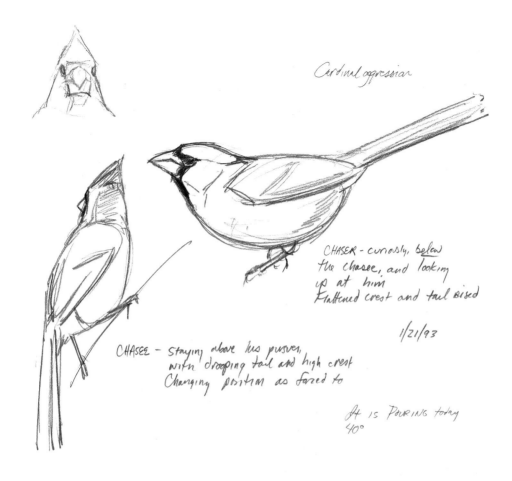

Cardinal aggression

CHASER - curiously, below
the chasee, and looking
up at him
Flattened crest and tail raised

1/21/93

CHASEE - staying above his pursuer,
with drooping tail and high crest
Changing position as forced to

It is Pouring today
40°

abundance of seed we provide. Winter feeding has been shown to enhance survival rates of black-capped chickadee populations; it might do the same for cardinals. Experiments with five supplemented and five nonsupplemented populations of blue tits in Ireland showed that birds that were fed all winter fledged more young come spring. Winter feeding may well have sped the dispersal of cardinals into the red-deprived northern tier of the United States, or at least encouraged the concentrations we see in backyards throughout the eastern half of the country.

The northern cardinal's range has expanded dramatically since the early 1800s. At the turn of the twentieth century, cardinals were common in Pennsylvania and New Jersey but stuck only a toe into southern New York. Massachusetts's first nesting was the year I was born (1958); Maine's in 1969. (I note with interest that these range expansions predate the explosion in bird feeding that started in the late 1960s.) The Midwest's invasion was faster; cardinals had flooded Ohio and colonized the Twin Cities of Minnesota by 1930; they reached Michigan's Upper Peninsula by 1994. For now, only southern Ontario boasts cardinals. But the species has blanketed the entire eastern half of the United States right up to the Canada border.

I've been feeding birds since I was about eight, four decades of hauling buckets of seed to waiting flocks. But only now am I starting to think about the larger impact of such a seemingly harmless pastime. A good snowstorm here in Whipple, Ohio, concentrates birds around the feeding station. Have you ever seen seventy cardinals in one backyard, against snow? I expect that, met with that sight, a European birder would have to sit down and breathe into a paper bag. When resident cardinal populations (and those of other feeder birds) build up to such heights, is the vision really as beautiful as it appears? What about the migratory birds that don't use feeders but still compete for the same resources? What about brown thrashers and gray catbirds, for instance, which spend the winter farther south, then return to northern latitudes to haunt the same shrubby habitat and eat the same crickets, grasshoppers, caterpillars, and moths that cardinals do?

What about common yellowthroats, yellow-breasted chats, and white-eyed vireos, also migrants that find themselves in competition with cardinals? Can it be good for migrant birds when our feeding programs flood their habitat with per-

ooo I would like some mealworms, now, please

She sits on windowsills and glares at me

Not much to look at—She's molting like mad Head, tail and wings

Meenah, the foundling cardinal—free-flying, but still coming in for mealworms and affection 10-20-99 She learned to shell sunflower seeds today!

Though she's been free for a month, she still likes to snuggle up under our chins

haps fifty individuals more of one species—a year-round resident—than might otherwise live there?

It's January now, and I've been pondering these questions even as I trudge out each morning to refill the sunflower and peanut feeders, spooking a whirring wave of birds from the backyard. The late, highly respected, popular ornithologist Roger Tory Peterson thought about such things, too, but he seemed to have come to peace with them. Asked about the proliferation of nonnative house sparrows, European starlings, and mute swans in his home state of Connecticut, Peterson reportedly replied, "How can more birds be a bad thing?" I've been scratching my head over that one for thirty years. Should I just sit back and thrill to the daubs of red dotting every tree and shrub in my yard? I've done my part to add to them.

In the summer of 1999, I took in a newly fledged northern cardinal that had been rescued from a cat-infested suburban backyard. The parents were nowhere to be found; the bird was flightless and unattended. The fledgling, a female, took to my kitten-chow-based, syringe-fed diet with alacrity, gaping lustily and growing visibly. Quiet and companionable, the little cardinal became a beloved companion to the then three-year-old Phoebe, who named the bird Meenah.

Meenah's transition from cuddling under a preschooler's chin to making her way in the backyard was surprisingly smooth; she took to the resident flock of cardinals, was courted by and mated with a wild male, and continued to visit her bowl on our deck railing through two succeeding winters for handouts of mealworms. Though she wasn't banded, we could always tell when Meenah had arrived, because she kept a habit from her fledgling days of landing smack-dab in the middle of the mealworm bowl without even bothering to pause on the rim first. We were thrilled to see this member of our family master the vigilance and skills she'd need to survive in the wild, to transfer her gentle affection to another of her species. All songbirds should be so easy to raise and release. But then all songbirds aren't quite as adaptable as the northern cardinal.

In the summer of 2004, a pair of cardinals chose to nest in a sprawling forsythia bush that hangs over our paved driveway. I could see the nest through the thick foliage as I stood on the cement. It was an ideal situation from which to observe the birds without disturbing them. Our scent was all around the driveway, so a potential nest predator would find nothing unusual in my presence there. I could stand on the pavement, lean over, and get a good view of the nest without touching the forsythia bush and leaving further scent clues.

On our eighty-acre sanctuary, we have a zero-tolerance policy for feral housecats, which inevitably are attracted to the throngs of birds in our yard and garden. Gray and fox squirrels, which will eat eggs, are rare, since our neighbors here in Appalachian Ohio eat *them*. Eastern chipmunks, avid egg and chick predators, are kept in check by our Boston terrier, who catches all the dumb ones and regularly routs the smart ones. Black rat snakes take perhaps the highest toll of songbird eggs and chicks here on the sanctuary. We host several large rat snakes in our garage all summer, where they help control the white-footed mouse population. In nesting so close to the garage in an easily climbed forsythia, the cardinals were highly vulnerable to snake predation. I peered into the forsythia, meeting the stoic gaze of a female cardinal pressed deep into her nest, and promised to do my best to protect her young. Did she know that nesting so close by my car might afford her an extra pair of eyes and swift action should a rat snake approach her nest? I'll always wonder.

The nest, supported by a shallow twig platform, was beautifully fashioned of purple-brown grape bark, fine twigs, dry straw, and grasses. The inner cup was tightly woven pine needles and fine blond grasses, and I marveled that the cardinal's heavy orange bill could loop, thread, and weave these diverse materials with such precision. In fact, the female masticates the twigs in order to bend and weave them as she wishes. No wonder cardinal nests withstand the worst winds of win-

An infant cardinal in the forsythia—I peek into its cradle when the hen is away.

ter, as frost and leaf drop reveal them perched in multiflora and honeysuckle tangles. I found the nest when the last forsythia flowers were falling from the twigs in mid-May and peeked over the course of a week while the female cardinal finished her clutch of three rufous-speckled, greenish white eggs. I checked only when she was off the nest, keeping my promise to protect her as well as I could and disturb her as little as possible.

One golden-slanted afternoon, I found the nest unattended and peeked to find a newly hatched nestling where an egg had been. Only twelve days of incubation had passed; I was amazed to think of the rapid developmental processes within that egg. Coral pink, with long, fine gray down, the grublike nestling raised its head and gaped, revealing pale yellow flanges around a red mouth lining. I quietly withdrew, smiling broadly to see that they'd made it this far without falling prey

Ten days old, this cardinal is out of the nest. It can't fly, can barely perch, but it's on its way. Its parents will feed it for up to two more months.

to a snake or chipmunk. By the next morning, a second chick had hatched. The third egg was infertile. Their growth was nothing short of stunning. Pinfeathers began sprouting, and by the time they were a week old, the twins looked like half-naked porcupines, with blood-filled blue quills bristling over their bodies, wings, and heads.

By Day 9, these quills had burst to reveal soft cocoa brown feathers, but their heads remained comically spiked with quills, with their bulging eyes giving them a froggy aspect. One chick left the nest on Day 9; the other was still crouched there on the afternoon of Day 10. My next check revealed it perching proudly in a gap in the forsythia foliage, looking out at its huge new world. I'd have to bid it, and my voyeuristic enjoyment of cardinal home life, goodbye.

It was hard to believe that the chicks' nestling period was over, only ten days after hatching. It's the enormous pressure from predators, in part, that so truncates cardinal incubation and nestling periods. It's this same pressure that causes nest failure for so many attempts, that keeps cardinals nesting and renesting into late August. Their low, open-cup nests are so vulnerable to snakes and rodents that the shorter the time they're occupied, the better. As soon as the cardinal young are able to perch and clamber, they vacate the scent-saturated nest. They're not truly mobile for another eleven days, sitting and waiting in the vicinity of the nest while their parents shuttle insects to them an average of eight times per hour. Even when the young begin to fly, they'll receive food for twenty-five to fifty-six days after fledging, mostly protein-rich insects, cut with increasing amounts of vegetable protein as they get older. It's then that most of us notice them, for their insistent pipping twitter becomes a constant background noise wherever cardinals are raising young. I've been known to shout, "Don't you *ever* shut *up*?" to the never-ending succession of cardinal fledglings in our yard as I weed and water the withering gardens of July and August.

Our sharp-shin has a penchant
for male cardinals. He strews
their bright feathers across the
snow.

And from early November until April, I keep toting seed, keep stoking the red fire. And I search for balance in the imbalance I have created. I laugh at myself, at the codependence I've created. For I depend on this oversize flock of backyard birds just as they count on me. They bring life and color and song to my habitat; they give me a reason to put on my coat in the morning, to glance, dozens of times a day, out the window to see who's visiting now. I willingly put on rubber boots and parka over my flannel pajamas, gladly haul heavy buckets of seed and smear my hands with suet, to welcome them into my yard and my life.

Lately, there's been a new visitor. He has blazing orange eyes and a sharp, hooked bill; knobby yellow feet tipped in ebony blades. Barely bigger than a blue jay, the color of rain clouds, the little male sharp-shinned hawk has a taste for cardinals—male cardinals. Five times this winter we've seen him slice through the air, execute a breathtaking jag and a loop or two, and neatly snag a redbird in midair, picking it up as if his talons were sticky with molasses and the cardinal were a floating feather. He corrects his course and swoops low into the woods, his crimson prize already limp in his grip.

He's part of a trend, one that follows the arc of bird feeding, too. Charles D. Duncan, a Maine ornithologist, looked at the precipitous drop in the number of sharp-shinned hawks counted migrating past Cape May, New Jersey, since 1980, and wondered if these hawks were disappearing or simply choosing not to migrate. He looked at eighteen years' worth of Christmas Bird Count data from New England for the answer. "Overall from 1975 to 1992, sharp-shinned hawks wintering in New England increased by more than 500 percent," Mr. Duncan wrote in the *Journal of Field Ornithology*. And why would those hawks choose to stay in New England? Anyone who's ever seen a yardful of birds freeze and then explode into flight, their peaceful flock shattered by a feathered bullet, knows why.

Like it or not, we're feeding the sharp-shinned and the Cooper's hawk from our feeding stations, too—they're getting seed, metabolized into blood, bone, and feather. Seventy cardinals festooning a single backyard is an undeniably beautiful sight, enough to make a seed-toting bird waitress proud. But that's a whole lot of cardinals in one spot, and it's anything but natural. Except for the seed I put out, they'd likely never congregate here. The quick talon, the appraising mind, the hard yellow glare of the sharp-shinned hawk; the rush of panicked songs and the drift of plucked feathers beneath the birch: that's natural. It's ours to accept, a balance to the imbalance we cheerfully create.

# Turkey Vulture

## The Unlikely Totem

THEY'RE BACK, circling the white sky of a gray March day, back from wherever they go all winter—to the chicken charnel houses of the Delmarva Peninsula? To the narrow passageway of Veracruz, Mexico, and then on into Central America? Turkey vultures are mysterious to me. I squint up at them and smile, always smiling when I see them. Like sun sparkling on water, these carrion-eating, conventionally ugly birds in their dark mourning jackets make me happy.

Along about 1981, when my life was in turmoil post-college and pre-commitment, I developed the habit of walking outside and looking to the sky for answers. And when I was at a crossroads, lost enough in the meanders of my own decisions to look heavenward, there would often be a turkey vulture overhead, looking down at me. Perhaps it was mere chance. Perhaps it's because they're common where I live. But signs, I think, are what you make of them. If I look to the sky for answers and usually find a turkey vulture looking down on me and take comfort in that sight, is that significant? Turkey vultures bring me solace, and I can't say why.

With almost three decades of vulture encounters behind me, I've recently

 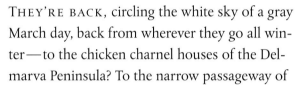

sought out the teachings of an assortment of Native American sources, developing a picture of the vulture as a personal totem. When vultures began to appear to me, I knew nothing of totems; Native American mysticism wasn't in fashion. It's in retrospect that I've become intrigued.

The process of discovering one's spirit guide, apparently, has an element of Zen (to mix religious philosophies just a bit). You do not choose your spirit guide or totem; rather, when the time is right, it appears to you. Knowing little of totems, I've never gone out looking for vultures, but I've seen them when I've sought guidance, more times than I can recall. Can a vulture smell turmoil and anxiety? It can certainly smell a ripe opossum. Do I emanate an aroma of indecision from time to time?

Reading further on totems, I learned that each animal possesses a number of characteristics that are open to interpretation. These seem fairly obvious overall, derived from the animal's appearance and behavior as commonly experienced by human beings. Not surprisingly, the owl is usually touted as a symbol of wisdom (although, having raised an owl, I'd much rather look to a corvid like a crow or raven for intelligence). Vultures, with their ability to soar on motionless wings, are described as demonstrating the efficient use of energy. Just as literally, the vulture totem is said to guide us to the cleanup of psychic messes. "If a vulture has flown into your life, you are being asked to remedy a messy situation and turn it into something positive." Well, all right. We tend to be in a bit of a mess at life's crossroads. From there, vultures are said to symbolize rebirth and transformation, as they consume putrefying flesh and gain strength and life from it. I especially like this one: "For those with this totem, you will be noticed more for what you do than how you appear." (A particularly comforting notion as I trudge past the half-century mark, undyed, unnipped, and untucked.)

The totemic significance of the vulture goes on and on, in flights of verbal fancy. From Starstuffs.com:

*Vulture teaches the power of purification of the mind, body and spirit. Vulture aids accomplishing tasks through great patience and vision, using your sense of smell and discernment, and how to glide and soar with your own energy. He teaches efficiency in actions and promises that changes are imminent. He shows how to restore harmony of thoughts and feelings so one can reach new heights with little effort.*

It all has the smell of augury about it, the newspaper horoscope kind of insight, in which a universal truth acquires sudden and special significance when applied to your current situation. And yet . . . I can't shake the conviction that vultures and I have a deep connection.

Just as the online mystics suggest, I have been making offerings to vultures in thanks for their guidance. The freezer, for me, is a place where good food goes to die. It lies in state, with occasional viewings, until a major power outage thaws it and gives me permission to toss it out. I load up a muck bucket and haul it out to the middle of the field, where turkey vultures have a field day sampling sausage, steaks, roasts, chicken thighs, and breaded nuggets. For the record, even a turkey vulture won't eat a processed chicken nugget. I stopped buying them for my son when I saw the vultures picking around them.

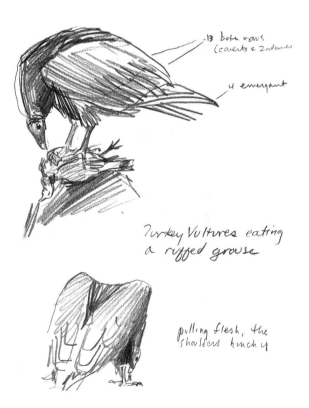

·13 both rows
(caverts & 2nderies

4 emergant

Turkey Vultures eating
a ruffed grouse

pulling flesh, the
shoulders hinch y

So perhaps there's more than a little chance involved when vultures drift over our land. They may be looking to give me spiritual guidance, but it's more likely that they're remembering the last freezer-burned pork roast they devoured here. And yet I don't mean to make too much fun, because the turkey vulture has manifested itself to me in unusual ways. Native American spirituality, virtually across all groups, holds that albino animals have spirit connections and are not to be killed. Hunting or killing them can lead to loss of hunting skills. White is associated not with purity but with wisdom and a connection to higher powers. White animals and birds hold powerful totemic significance for Native Americans.

We had lived in our Ohio home little more than a year when, on a gray, dreary day, turkey vultures came tilting over the snow-streaked hills. I was working in a small back bedroom studio, glancing out the window from time to time, enjoying the slow return of spring on their dark wings. My macaw, Charlie, was perched near the north window, watching the vultures, when suddenly he voiced a startled *raaaaawk!*—a low, guttural sound he makes when he spots soaring raptors. There was such emphasis in the call that I looked up from my work. There, over the gray-blue hills, was a snow-white turkey vulture, tilting and riding the March winds with the rest. It was a moment that, had it happened now, I'd have recorded forever with a telephoto lens. But I had no camera, so I grabbed a sketchbook and swiftly sketched the bird, with three black primaries on its right wing, a scattering of black secondaries, a few black tail feathers, smudges of black on its secondary coverts, and a charcoal gray head. I believed that I would never see such a thing again.

When the bird had passed by, headed north, I began a quest for information. Had anyone ever recorded a white turkey vulture before? I painted a small study from my detailed sketches and sent it off to Hawk Mountain Sanctuary in Kempton, Pennsylvania, hoping that the bird's pattern of black feathers would prove distinctive enough that someone else might have reported it. And that fall, a turkey

a vision over Whipple,
Ohio March 11 1993
12:20 -12:28 p.m. - a leucistic
turkey vulture with perhaps 30
companions. Attacked by a crow, it
settled for a few minutes in a tree, preened,
then took off on snowy wings to the north.
This painted hurriedly, from memory, as soon as it left.
I can only think it was sent - what made me look up?

vulture matching its description was spotted by Hawk Mountain observers as it migrated through Veracruz, Mexico!

I savored that contact with the white bird, caught up in the magic of having seen a vulture that was perhaps one in several million. In the early summer of 1994, I drove to Pittsburgh to give a talk. I'd traveled less than an hour north when I spotted a turkey vulture, white, with precisely the same black feathering on its right wing and tail as the bird I'd seen over my house. I can't begin to estimate the odds against seeing a white vulture in the first place, much less encountering what was undoubtedly the same bird a year later. Word of my initial sighting had spread, and a fellow member of the Wheeling-based Brooks Bird Club called that summer to say that he had repeatedly seen the white vulture at a roost near my second sighting in Woodsfield, Ohio. Signs, signs, everywhere are signs, and this one, perhaps the most powerful spirit totem one could imagine, had appeared to me unbidden not once but twice.

But I have sought them out, too, the turkey vultures, hiking through the Connecticut woods to a well-hidden rock outcropping where I'd heard they were nesting. The climb to the cavelet wasn't bad, but, as my head topped the ledge, I heard a deep and guttural hissing sound—as if Darth Vader himself was lurking in its farthest recesses. It went on and on without a break for breath, making me wonder if vulture chicks were capable of circular breathing, like some saxophone players I've heard. A low, resonant exhalation that one might expect from a huge anaconda or Komodo dragon, the sound scared me in a primal way, the way my first bear sighting did. I suddenly wanted to get out of there. Peering back into the cave, I found two almost spherical chicks covered with filmy gray down, hunkered back on their heels and hissing for all they were worth. I knew enough not to press it and took a quick look at them with my binoculars, lest I be covered in a projectile presentation of their last meal. Jitters and all, it was a never-to-be-repeated thrill to visit a vulture nursery.

Years later, I was driving the familiar path to home over the low-lying area in southern Ohio that we call Whipple Flats. There, near the banks of Duck Creek, I saw a turkey vulture standing on the gravel shoulder with no explanatory carcass nearby. Its head was hanging down; it was a picture of dejection. I pulled over and went to its side. The vulture's eye rolled, but it moved not a centimeter when

A turkey vulture prepares to deliver a load of pre-digested roadkill to its young.

I knelt beside it. "What's wrong, hon?" I asked. The vulture sighed a tiny, low sigh and looked at me, making no effort to walk or fly away. "I'll take you home and we'll figure it out, okay?" I tucked the unresisting bird under my arm and rode the rest of the way with it lying on my lap like a tame hen.

When we got home, I stood the vulture on our picnic table and stretched first one wing, then the other. I felt all the long bones of the wings. There were no breaks, no bruises. The legs checked out, too. But the vulture's keel stood out on its breast like a blade, the muscles on either side wasted. This bird was starving.

I took it out to the vegetable garden, which is protected by an eight-foot fence, and spread a blanket of clean straw. I built a shelter with lawn chairs and a tarpaulin and placed a dog dish of clean water inside. I cut up some raw chicken, bone and all, and knelt by the vulture's side. Its eyes brightened when it saw the food, and it gently took several pieces from my fingers. I laid the rest of the chicken down and left it alone. When I returned an hour later, the food was untouched. I offered more from my hand, and the vulture eagerly ate. It was to accept food only from my hand for the rest of its ten days of recuperation.

The bird continued to eat and gain a little weight and strength, but it never lost its docility. I became concerned that it did not attempt to fly, and a summer trip was approaching, so I decided to take it to the Ohio Wildlife Center in Columbus on our way to the airport. As we were loading the car, my husband, Bill, asked, "Hey, what are you going to do with that vulture while we're gone?" I hesitated before answering. "Well, I was hoping to drop it off at the bird hospital on our way to the airport." Bill blanched visibly, knowing what might await us.

"You're kidding, right?"

"No, I'm not. It'll be okay. It's really tame."

And it *was* okay for the first ten miles, riding quietly in a dog carrier in the back of our van. I started to relax. Maybe this was going to work. I had called ahead; the veterinarian was waiting to give the bird a thorough exam and place it with a raptor rehabilitator who had experience with vultures. And then it became apparent that the bird was not okay, and neither were we. Although I pride myself on coming up with evocative prose, the awesome stench of vulture vomit defies description, especially when confined to a closed vehicle and recirculated in its air-conditioning system. Gagging, we

pulled over, and I set about removing the noisome bolus from the pet carrier without further upsetting our passenger. I have blocked the memory of what Bill said about the advisability of transporting a vulture in the *Bird Watcher's Digest* company van, but the smell lingers in my brain's most primitive centers, doubtless an adaptive trait, to prevent my ever trying to transport a well-fed vulture by auto again.

We made it to the hospital and gladly turned our cargo over to people more used to vulture vomit than were we. It recovered uneventfully; the only thing the veterinarian found was a heavy parasite load, which could conceivably have sapped its strength enough to render it flightless. Deloused and built up, it was released, I hope never to find its way to a roadside, hanging its head, again.

I always wondered if that bird consciously sought help by standing by the roadside when it lost the strength to fly. I told its story to my friend Charles Kennedy, then president of the Louisiana Ornithological Society, and Charlie told me a story of his own.

While out gardening in his yard one spring day, Charlie heard screeching brakes and the thump of a collision on the road. He paused, then resumed his labors, figuring a car had hit a rabbit or woodchuck. Some time later, a turkey vulture came walking through the trees into Charlie's yard, dragging one wing. "Looks like you've got yourself in a fix, old son," Charlie said. "Go on back into the woods. There's nothing I can do for you." The vulture stood looking at Charlie as he turned the soil. Needing to fetch a tool, Charlie headed for the garage, and when he turned around to come back out, the vulture was standing right behind him, having followed him from the garden.

 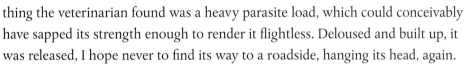

Charlie considered the bird. "Well, all right, I'll make some calls and see if we can find somebody to fix you up." He headed for the house, vulture hobbling right behind.

I wish the story had a happy ending, but despite the efforts of a veterinarian and rehabilitator, the vulture didn't make it. Still, it left Charlie and me with the slightly spooky conviction that these two vultures had deliberately sought our help when they were in greatest need. Tables turned on the totem.

I watch the sky as I walk these Appalachian foothills, and I still lift my eyes to the heavens when I'm wondering and worrying. But I don't wonder anymore if the vultures come to me for a reason. I know there's no answer, and it doesn't really matter why they come; it's enough that they do. Vultures make me smile, like sun sparkling on water.

a titmouse gathered hair
from the raccoon wreck
while the vulture tore it apart
4/29/91 West Rd

# Chestnut-fronted Macaw

## First Comes Love . . .

AS I WRITE, the emerald green head of a macaw emerges from under my desk. He has crawled up my leg from a favorite perch on my foot. He's been doing this for nineteen years, and I expect him to be sitting on me, giving creaky calls and showering me with feather dandruff, for at least the next twenty-five. He's the relationship I can't get out of.

I bought this parrot in 1989, the first time my biological clock rang. I needed something young and helpless to care for, but since I was living hand-to-mouth as a field biologist, a baby wasn't in the cards. It was one of the moments in my life when a crystal ball might have been helpful: to look forward nineteen years and see myself still fixing a hot breakfast every morning for a bird; to see that sweet, cooing baby parrot morph into a crotchety tyrant, not averse to sinking his powerful beak into flesh to make a point.

And yet, Charlie speaks a few words; he has a flair for slapstick. In the company of people, he listens to the conversation and laughs loudly at precisely the right moment. He waddles around the house, toenails clicking on linoleum, looking for a nice closet where he can hole up. The bare skin on his cheeks is soft and warm. He likes to be hugged.

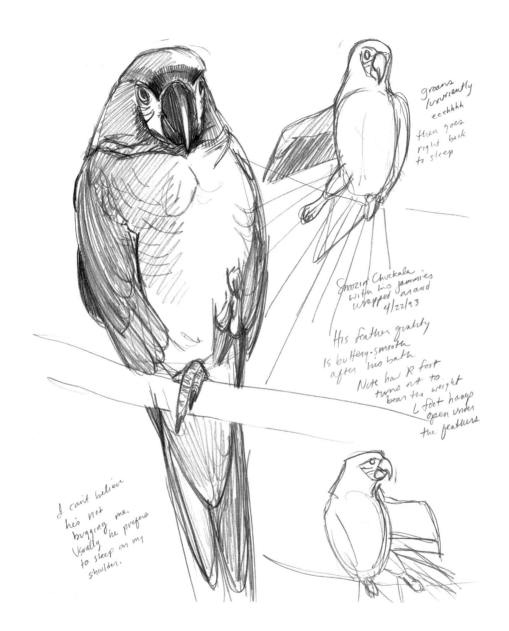

groans
luxuriantly
eechhhh
then goes
right back
to sleep

Snorzin' Chuckala
with his jammies
wrapped around
4/22/93

His feather quality
is buttery-smooth
after his bath

Note how R foot
turns out to
bear the weight
L foot hangs
open under
the feathers

I can't believe
his not
bugging me.
Usually he prefers
to sleep on my
shoulder.

A captive parrot selects the only mate it can find (in this case, Charlie's picked me), but I just refuse to follow the plan he's laid out for me. I share my affections with another of my species, even when Charles punctures my skin to prevent this perceived infidelity. I won't eat the breakfast he regurgitates for me, no matter how tenderly proffered. Occasional furtive copulations with my sock-clad foot net him nothing but a temporary release. He points out and protects his chosen nest site, a grotto under the sink, with cracked squawks and sudden rushes at passersby. But I can't succumb to his will, crawl under the sink, and lay the two round white eggs that Charlie believes I must have in me, which he so longs to incubate and protect. He crouches in the half darkness, looking up at me with a Don King wig of feathers over crazed golden eyes. *Come on in, baby. You know you're ovulating.*

Every once in a while, I look down on myself, a middle-aged woman with a middle-aged parrot dropping dandruff and worse on her shoulder. Sometimes, after he has perforated my finger or lip in a fit of pique, it occurs to me that I might just surrender Charlie to a parrot rescue group. Just as quickly, I discard the idea. Who am I to dump this slightly mad bundle of idiosyncrasies and multicolored feathers on anyone else? We have a history together, forged in stone on that fateful December day in 1989 when I gathered a baby macaw in my arms and said, "I do."

Parrots can be delightful. But they are raunchy, awful pets. I'll probably be an old, old lady before I figure out what has kept Charlie and me together all these years. And I'm sure Charlie, that tatty old rotter, will be sitting on my shoulder when I do. Maybe it's love. But it feels a little more like marriage.

The essay printed above aired on National Public Radio's *All Things Considered* on Friday, March 14, 2008. Three days later, it was still the number one most e-mailed story on NPR's website. Only a speech on race relations by the presidential candidate Barack Obama finally displaced Charlie from his virtual throne. Do millions of listeners keep aging parrots in a corner of their living rooms, or did the commentary strike a chord with anyone who has entered into the human-animal bond of love, tolerance, and codependency?

It's possible to grow old along with one's parrot, and that makes parrots unique in the pet world, with the possible exception of tortoises. I am growing old with Charlie, in sickness and in health, for richer and poorer, for better or worse. He is perched on my foot as I write, singing a low song of contentment to it, to me. He preens, rouses, feather dandruff flying and settling on the newspapers below. I have tailored my life and home, my travel schedule, my grocery list, and my daily routine to the needs of this tame but wild, familiar but alien green being.

*Charlie, just getting his tail*
*4/11/88*

If I am sure of anything after twenty-three years of living with a macaw, it's that parrots are wild birds, that they show no signs of becoming domesticated, no matter how many generations have been raised in captivity, and that this simple truth makes them singularly lousy pets. Parrots and people can bring out the worst in each other. None of this is the parrot's fault. The blame's on us for so admiring their colorful plumage, ardent sociability, and lively intellect that we feel the need to cage, possess, and even collect them.

I came of age in the 1970s, when pet shops were filled with wild-caught, imported parrots, young and old, healthy and ill, common and endangered. The trade in wild birds was uncontrolled; nesting trees were felled, the nestlings stolen; baby parrots were drugged and smuggled in suitcases, blouses, car trunks, even the hubcaps of cars. Survivors of such insults showed up worldwide in pet shops and at bird fairs, huddled on perch stands. Fed monkey biscuits and sunflower seeds, they were the pitiful wrecks of what had once been free-living members of social flocks. And these refugees were to become the cheaply acquired foundation stock for a booming captive parrot breeding industry.

When fines and jail terms finally caught up with wild bird smugglers, trade in captive-bred baby parrots began to take off. Nestlings were close-banded, fitted with seamless aluminum rings that could be slipped only over the foot of a small nestling, to be worn for life as badges of their legal provenance.

Having had a lifelong love for parrots, and being young and foolish and flush with a little money from my first real job, I became convinced that I needed a baby parrot. With the perspective of twenty-three years, having given birth to two children, I understand the root of that urge and why I unconsciously chan-neled it into a desire for a pet bird. I wasn't married; I lived hand-to-mouth and moved every few months, but I needed something young and helpless to care for. I'd lost a treasured pet budgie to cancer after only three years, and I wanted a pet bird who would live a long, long time. Oh, be careful what you wish for.

The problem with kittens is that they grow into cats. And the problem with baby parrots is that they grow into adult parrots. Baby parrots give quiet, nasal feeding calls; they bob their heads endearingly, fluttering pin-feathered wings. They snuggle and burrow into your arms, looking for warmth and comfort. They explore your face with soft, rubbery tongues. Their emerging feathers stand up in crazy, spiky wigs; their young

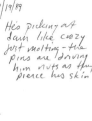

1/19/89

He's picking at
dam like crazy
just molting — the
pins are driving
him nuts as they
pierce his skin

beaks are still soft and weak, as yet unfit for rending and piercing. To a young, aspiring ornithologist, a baby parrot seemed like a rather pricey answer to a prayer.

In my own defense, Charlie picked me. Known to the home breeder-dealer I dealt with as a rather insular and persnickety bird, Charlie wouldn't warm up to just anyone. So when he eagerly leapt onto my wrist and swarmed up my neck to preen my hair and whisper in my ear, Charlie made an impression. "He loves you! He's never done that with anybody!" It never occurred to me to wonder whether she told all prospective buyers the same thing.

She told me that Charlie wasn't for sale, because she wanted to keep him for breeding, if surgical sexing bore out her suspicion that Charlie was a female. Reluctantly, I peeled myself away from the small stub-tailed bundle of green and red feathers, but not before he attempted to copulate with my hand. "If this bird's a female, I'll eat my hat," I told the dealer.

Two weeks later, she called me. "I just had him surgically sexed. Charlie *is* a male! You can have him if you want him. He needs a really good home, and I know he loves you." What she'd seen and noted was the nickel-size patch of bare skin on his abdomen that Charlie had already, at four and a half months of age, begun to pluck. To an experienced parrot handler, this bespoke an emotional sensitivity that could make him a poor pet prospect. He'd need a solicitous caretaker, lots of attention, a "really good home."

Were the dealer a Realtor and Charlie a home, she'd have described him as "loaded with potential." He was a handful, a fixer-upper from the start. Blinded by parrot lust, I couldn't wait to hand over a month's pay and begin our life together. On his first vet check, it was apparent that Charlie had never been surgically sexed, a noninvasive procedure wherein a tiny incision is made near the last rib and spine for a quick peek at the left gonad, be it testis or ovary. Doubt at the dealer's honesty began to pluck at my psyche, but all that was moot. I had wanted this bird desperately. I had bonded with him. Charlie was mine now to love, feed, and care for.

I fed him warm parrot chow from a spoon, let him burrow under the bedcovers, cuddled him in the evening, gave him exotic nuts to crack, a golf ball to roll around the living room. I cleaned up copious droppings and quickly decided it would be expedient to toilet-train him. I noticed that, when I approached his cage, he often defecated in excitement, so I began to give a simple command each time that occurred. When he complied, I'd immediately take him on my wrist as a reward. It didn't take long for him to catch on. Before two days had passed, Charlie would defecate on command, and not on my shoulder. Even if he didn't need to, he'd squeeze out a tiny dropping when asked. And he'd knock the back of my neck with his beak when he felt the need. I'd hold him over newspaper, wastebasket, even the toilet, and he'd release, sometimes having held back for an hour or two. To this day, he remembers both to defecate on command and to warn me with a knock or nip when he needs to relieve himself.

I soon discovered that keeping this bird in the style to which he'd become accustomed took a bit of work. I prepared him a fresh fruit, vegetable, pasta, and rice breakfast every morning. He liked to eat whatever I was eating, including chicken, beef, fish, cheese, yogurt, eggs, toast, pasta, nuts, peanut butter, cake, cookies, dried fruit, and occasional sips of juice, beer, and wine. He often shared dinner with me, asking for bites of whatever I might be eating. He'd wave a chicken bone in his foot as he split it end to end, extracting the marrow. I'd read that wild parrots had been spotted feeding on carcasses, and Charlie seemed to know just what to do with bones. In those first months, parrot ownership was going pretty well. Never mind the three-square-foot cage that now dominated my tiny living room; forget the newspapers that covered key sections of the floor. Charlie was some parrot.

When his wing feathers had fully grown in, Charlie began to fly around the cottage, and a not-very-subtle shift in his attitude became apparent. True to his bird nature, he favored high places—especially curtain rods and mantels—where he could knock knickknacks off shelves and chew woodwork. He began to nip, then to bite, and to take flight before I could return him to his cage. Taken outside, he'd feel a gust of wind and lift off for the tallest tree. As much as I hated to deface his sea blue wings, I was forced to clip his primary feathers or lose control of him altogether.

I realize now that this is where the real trouble began. Released from the towel in which I'd wrapped him to commit the insult, he stared at his clipped wings in seeming amazement. And he commenced to shred the shafts of the cut feathers. This progressed to overpreening both wing and tail feathers, and the nickel-size spot of plucked feathers on his belly expanded to include the insides of his legs. Charlie wasn't even a year old, still coming into adult plumage, and he was removing the feathers as fast as they grew in. From that day on, he never allowed a wing feather to fully emerge before chewing it off. I was distraught, knowing I'd done the wrong thing but helpless to reverse Charlie's predilection. I showered him with attention, with flossy, fibrous toys, stuffed animals. He shredded them and kept working on his feathers, plucking even every emerging blood feather with a sharp "OW!"

Self-mutilation is a common response to captivity in both birds and mammals. Look closely at older animals in some zoos and you'll see bare patches on the forelegs where neurotic tongues have licked too often, missing toenails, bald patches where they've rubbed themselves raw on cage bars. There's even a term for it: neurodermatitis.

I couldn't believe that Charlie, my constant companion, would be subject to sufficient emotional disturbance to result in feather plucking. I thought back to the bare patch I'd seen on his belly when he was a nestling, to the dealer's allusion to his need for a "really good home." He had the best environment, the best fresh food I could give him. Repeated tests by his avian veterinarian hinted at nothing organic as a cause for the mutilation. Charlie's plucking seemed to be a response to myriad emotional and physical needs left unfulfilled in his highly artificial life with me. I would have to accept that fact, care for him, and love him as he was. Two decades later, he's still plucking his belly, leg, and wing feathers, and he has two bare epaulets on his shoulders. I'm thankful he leaves as many feathers as he does; he still looks pretty good from the back. Feather plucking, two different avian veterinarians have assured me, is part of his psychic makeup, just as pacing and weaving seem to suit the captive bear and tiger. Just as captivity suits none of them.

Parrots are vocal; some turn that aptitude into imitation of human speech. Charlie learned eight words, then ceased to pick up any more. Chestnut-fronted macaws aren't known for talking, but they're affectionate, funny, and personality-packed. They're also aggressive as macaws go. Several breeders have told me that there are few birds as dangerous as territorial chestnut-fronted macaws. One man said he enters the aviary of his breeding pairs with a metal garbage can lid as a shield. The macaw researcher Charlie Munn, for whom my bird is named, reported that he saw a pair of wild chestnut-fronted macaws win a standoff over a nesting cavity with blue and yellow macaws four times their size.

Like all parrots, chestnut-fronts are very, very loud. In the wild, parrots squawk and scream to maintain contact with their flocks. They fly fast, wings flicking shallowly, avian storm troopers, screaming all the way.

In captivity, parrots scream to welcome human companions back home and to augment conversations with their own vocalizations. In my tiny Connecticut cottage, where I was alone in the living room–aviary for most of the day, Charlie chipped in whenever the phone rang. "Hellooo? Yeah!" he'd say when I picked up the receiver. From there, he'd escalate his conversation to deafening levels, and I had to shut myself in the back room to hear or be heard. I took to giving him toys and treats whenever the telephone rang, which helped keep him occupied but also rewarded the screaming behavior. Such was the tug o' war, the coevolution, the clumsy daily merengue I danced with this bird.

When I met my soon-to-be husband, in 1991, Charlie took an instant but not unexpected dislike to Bill. He'd sit on my knee, preening happily, then, a look of resolve crossing his face, climb methodically down, waddle across the room, climb up Bill's leg, bite him sharply, and waddle back to me, his mission accomplished. Suggestions were made about finding a new home for this pretty tyrant. Charlie moved with me from Connecticut to Maryland, where Bill built him an enormous rope jungle gym, suspended from the rafters of my studio. Over time, we modified Charlie's behavior by sequestering him whenever he bit Bill. If he was to get corn chips and the occasional sip of Heineken, he needed to play nicely. It's been years since he's bitten Bill. To this day, though, embracing in Charlie's presence produces a salvo of screeches, raised feathers, and wickedly pinned pupils.

He remains my bird, or, from Charlie's perspective, I remain his person. It can be a drag to be owned by a macaw. It is also expensive.

In order to continue cohabiting with such a creature, Bill and I had an eight-by-ten-foot aviary built onto my studio when we added on to our Ohio home in 1999. Sliding glass doors allow me to control Charlie's enthusiasm for adding to our conversations or ruling on our social interactions. Having lived at the aural mercy of a parrot ensconced in the living room, I believe that anyone considering investing in a pet parrot should also plan to build it a separate room, handy to a busy part of the house, with sliding glass doors. The month's pay I surrendered to buy Charlie in 1989 was a thin glaze of frost on an iceberg of investment made since, providing for our mutual welfare and sanity.

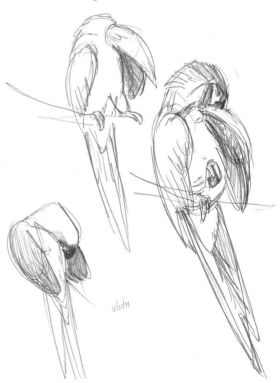

Most birds are not particularly tactile creatures. Parrots are exceptions. Because they mate for life, they engage in complex social behaviors that help maintain the pair bond. Among these behaviors is allopreening, in which one member of the pair gently sorts through the other's head feathers, removing feather sheaths. Parrot owners often provide allopreening for their pets, gently rolling emerging feathers between their fingers to remove the sheaths. Parrot and owner enjoy the exercise. Charlie enjoys having his head preened and the oil gland at the base of his tail massaged. He likes to cuddle up under my chin and nap. From his perch on my shoulder, he watches out the window for soaring raptors, giving voice to a low rattle when his sharp eyes discern one. To Charlie I owe three eagle sightings and a flabbergasted view of the only albino turkey vulture I've ever seen. I've often thought that a parrot would be a great asset at a hawk watch site, if it weren't so traumatic for the predator-spotting bird.

Being cavity nesters, parrots feel comfortable in dark, confined spaces. On cold days, Charlie dives down the front of my sweater or jacket and chuckles in the warm darkness. I have answered the door wearing Charlie like a joey in a kangaroo's pouch, only to have him suddenly poke his head out at my collar, to the surprise and consternation of the delivery person who rang. The other side of this tactile nature is a nippy bossiness, which presents few problems when two wild parrots spar with their hard beaks and tough, scaled feet. Charlie's perfectly capable of giving soft "play nips." We play a game called Bite This, in which I offer my finger to him, saying, "Bite this!" With a loud growl and a great show of ferocity, he gives it the softest of nips, following it with a startled "OW!" and a cackle of laughter. It's fun for both of us. Unfortunately, parrots in the grip of excitement lose the ability to calibrate their nips to vulnerable human flesh. Lacking shield-like beaks, people take the brunt of such passionate bites on tender lips, ears, and fingers. Living with a parrot is all about reading the lightning-fast changes of its moods and being aware of the potential releasers of aggression. It's about trying not to get perforated.

It took me nineteen years and innumerable bites before I learned a simple lesson: Charlie was most likely to bite me when there were strangers near his cage. It's natural for a proud parrot owner to want to introduce guests to the bird, and that usually involves taking the parrot from the cage to the owner's hand or shoulder. As often as not, this move results in aggression from the parrot, directed to-

Charlie sleeping
10/4/88
Echefoose

ward the bewildered owner. Over time, a parrot becomes protective of its territory (its cage) as well as its mate (the owner). Strangers crowding around a parrot's territory and mate often evoke a violent response from the bird. It attempts to drive its partner away from perceived danger by striking with its beak. In the wild, such action would prevent its mate from pairing with another bird. In a captive situation, this natural psittacine behavior causes the owner to curse, flail her arms, grope for a tissue to stanch a bleeding lip, and make feeble excuses to shocked guests about her excitable, unsuitable, still thoroughly undomesticated pet.

Charlie sits on my shoulder for much of every day, gently preening my hair, eyebrows, and ears. I kiss the soft white skin of his cheeks and play with him as if he were a tiny dog. He is preening on my shoulder as I proofread this manuscript, a beloved, calming presence, a fusty scent in my nostrils that I miss when I'm away from him. Yet Charlie has pierced my lower lip twice, and put countless deep, crescent-shaped holes in my hands and arms when strangers were present. He strikes like a snake, bringing the force of a beak that can crack Brazil nuts to bear on my vulnerable skin. After eighteen years of such mortifying incidents, I finally put a sign up in his aviary to remind me: NO KISSES NEAR CAGE! I now ask him to step on a long dowel when strangers are present—I don't permit him to climb to my shoulder in such a charged situation. The embarrassing mate-guarding bites have virtually ceased.

Charlie's a parrot. He'll always bite, because parrots bite in a number of situations. They bite not because they're inherently vicious but because biting is what they'd do in a similar situation in the wild. Biting works for parrots. Concern for the owner's welfare, a consideration one expects and even demands from a pet dog, cannot be instilled in a parrot; it is not so much as a glimmer in the bird's mind. Yes, there are parrots who imitate smoke detectors when they perceive a fire, saving the family from asphyxiation; there are parrots who scream their owners awake when burglars invade. But those birds likely still nail their owners with a bite when it suits them to do so. Even Alex, the celebrated African gray parrot with the astounding vocabulary and well-substantiated keen intellect, bit his beloved labmates. You'd think that a parrot who could count, distinguish colors, coin words, and murmur endearments might drop biting from his repertoire. But parrots seem to lack the capacity to override their powerful mate-protection instinct with anything resembling reason or empathy. The onus is on the parrot's owner to figure out how to work around the natural behavior of the wild thing in her house.

How many among us would keep a dog that tries to bite when its food dish is refilled, that lunges at us when we tidy up its bed? In the parrot's mind, when we clean up after it and offer it food in its cup, we're invading its territory. Defense of territory and mate guarding are the two strongest instincts parrots possess, and they make life interesting for those of us who look after these birds. Such behaviors keep us on our toes. Charlie goes into breeding mode in January, and he can be downright dangerous for a month or more while his testosterone is flowing. People who keep the pet pact with parrots for their entire life spans are few and uniquely dedicated.

Many pet parrots, quite understandably, wind up in foster homes and rescue organizations when their owners decide to have children. We look with new eyes at this wild pet when dimpled baby hands enter the picture. I'd had Charlie for nearly a decade when our daughter, Phoebe, was born, in 1996. His golden eyes nearly popped out of his head when he beheld our infant daughter for the first time. His beak fell open, and his rubbery black tongue wiggled.

He sputtered in seeming astonishment, consumed with the desire to get closer to this writhing, reddish infant. Sorry, Charlie. Though I read no aggression in his eyes or posture, it would be a cold day in hell before he'd get close enough to touch or taste our new baby.

The Wig expresses amazement.

As time went on, we worked around Charlie's intense attraction to Phoebe, allowing him near her without having actual contact. She slept peacefully through his worst screaming bouts, having heard them in utero. Slowly it became apparent that Charlie's interest in her was just that. Though jealousy is what parrots do best, he bore no malice toward the baby. By the time Phoebe was pulling up on the side of her playpen, Charlie was perching on its railing next to her, preening and cooing. As a toddler, she rolled him in her blanket and carried him in her arms like a doll. They giggled and played among the towels in the linen closet together, Charlie rushing out to defend his new companion from me. It was all fine with Charlie, and I was amazed at the bond they forged. That changed completely with Liam's arrival, in 1999. Charlie's focus shifted to the new infant, and he began chasing Phoebe with an unmistakably wicked look in his eye. I was distressed and mystified, but I shouldn't have been. A conversation with the bird-keeper at a zoo in Victoria, Texas, made it all clear. She asked me a few questions.

"How long have you had Charlie?"

"Ten years."

"Does he consider you his mate?"

"Well, he copulates with my foot, bosses me around, and attacks me when strangers are near, so I'd say yes."

"When did he start acting aggressively toward Phoebe?"

"Right after Liam was born. How could he be so sweet to her for three years, and then turn on her?"

The aviculturist explained that, in all likelihood, Charlie considered both Liam and Phoebe to be his offspring. In parrot society, when the second brood hatches, it's time to oust the fledglings from the first brood, to drive them from the home territory and encourage them to set up a place of their own. This allows the parent birds to focus their energy on the new nestlings. Charlie was genetically programmed to be a serial parent. Once again, his obvious affection for a person was eclipsed by his desire to maintain proper order in his parrotcentric world. Analyzed through a parrot's unique point of view, everything Charlie did to guard his territory, mate, and putative offspring made perfect sense. The trick was keeping his psittacine perspective in the front of my mind, trying to make sense of his behavior toward us by divining the instinctual blueprint in his mind. Judging this engaging, sometimes dangerous creature by human standards, branding him "vicious" or "jealous," would get us nowhere.

As Phoebe and Liam have grown up, Charlie has maintained a kind of détente with them, neither pursuing their affections nor discouraging them. They're simply flockmates now. He'll go out of his way to perch on the backs of their chairs; he'll delicately take treats from their fingers; he'll gladly accept a lift from Phoebe's outstretched arm; but he allows only

Bill and me to pet, preen, and touch him. Given the spectrum of behavior in older parrots, I feel grateful that Charlie is as tractable and pacific as he is.

To live with a parrot for twenty-three years is to develop an intricate understanding of and empathy with his unique plight—that of a monogamous, intensely social creature plunged into a world that makes no sense and does not fulfill his emotional needs. People reach into his sanctum sanctorum—his cage—to change papers or replenish food, continually annoying him. A parrot is frustrated by his human companion's inattentiveness, her habit of leaving him alone for hours at a time. He screams to make contact, to call her back. He bites her to drive her away from potential rivals or enemies. He attacks her human mate, refusing to acknowledge his place in the flock. Everyone should know she belongs with the parrot, should be his constant companion, but no one seems to understand such a simple thing.

I have made peace with Charlie, because I love him and believe that the pact we forged in 1989, however star-crossed, is to be honored. Scanning parrot rescue websites, all of them flooded with rejected pets, I know I'm in a distinct minority. I stay away from pet stores, because I can't bear to see the bright, dark eyes of the latest crop of hand-fed nestlings, knowing the life of misunderstanding, alienation, and loneliness most of them will face once they grow up to be parrots. I wonder how parrot breeders reconcile their proclaimed love for birds with the abysmal conditions to which they send so many of their hand-raised babies—a small cage in a back bedroom, where no one can hear their screams, passed from owner to owner via want ads. Meanwhile, hundreds of thousands of unwanted adult parrots languish, are put up for rescue and adoption, die alone. I can see no reason to keep breeding parrots for the pet industry, other than to support the industry. A prospective parrot owner will enjoy a year or two of its cuddly babyhood, with decade after decade of true parrothood—ear-piercingly loud, spectacularly messy, often uncuddly, and occasionally dangerous—to follow.

I hope for a collective awakening to the understanding that parrots can truly be parrots only in the wild, the kind of enlightenment that is slowly creeping in about chimpanzees, dolphins, and elephants. Highly intelligent, social, long-lived, and emotionally complex, parrots deserve so much better from us than solitary confinement. They belong with their flocks in the wild, where their numbers continue to dwindle. I can't repatriate Charlie—old, flightless, and half-naked as he

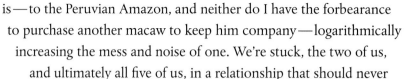

is—to the Peruvian Amazon, and neither do I have the forbearance to purchase another macaw to keep him company—logarithmically increasing the mess and noise of one. We're stuck, the two of us, and ultimately all five of us, in a relationship that should never have been initiated. The dealer got her $750, and I, and then we, took on a lifetime commitment to living with a wild macaw in our house. Had I known what lay ahead, the tens of thousands of dollars we'd spend on specialized foods and equipment, on building a glassed room for him and paying a pet sitter to visit every day whenever we travel, I'd have set up an endowment fund before I purchased him.

I sometimes wonder if Charlie will outlive me, if I will have to hand him down to Phoebe or Liam. I don't know where to put my thoughts about Charlie, because, like him, they don't fit neatly under any particular heading. He's not a pet, exactly; he's a presence in my life, one that must be accommodated, tolerated, cleaned up after, worked around, provided for, and dearly loved; more like a quirky, crotchety relative who's come to stay . . . for good. Yes, I got what I wished for in 1989, a pet bird who would live a long, long time.

# Epilogue

CHARLIE SAVED his greatest secret for last. As this book went to press, my little green macaw entered a two-month period of frantic nesting behavior—backing into corners, throwing food from dishes, tearing stacks of newspapers and catalogues into bushels of confetti, possessed by a hormonal surge I'd never witnessed in twenty-three years. On a Monday evening, he shared a roast chicken dinner with us. Three hours later, Charlie was in great distress, straining to pass an enormous egg. I held my little hen macaw in my arms past midnight, then, before dawn, rushed her to an avian veterinarian three hours distant. Despite heroic efforts to save her, a massive infection had set in, and Charlie left us on August 9, 2011.

We'd built a sunny, climate-controlled room onto my studio just for Charlie. We were in it for the long haul: the loud screams, the thrown seed, and the chewed walls. And now I find that Charlie had built an annex on my heart. The studio is terribly quiet now—my shoulder aches for her familiar weight, my ear for her whispered confessions. But I won't fill the void she left with another parrot. Charlie redefined "pet" for me. A pet, I've come to believe, is an animal whose emotional needs can be met by a human being. However much I loved her and tried to keep her engaged and happy, this little blue and green bundle of unmet needs was more inmate than pet, as are, I'd submit, all captive psittacines. Without mate and flock, without the joy of flight from flower to fruit to roost to nest, captive parrots are just marking time, time that felt at once too long and much too short to me.

I still can't grasp that rowdy, swaggering Chuck was a hen the whole time, and I don't miss the irony of a bird whisperer being taken in for two decades by a dealer's lie and a little aberrant sexual behavior on Charlie's part. What I miss is Charlie: loud, bossy, tender, funny Charles, dearly loved and, like all captive parrots, misunderstood to the end.

# Notes

20 *studies in Michigan have shown:* Michael P. Lombardo, Ruth M. Bosman, Christine A. Faro, Stephen G. Houtteman, and Timothy S. Kluisza, "Effect of Feathers as Nest Insulation on Incubation Behavior and Reproductive Performance of Tree Swallows *(Tachycineta bicolor),*" *Auk* 112, no. 4 (1995): 973–981.

25 *"A little fool lies here":* In Otto Erich Deutsch, *Mozart: A Documentary Biography* (Stanford, CA: Stanford University Press, 1965).

34 *"the softest of beds":* Theodor Geisel, *Dr. Seuss's Sleep Book* (New York: Random House Books for Young Readers, 1962).

39 *fully 7 percent more birds survive:* M. C. Brittingham and S. A. Temple, "Impacts of Supplemental Feeding on Survival Rates of Black-capped Chickadees," *Ecology* 69 (1988): 581–589.

58 *case of suspected polygyny:* T. M. Haggerty and E. S. Morton, "Carolina Wren *(Thryothorus ludovicianus),*" in *The Birds of North America,* no. 188, ed. Alan F. Poole and Frank B. Gill (Philadelphia: Academy of Natural Sciences and Washington, D.C.: American Ornithologists' Union, 1995), 8.

74 *fledging occurs around Day 20:* T. R. Robinson, R. R. Sargent, and M. B. Sargent, "Ruby-throated Hummingbird *(Archilochus colubris),*" in *The Birds of North America,* no. 204, ed. Alan F. Poole and Frank B. Gill (Philadelphia: Academy of Natural Sciences and Washington, D.C.: American Ornithologists' Union, 1996), 10.

93 *Ninety percent of the ospreys nesting:* A. F. Poole, *Ospreys: A Natural and Unnatural History* (Cambridge: Cambridge University Press, 1989), 209.

95 *R. C. Szaro observed adult ospreys:* R. C. Szaro, "Reproductive Success and Foraging Behavior of the Osprey at Seahorse Key, Florida," *Wilson Bulletin* 90 (1978): 112–118.

101 *he quotes the ethologist Donald Griffin:* A. F. Poole. *Ospreys: A Natural and Unnatural History* (Cambridge: Cambridge University Press, 1989): 9. Poole is quoting ethol-

ogist Donald Griffin from his book *Animal Thinking* (Cambridge: Harvard University Press, 1984).

104  *In the fall of 2004:* Tom Baptist, personal correspondence with the author.

118  *a single chimney sweep has been known to kill:* Paul Kyle and G. Kyle, "Environmental Tips for Homeowners and Professional Chimney Sweeps," http://www.tpwd. state.tx.us/huntwild/wild/birding/pif/chimney_swift/homeowners_sweeps/.

122  *showing that edible bird's nest extract:* Chao-Tan Guo, Tadanobu Takahashi, Wakoto Bukawa, Noriko Takahashi, Hirokazu Yagi, Koichi Kato, Kazuya I-P Jwa Hidari, Daisei Miyamoto, Takashi Suzuki, and Yasuo Suzuki, "Edible Bird's Nest Extract Inhibits Influenza Virus Infection," *Antiviral Research* 70, no. 3 (2006): 140–146.

161  *Experiments by Donald Kroodsma showed:* Donald Kroodsma, *The Singing Life of Birds* (Boston: Houghton Mifflin, 2005): 84–85.

198  *"Everyone knows . . . that the autumn":* Aldo Leopold, *A Sand County Almanac* (New York: Oxford University Press, 1949).

242  *James Tanner's elegant treatise:* James T. Tanner, *The Ivory-billed Woodpecker* (1942; repr., Mineola, NY: Dover Publications, 2003).

244  *"We, the woodpeckers":* James T. Tanner, unpublished MS, later published as "A Forest Alive," *Living Bird* 24, no. 3 (Summer 2005): 37–41.

246  *"We didn't know the ivorybill":* Richard M. Saunders, *Carolina Quest* (Columbia: University of South Carolina Press, 1951).

251  *"She came trumpeting":* J. K. Terres, ed., *Discovery: Great Moments in the Lives of Outstanding Naturalists* (Philadelphia: J. B. Lippincott, 1961).

260  *a book on the species:* Jerome A. Jackson, *In Search of the Ivory-billed Woodpecker* (Washington, D.C.: Smithsonian Books, 2004). Quote by Don Eckelberry.

270  *lowest recruitment rate of any bird:* R. C. Drewien, W. M. Brown, and W. L. Kendall, "Recruitment in Rocky Mountain Greater Sandhill Cranes and Comparisons with Other Crane Populations," *Journal of Wildlife Management* 59 (1995): 339–356.

270  *Over the two decades:* Kammie L. Kruse, J. A. Dubovsky, and Thomas R. Cooper, "Status and Harvests of Sandhill Cranes: Mid-continent, Rocky Mountain, Lower Colorado River Valley and Eastern Populations 2011," Administrative Report, U.S. Fish and Wildlife Service, Denver, Colorado, 2011.

273  *it's estimated that there are one hundred:* Rex Sallabanks and Frances C. James, "American Robin (*Turdus migratorius*)," in *The Birds of North America Online,* ed. A. Poole (Ithaca: Cornell Lab of Ornithology, 1999).

285  *The researcher David Blockstein outlined:* David E. Blockstein and D. Westmoreland, "Reproductive Strategy," in *Ecology and Management of the Mourning Dove,* ed. T. S. Baskett, M. W. Sayre, R. E. Tomlinson, and R. E. Mirarchi (Harrisburg, PA: Stackpole Books, 1993), 105–116.

285  *According to the 1989 North American:* S. Droege and J. R. Sauer. "North American Breeding Bird Survey Annual Summary 1989," *Biology Report* 90, no. 8 (1990).

297 *A. C. Bent's elegant:* Arthur C. Bent, *Life Histories of North American Cardinals, Grosbeaks, Buntings, Towhees, Finches, Sparrows, and Allies,* U.S. National Museum Bulletin 237 (Washington: Smithsonian Institution, 1968). Original Source: Arthur Cleveland Bent and collaborators (compiled and edited by Oliver L. Austin, Jr.), Smithsonian Institution United States National Museum Bulletin 237, Part 1 (Washington: United States Government Printing Office, 1968) 1–15.

298 *Winter feeding has been shown:* M. C. Brittingham and S. A. Temple, "Impacts of Supplemental Feeding on Survival Rates of Black-capped Chickadees," *Ecology* 69 (1988): 581–589.

307 *Charles D. Duncan . . . looked at the precipitous drop:* C. D. Duncan, "Changes in the 307 Abundance of Sharp-shinned Hawks in New England," *Journal of Field Ornithology* 67 (1996): 254–262.

310 *"If a vulture has flown":* http://www.linsdomain.com/totems/pages/vulture.htm.

311 *"Vulture teaches the power":* http://www.starstuffs.com/native_spirituality/.

# Index

vocalization, 116, 126, 130; Willa, *136*; Yellow, *131*
Szaro, R. C., 95

tanagers *(Piranga),* range and diversity, 149, 151, 153
tanagers, paradise, 151
tanagers, scarlet, *150, 152*; description, 151, *155*; diet in the wild, 151, 154; fledglings, 154; home range and habitat loss, 152; mating behavior, 153; migration, 149, 151–52, 153, *155*; nestlings, 154; nest parasitization by cowbirds, 152–53; nests, 153; population dynamics, 152–53; predators, 151, 154; reproduction, 153–54; sexual dimorphism, 154; Tangee, 154, 156, *156, 157,* 158; vocalization, 149, 153, 156; winter plumage, 151
Tanner, James, 242, 244, 252–53, 260
Tanner, Nancy, 242–43
Teale, Edwin Way, 232
temperature control: in captivity, heat, 119, 123–24; in the wild, 19
Tennessee Wildlife Resources Commission, 277
terns, 272
terns, common, 109, 190
terns, least, *183, 184*; foraging, *177*; on Great Gull Island, 190; habitat conservation, 178–85, *179,* 190, 192; human depredation, 180–81; on Menunketesuck Island, 186–87, *188,* 189; nest, 178; nest defense behavior, 186; nestlings, *180, 186,* 189; parental behavior, 180–81, 187; predators, 186, 187, *188,* 189; recognition of individual people, 185, 186; reproduction, 178, 183; threatened/endangered species, 190; vocalization, *177*
terns, roseate, 189, 190
territory, competition for, 41. *See also* nests, competition for nest sites
Thomas, Elizabeth Marshall, xxiii

Thompson, Bill, III (husband): bird labeling technique, 128; and Charlie the macaw, 328, 336; and chimney swifts, 128, 134; Duck Stamp purchase, 276; and eastern bluebirds, 2–3, 12; and eastern phoebes, 173; editor and publisher of *Bird Watcher's Digest,* x; magazine cover art, 237; and ruby-throated hummingbirds, 90; and sandhill cranes, 267; and a titmouse, 112; and a turkey vulture, 316; wedding, 221
Thompson, Liam (son): and Charlie the macaw, 334, 335; and chimney swifts, 130, 134, 136; and eastern bluebirds, 12; and eastern phoebes, 62; and European starlings, 30; at Festival of Cranes, 267; life with a bird rehabilitator, 228, 267; "preening," 120; and ruby-throated hummingbirds, 72
Thompson, Phoebe Linnea (daughter): and Charlie the macaw, 333–35; and chimney swifts, 134, 136; and eastern bluebirds, 15; and eastern phoebes, 160, 165, 170, 173, *175, 176*; at Festival of Cranes, 267; and grouse, 194–95; life with a bird rehabilitator, 267; and mourning doves, 286, 287; and northern cardinal, 301; and ruby-throated hummingbirds, 69, 72, 81, 87
thrashers, brown, 299
threatened species. *See* endangered/threatened species
threats to birds: cars, 22, 230, 317; cats, 111, 112, 186, 209, 213–14, *214,* 219–20, 220; dogs, 203; electrocution from power lines, 96; flying into glass windows/doors, 5, *77,* 145–46, 291; high tide, 183–84; human (*see* food, human; habitat degradation; hunting; intervention and interference); illness (*see* disease and illness; parasites)
thrushes, 273
thrushes, hermit, xvi, 195

thrushes, wood, 219–20, *220*

*Thryothorus*, 54, 55. *See also* wrens, Carolina

titmice, *318*

titmice, tufted, *110, 112*; arrival, 111, *112*; competition for territory, 41; departure, 113, *114*, 115; description, *113*; feeder, yard, *114*, 115, 173; feeding in captivity, 112; predators, 112, 145; vocalization, 112, 126, 145

tits, blue, 298

toenails, clipping, 215

totems, 309–12, 314

touchstone species, 278, *279*

tourism, 279

tracking, satellite, 104, 107–8, *108–9*

transport of birds, 72, 76, 167, 168, 316

Troyer, Andy, 7

Truslow, Fredrick Kent, xviii

turkeys, ix

turkeys, wild, 195, 197, *198*

U.S. Fish and Wildlife Service, 229, 260, 263, 277, 278

vigilance behavior, 140–41

vireos, red-eyed, 154

vireos, white-eyed, 147, 299

vultures, turkey, *309, 316, 317*; albino sightings, 312–14, *313*, 330; arrival, 314–15; description, 309; diet in the wild, 309, 310, *311, 318*; feeding in captivity, 316; feeding young, *315*; flight, 310, *313, 318*; hit by car, 317–18; at a landfill, 200; migration, 309, 313; nestlings, 314, *315*; as predator, *311, 318*; starving and lethargic, 315–18; stench of vomit, 316–17; as totem, 309–12, 314; vocalization, 314

warblers, 28, 154

warblers, Blackburnian, *53, 54*

warblers, blue-winged, 48

warblers, prairie, 48

waxwings, cedar, 64, 83, 154

Weidensaul, Scott, xiii, xiv–xvii

whip-poor-wills, 45, 198, 290

wildlife rehabilitation facilities, bird, 64, 65

wildlife rehabilitators: emotional challenges, 77–79, 109, 162, 174, 204, 226; euthanasia decision-making process, 66, *77–78*, 215, 217, 220; joys, 84, 88, 134, 146, 158, 171, 212, 233–35; knowing when to release a bird, 113, 134, 170, 210–11; naming an animal, 209; permit, 64, 111; referred by *Bird Watcher's Digest*, 228; responsibilities, 64, 76, 111, 124, 168–69, 209, 215; time and costs, 126, 235

windows and doors, birds hitting glass, 5, *77*, 145–46, 291

woodpeckers, 120, 145

woodpeckers, downy, 32

woodpeckers, hairy, 5

woodpeckers, ivory-billed, 234, 239, 242, 245, *247*, 260; author's artwork and writing, 242, 264; in Cuba, 254, 263; description, 240; diet in the wild, *250, 252, 253*, 263; extinct status, debate, 237–38, 249, 252, 259, 261, 263, 264; fledglings, 245; flight, 248–49, *248, 251*, 254–55, *255, 257*, 261, *262*, 264; foraging, 248, *252, 254*; habitat and habitat loss, 238, 243, 249, *252–53, 257, 258*, 263, 264; life span, 259; locomotion, 240–41; nest, 245; research on, 242, 244, 253, 260–64; search for, 238–39, 256; sightings, 238–39, 241–46, *247, 248*, 249, 251–59, 263; sound of bill hitting wood, 239, 243, 251; and Thomas Murray, 244; threat display, 255; vocalization, 239, 243, 248, 250, 256

woodpeckers, pileated: on author's property, 249; description, 256; generalist, 254; population increase, 252; tongue, *73*

woodpeckers, red-headed, 29

World Wildlife Fund, 254